# HELP! from
## Heloise

*Other Avon Books by*
**Heloise**

HINTS FROM HELOISE

# HELP! from Heloise

by HELOISE

AVON BOOKS ◆ NEW YORK

AVON BOOKS, INC.
1350 Avenue of the Americas
New York, New York 10019

Cover photograph by Craig Stafford
Text illustrations by Graham Halky
Published by arrangement with Arbor House Publishing Company
Visit our website at **http://www.AvonBooks.com**
Library of Congress Catalog Card Number: 80-70453
ISBN: 0-380-79184-6

First Avon Books Trade Printing: April 1997
First Avon Books Mass Market Printing: October 1982

Printed in the U.S.A.

OPM 10 9 8 7 6 5 4 3 2

*To the homemaker, no matter what gender, age or marital status.*
*We all need help at one time or another.*

*And to my dear mother, who in 1959 started "Hints from Heloise"*
*and the idea of sharing hints with each other. She taught me at an*
*early age to care about you, the ones that have helped make Heloise*
*a household word.*

*A special thanks to my daddy, I couldn't have done this without*
*him.*

# Contents

# General Introduction

Hello, this is your friend Heloise. Since you're reading this book, I figure you could use some help!

Actually, we *all* need help. No matter how efficient and organized we are, the moment sometimes arrives when nothing is more important than knowing how to get ball-point ink out of a shirt, or how to remove a plastic bread bag that's gotten stuck to your toaster. What then?

Since my first book, *Hints From Heloise,* was published, I've found out from thousands of people in every corner of the country that sometimes the littlest things going wrong make for the most frustrating problems. I started making a list of them. The list grew. Boy, do we have problems!

Well, now *Help! from Heloise* is here, with solutions to those problems that seem to pop up most. Whether you need an ounce of prevention or—sometimes it happens!—a pound of cure, *Help!* is at hand.

*How to Use This Book*

If you turn back to page 7 and look at the Table of Contents, you'll see what's in this book. There are three parts—one each for inside, outside, and all around your house—and twelve chapters.

I almost called this book "P.S. from Heloise"—*P* for the Problems we plan to avoid, *S* for the Solutions we sometimes have to have ... in a hurry! Well, fact is, each chapter in this book contains dozens of *P*'s and *S*'s—solved problems, questions with their answers—all organized under alphabetical headings so you can find 'em fast. And I often find that one good idea leads to another, so I've put in lots of cross-references to help you on to greater things.

In addition to these *P*'s and *S*'s, every chapter is stuffed full of additional tips that may help you from having some problems in the first place. Wouldn't you rather pour a cup of water into the broiler pan *before* broiling hamburger patties than spend time scrubbing and scrubbing the pan *afterwards*?

At the back of this book is an Index to everything—Problems, Solutions and all the hints. It's the best way to find what you're looking for—and to find related things you didn't realize you needed to know, too.

*Heloise's House*

Before you start turning to find the "helps" you need, you may be wondering about something people ask me all the time: Where does Heloise find these hints in the first place? The answer, of course, is that most of them are found by *you*, and shared with me when you write in, and shared *by* me with everyone who reads this book.

I also have a "test house," my home in Texas, where my staff and I combine and carefully test the best suggestions America has to offer —and we even invent quite a few of our own!

*The Heloise Philosophy*

You know, lifestyles are changing, and family units have changed from the "perfect" family with mother, father, 2.5 children and one pet with a two-car garage, to almost anything-goes. Men are now getting custody of the children. Women are working full time and spending more time away from home.

I feel that today the term "homemaker" means anyone who has to do some laundry, wash his or her own hair, take the garbage out, or even fix that first cup of coffee in the morning. (In my family, we were taught that if you were old enough to walk then you were old enough to help out around the house. It may be only carrying the napkin from the dinner table to the kitchen, but it's a start.) *Every* homemaker who helps around the house can use *Help! from Heloise.*

So the hints and solutions in this book are for everyone, and they're for everyday problems. Some of the hints you may know already, but if you're like me, some of them you'll absolutely flip out about. How smart we all are when we all put our heads (and our hints) together!

I'm constantly learning from the readers of my newspaper column and from people who read my books, who send in their best ideas to me to share with others. Often the most obvious-sounding solution is the one everyone has been searching for. That's what the entire Heloise philosophy is—Caring and Sharing.

My best wishes to you, may all your problems be very small and easily cured. If not, remember I am here to help whenever I can with those big ones too. If I can't, I can listen to you and let you know that there are millions of others with the same or worse problems, and I love each and every one of you!

—Hugs, Heloise

How to reach me:
Fax: 210-HELOISE (435-6473)
E-mail: Heloise@CIS.CompuServe.com
Mail: P.O. BOX 795000
      SAN ANTONIO TX 78279-5000
Internet: http://www.HELOISE.com

# PART ONE

# Inside the House

## INTRODUCTION

A house, a home or an apartment—no matter where you live, the inside is your domain.

The trend in housing seems to be more and more towards the compact, the easy-to-care-for. More people are moving into condos, into smaller houses with little tiny yards (we call them garden homes here in Texas). The whole world seems to be going for "smaller is better," even in our cars.

The first section of the book is just what the title says, "Inside the House"—the things that go on inside, the things you must care for and the things that you do for yourself.

I have broken this down into five major areas of the home.

The first and foremost is the kitchen. We all know how important the kitchen is to any family. You can live without a dining room or a living room, but it sure is hard to live without a kitchen.

Your kitchen may be very large with all the gadgets in the world, or it may be just a sink, coffee pot and a hot plate. No matter, it's still the place that is the heart of the home.

I don't care what you do, how large your living room is, or your den or the area you entertain in, it seems everyone always ends up in the kitchen. Right? When I lived in my tiny apartment I would carefully plan things so that no one had to go into the kitchen to get anything. Food was already out, drinks and ice and glasses were on the patio, etc. There was no reason for even me to go in there.

You guessed it. Out of twenty people that came over one night, fifteen of them ended up in that tiny kitchen, shoulder to shoulder. So I gave up. If that's where everyone is going to end up anyway, let's make the best of it.

In my home now, the kitchen is large, and we even have a center island that is three feet by four feet and forty inches high. I put chips, dips and cheese out and make my kitchen a real entertainment area. Everyone likes it and so do I.

The next chapter is about probably the second most important room in the house. The bath. Unless you live in the backwoods, or have a roughing-it type of retreat, you have indoor plumbing and at least one bathroom, if not several.

That old bath sure does get a work out, doesn't it! If there are children or teenagers in your family, I bet you never thought anyone could spend so much time in there.

If you are lucky enough to have your own bath that you don't have to share with anyone, I would say that is really a luxury. If you are like most people, you have to share the bath area with someone. This section will give you good advice on coping with the problems that arise.

Laundry problems have got to be some of the most-asked questions that I get in my column. We are all stuck with doing a little laundry now and then, even if it's only hand washing those special garments in the bathroom sink, or trying to sort socks. Yuck. Sometimes I wish all socks came in only one color. Even though some might say it would be certainly boring, it sure would make laundry day a heck of a lot easier!

The problems and solutions in this laundry section are the ones I get asked, over and over and over. Simple, tried and true, but the hints will make your laundry day a bit brighter and lighter.

Inflation has become a way of life. With the cost of clothing going up like everything else, more and more readers are sewing and repairing, rather than discarding and buying new. Sewing and mending and taking better care of clothes is very important. I think you will see from this chapter that if you will take a few minutes to do it correctly, then it will save you time and money in the long run.

If you aren't a seamstress, you still may have to sew on a button, or at least pin it on for the time being. There are a lot of short cuts and easy ways to do these things, and I hope you will remember them when you need the help.

Last but not least in this section is my favorite chapter: Miscellaneous. If I could put everything under this heading, wouldn't you have a time finding what you want!

Miscellaneous covers things like carpets, closets, furniture care, and some real good information on storage.

Welcome to my world—and may this section on "Inside the House" help when you need it!

—Hugs, Heloise

# ☐

# *Your Kitchen*

Let's pour a cup of coffee and talk a few minutes about a very special place.

A kitchen is just a room in the house until folks move in, and then it becomes the heart of the home. People lend the warmth and glow that make your kitchen that very special place.

On a cold rainy day, there's no better gathering place than the kitchen table for coffee with a friend. When the kids come home from school tired and hungry, you know the first place they go. And, of course, the kitchen's a very special place when the kids are all in bed and you and hubby can share a cup of hot chocolate and the news of the day.

Your kitchen tells others a lot about you. It says, "I like bright colors and I'm a gregarious type," or "I like cool, refreshing greens," or "I like a quiet cozy nook," or "I prefer uncluttered, modern, functional things," or "I'm a soul who loves the beauty of yester-day." And, though we are all different in our likes and dislikes, we all want our kitchens to be a happy place for ourselves and our families.

We all know how much activity is connected with this heart of the home, and it seems as if all the chores that begin there never get done. I can remember mother saying so many times, "Just top clean and do what you have to do and then when you really feel like it, do the heavy cleaning."

Well, one thing about the kitchen that bugs me is cluttered counters. I don't know about you, but if my kitchen is presentable I feel like a million dollars and my day goes much smoother. Have you noticed that the mood YOU are in is the mood that the whole household gets into? T'ain't fair but it's true.

The rest of the house somehow doesn't seem insurmountable after I've gotten the kitchen done. I always clean the counters and table off first; that way, if unexpected company drops in at least you have a place to sit down for coffee. However, you need to do what suits YOU best. Don't do something a certain way because it works for your neighbor, unless it works for you.

Success in running a kitchen efficiently does require a little planning and a little organization. I love a little saying that someone passed on to me—PLAN YOUR WORK and WORK YOUR PLAN!

There are three things that really have helped me manage in my own kitchen, and that's (1) having a telephone with a l-o-n-g cord so I can keep on working while I talk (sometimes I just sit down and scoot along the floor washing cabinets); (2) writing a menu and shopping list out and posting the menu for the week on the fridge so I know at a glance what to thaw and what to cook; and (3) writing my most-used and favorite recipes on cards and taping them to the inside of my cabinet near the place where I store my staples and do my mixing.

We are all in this kitchen thing together! All of us have to clean ovens and refrigerators. All of us have to mop spills. All of us have to get the cabinets "back between the fence posts." So I have compiled this special chapter. We'll lend each other a helping hand and get our kitchens shipshape. We'll go from Rags to Dishes!

## ACCESSORIES

### Bulletin Board

**Problem**  *I don't have space for a kitchen bulletin board.*
**Solution**  Purchase some "chalkboard paint" and chalk paint the inside of a cupboard and you'll have an instant message center!

\*   \*   \*

Tape lists of birthdays and anniversaries to your bulletin board and they will be less likely to slip your mind.

\*   \*   \*

An "inspirational board" will turn a gloomy day into a sunny one and turn a frown into a smile. Clip poems, sayings, cartoons, pictures of loved ones, whatever gives you a lift, to this special bulletin board that you can go to when needed. Try it, it really works!

### Canisters

Silver cleaner will make your aluminum canister sets shine like new!

\*   \*   \*

P        *The aluminum canisters I have leave black marks*
              *on my cabinet.*

S        Glue pieces of moleskin or little pieces of felt on
              the bottom.

*   *   *

If you break fingernails trying to get canister lids off, glue some knobs on the lids.

*   *   *

P        *I use apothecary jars for canisters. I detest filling*
              *them because it is so difficult.*

S        Try this: Cut a small hole (about the size of a
              nickel) in the corner of a plastic bag. Put the bag
              in the canister and pull the top of the bag around
              the neck of the jar; now you can dump "whatever"
              in the bag and it will flow through the hole into
              your apothecary jar.

*   *   *

P        *I have a gorgeous set of ceramic canisters but the*
              *lids won't fit tightly.*

S        Go ahead and use them, but put your ingredients

in plastic bags, twist them closed with a twistie, and place them in your canisters.

\* \* \*

To clean ceramic canisters, use a mild ammonia-and-water solution or a commercial window spray.

\* \* \*

The jars that freeze-dried coffee comes in are super as canisters for those folks who live alone and don't want or need regular-size canisters.

\* \* \*

Use small jars to store quantities of one or two cups of flour, sugar or coffee to use in a pinch.

\* \* \*

**P**     *What can I do with an old canister set?*
**S**     Put the canisters in your bath to store hair rollers, cotton balls, cotton swabs, makeup, etc., or put them in a child's room to store crayons, puzzle pieces and small toys. In your kitchen you could remove the lids and use the canisters to store long spoons, spatulas, etc.

\* \* \*

**P**     *I have some new canisters of dark wood. I'm afraid that water and spills on the cabinet will mar them.*
**S**     Why not glue some garden hose washers underneath them to raise them slightly out of the path of spills?

*Curtains*

P       *How can I restore body to limp dacron curtains?*
S       Soak them in a solution of 1 cup Epsom salts and
        1 gallon of lukewarm water; rinse by hand.

\*    \*    \*

P       *My curtains snag when I slip them on the rod.*
S       Put a piece of transparent tape over the end of the
        rod, or slip a small plastic bag over the rod and
        secure it with a rubber band before putting your
        curtains on the rod.

\*    \*    \*

An old pair of cafe curtains with rings, stitched face to face and
turned inside out, makes a great laundry or storage bag. Thread a
piece of rope or cord through the rings.

\*    \*    \*

P       *The curtain over my kitchen sink constantly looks
        bad because of water spots.*
S       Some folks with this problem have switched to
        terry cloth curtains over the sink. When dirty or
        spotted, just toss them in the washer and dryer and
        rehang. Shutters that can be opened while your
        sink is in use are a solution, but unfortunatley will
        cost you something.

\*    \*    \*

To cover an unsightly kitchen shelving area, place a tension-type
curtain rod to hang a curtain over the opening. Match your kitchen
colors.

*Place Mats*

P       *How do I get the grooves clean on my patterned
        place mats?*
S       Use an old toothbrush and scrub them with deter-
        gent.

**P**    *I love the look of place mats on my wood table, but I worry that they aren't enough protection from spills.*

**S**    Cut a pad the size and shape of your place mat out of an old quilted mattress cover or those flannel-backed moisture pads that can be found in the baby department of your store. Put this pad under your place mat. This extra pad will surely solve the spill problem, but I would check to see how much protection they offered before placing anything really hot on them.

\*    \*    \*

**P**    *How can I keep my plastic place mats from sticking to my table?*

**S**    Glue felt strips on the back, or line them with nylon net.

\*    \*    \*

**P**    *I get so tired of hunting through drawers for place mats; I think I would use them more if they were handier.*

**S**    A multi-skirt hanger will hold mats in your pantry. You can even store them under the sofa cushions (at least they'll stay flat!) If you do have to put them in a drawer, be sure it is one that is close to the table and easy to get to.

\*    \*    \*

Fingertip towels make washable, practical place mats for small children.

### Potholders and Oven Mitts

Crocheting pot holders? Use rug yarn for durability.

\* \* \*

A child's toy rolling pin makes a darling holder for pot holders. Screw two cuphooks in the pin and attach it to the wall; or, take a wooden spoon (paint if desired) and screw two cuphooks in it and attach to wall.

\* \* \*

Pot holders can be made out of worn-out silicone ironing board covers, old mattress pads and stretched-out thick socks, just to name a few materials.

\* \* \*

P     *What can I do with worn-out oven mitts?*
S     When the oven mitt loses its protection, give it to
       hubby to wash the car with.

### Scrubbers

The nylon net bags that onions and potatoes come packaged in make fantastic scrubbers. Just fold the bag into a square and stitch along the edges. Slip a washcloth or a sponge inside one of the bags and it makes a super dishrag scrubber.

\* \* \*

You'll wonder how you ever did without these wonderful scrubbers. Stuff a sponge into the knee area of an old, clean, nylon stocking. Cut and tie knots in the ends. Keep one in the kitchen, one in the bath, and one in the car for those trips to the car wash.

\* \* \*

P       *I have seen nylon net scrub brushes made by using a plastic bleach bottle. Can you tell me how it's done?*

S       Take 72-inch-wide nylon net and cut it into six strips three inches wide. Then, lay one strip on top of the other until all six are in a pile. Now, gather them all together through the middle. Next, cut out the handle from your empty bleach jug; be sure and leave about one-half inch or so of the bottle along with it. Now, use a hole puncher and punch holes about every one-half inch along the plastic edge.

       Get a strong string and stitch the net to the plastic by going through the center line of the net, then through the holes of the plastic, and finish by separating each row of net so it will be "bushy" and stand out.

## Spice Racks (Also see Spices, p. 79)

P       *I just got married and received several spice racks. Any suggestions for making use of the duplicates?*

S       Lucky you! Some of us scrounge around at garage sales and such trying to pick up the old ones because they're so handy! Put one in your bath or bedroom to store makeup in or fingernail polish and remover. You can store straight pins, needles, and other small sewing items. Hubby probably would love to have one to store his nails, thumbtacks, screws, etc., there.

\*    \*    \*

P       *I would love to have a spice rack but I'm really on a tight budget. Any ideas for a homemade one?*

S       You bet your boots I've got some ideas! A 2-pound

cardboard cheese box covered with shelf paper or adhesive-backed paper will hold six cans of spices.

*    *    *

If you don't have a spice rack, a lazy Susan is great for holding your spices in a cabinet.

*    *    *

Alphabetize your spices in their storage space to save time locating them.

### Towels (Also see Towels for the bath area, p. 126)

Plan on doing a lot of cooking or baking? Pin a washcloth or small towel to the belt of your clothing or apron, and you'll have a handy cloth to wipe your hands on.

*    *    *

A really handy item in your kitchen is a "refrigerator" towel. This type of towel buttons together and can be hung over the door handle of your refrigerator.

*    *    *

P    *How can I keep a kitchen towel from falling off the towel rack?*

S    You can sew gripper snaps on the towel, or you can pin the ends together with a safety pin or clothespin. If you have a paper towel holder, sew two towels together (all ends), slip the towel over the dowel, replace the dowel and you have a "rolling" towel.

## APPLIANCES, LARGE

This section was written to help you with problems encountered cleaning appliances as well as to give a few hints for making your appliances do "double duty"!

Be sure to make a file folder or an expandable envelope to store all your instruction books, warranties and sales tickets. Keep all of this information together in one file; it sure beats digging through a dozen drawers and tearing the house apart.

Before you call a repairman or take an appliance to a serviceman, be sure to check to see if it is plugged in or if you have blown fuses or tripped circuit breakers.

\*   \*   \*

**P**     *I'm a bride-to-be and I'd like some suggestions in choosing appliances.*

**S**     Best wishes for a long and happy life! I'd be happy to give you a few hints . . . first of all, ask yourself, how often will I use it? Where will I store it? How will I clean it, and also, how heavy is it to move? If you don't know what features to look for or what prices are reasonable, pick up a copy of a major store's catalog and look through it. You can get an idea of what the basic features and capabilities are, as well as what "like-to-have" (I call them "gingerbread") features are available. You can also get a pretty good idea of what price you'll have to pay.

\*   \*   \*

When you move, leave the instruction books and warranties to those appliances that will be left in your home for the new owner.

## Dishwasher
*(Also see Cleaning dishes and glassware, p. 63)*

Judging from the letters I get, some of you are having problems with your dishwashers. That's a shame because your dishwasher was built to be a boon to you. Once you master a few "basics" you'll realize the full benefit your machine was designed to give you.

Number one, the water needs to be hot enough to do the job. If your dishes aren't getting clean, or film and water spots are left, this is probably the reason. Some machines have built-in "boosters" that heat the water to the correct temperature once the water is in the machine. If yours doesn't have boosters, you can check the temperature by letting the water run out of your faucet until it's as hot as it's going to get. Fill a tall glass with the hot water and drop a tablespoon of your dishwasher detergent in there. If the detergent mostly dissolves before it reaches the bottom of the glass, the water temperature is hot enough. If not, you may need to turn up your water heater a bit. The temperature should be around 120°F. A word of caution: Small children are easily scalded and some have even died from scald burns due to water that was between 140°F and 160°F.

If you're sure your hot water heater is at the right setting, it may be that you're trying to run the dishwasher right after baths or while doing laundry, and there's simply not enough hot water available. Try rescheduling your dishwashing time to make sure you have really hot water on hand.

Another problem can be the dishwasher detergent itself. You should pick up that box *at the store* and give it a good shake. Don't put it in your basket if it doesn't sound loose and powdery. Old, lumpy detergent just won't get the job done.

Where do you store that box of detergent once you get it home? I used to store it under the kitchen sink until I found out that it's far too warm and moist under there. Find a cool, dry shelf and keep the box spout closed tightly.

If you'll check that filter in the bottom of your dishwasher regularly and keep it free and clean, your dishes will come out cleaner. Face it, if there's guck and pieces of food in that filter, it's just going to recirculate over your clean dishes until you get that filter clean.

Slivers of broken glass, spoons that have fallen to the bottom (I have even found matchsticks) that get under the waterflow arm or in the filter can mess up the whole works!

Another tip is to load dishes properly. If you block the spray of water from reaching all the dishes, you simply can't expect sparkling dishes.

I have found that some brands of detergent unfortunately do not work as well as others. Try changing brands and see if that helps get your dishes cleaner. Also, if you are not filling the detergent cup to the manufacturer's suggested level, especially if you have hard water, that could mean the difference between so-so clean and *really* clean and sparkling dishes.

Folks who prerinse dishes before putting them in the dishwasher (lucky me, mine come out clean without prerinsing!) have problems with other members of the family not knowing whather or not the dishes in the machine are ready to use or ready to wash. Some readers have made little signs saying "Wash me" or "I'm washed" which they attach to their machines with little magnets.

If etching is a problem, try not to overload your dishwasher and do use the right amount of detergent. Etching is caused by a combination of things; mainly it's because the water is too hard or too soft and because the dishes are not thoroughly rinsed. This causes a silica film to build up on the glassware. To be on the safe side, always hand wash fine crystal. Also, be sure and see if your fine china is specified dishwasher-safe. Gold-plated flatware should *never* be placed in a dishwasher.

\*        \*        \*

Remove the entire flatware basket to unload flatware—saves steps!

\*        \*        \*

If you want to wash small items in your dishwasher, tie two pint-size plastic baskets (like the ones you get from the grocery store with strawberries) together with twisties.

\*        \*        \*

P       *I have trouble with small forks and such falling to*
        *the bottom of the dishwasher.*
S       Place a plastic scrubber in one of the sections of
        the silverware basket and stick those small items
        through it.

\*        \*        \*

Put nylon net in the silverware basket to prevent small flatware from falling to the bottom of the dishwasher.

\*        \*        \*

**P**          *The inside of my dishwasher is discolored.*
**S**          This is probably due to hard-water lime deposits.
               With an empty dishwasher, set one cup of bleach
               in the bottom rack and run through a wash cycle
               (do not run dry cycle). Then, run one cup of vine-
               gar through an entire cycle. NOTE: Do not try to
               "short-cut" it and run both the vinegar and bleach
               through at the same time. Bleach should not be
               mixed with other substances due to poisonous
               gases that can form. Read the labels!

*       *       *

If you normally wash small loads, why not wash seldom-used dishwasher-safe glassware each time you run a load? You won't have
such a chore to do when you need it.

*       *       *

If you only run a load through your dishwasher every two days or
so, place a glass of water on the bottom rack and put the flatware
in it to soak until "wash time." You won't have any hardened,
stuck-on food on your flatware.

*       *       *

If you want to sweeten the smell in your dishwasher, add a half a
box of baking soda and run the machine through a rinse cycle.

*       *       *

Do not place gold-decorated china, hand-painted dishes, hollow-
handled silverware, wooden ware or heavy glass such as lead crystal
in your dishwasher.
(Also see Cleaning Dishes, p. 63)

*       *       *

**P**          *The racks on my dishwasher won't slide freely.*
**S**          Take a soap pad and vinegar and scour the metal
               part the rollers glide on.

*       *       *

P       *How can I keep the water from splashing all over?*
*I have the portable dishwasher that drains in the*
*sink.*

S       You can cut the bottom and top off of a bleach
bottle, and the handle, and then place the dis-
charge hose through the handle slot. Or, you can
let the water drain into an empty shortening can;
the water will fill to the top and then overflow into
the sink drain without splashing.

\*    \*    \*

If your dishwasher goes out, remember you can use the racks for
draining dry (your dishes will still be out of sight, too!).

DISHWASHER—OUT OF ORDER?
Check the following before calling repairman:

1.  Is it plugged in?

2.  Is there a fuse blown or a breaker tripped?

3.  Is it clean under the filter-strainer? No food, spoons, or gook
    under there?

4.  Is the detergent flowing freely in the box? Shake the box—if it's
    lumpy the soap won't clean good.

5.  Is the water hot enough? Check your hot water heater tempera-
    ture.

6.  Is there something lodged in the solenoid that won't allow the
    washer to fill or drain?

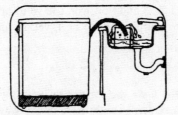

*Freezer*
*(Also see Refrigerator, p. 41)*

Full freezers are more economical to operate than empty ones. You can even stock your freezer with rolls of paper towels, macaroni, crackers, cookies, and so on to fill up those empty spaces.

\* \* \*

P        *Do you know of a simple way to inventory freezer contents?*

S        I think I have two really good ways to do this. The first is to make a list and place it in a zippered plastic bag that you've taped upside down on your freezer door. You can mark off items used and add new items. Keep a pencil handy by your list.

Another way that will be well worth the time and effort is a peg board. Make a peg board about two feet square and space nails two to three inches apart and in rows about four inches apart. Write above each nail the items you freeze such as corn, peas, beans, pork, chicken, etc. Hang a tag under each item—one tag for each package you have in your freezer. When you use an item take a tag down; when you put an item in your freezer add a tag.

\* \* \*

You don't have to have tape to mark plastic freezer containers. A black crayon or marking pen works super.

\* \* \*

Color-code your meats and you won't have to open or dig through your freezer: For example, red for beef, yellow for chicken, blue for pork, etc.

\* \* \*

P        *I need some suggestions to make defrosting easy.*

S        Hon, I don't think there is any way to make defrosting "easy," but there are a few tricks to make it less hard!

First of all, as a safety measure, unplug your refrigerator from the wall. Place a thick layer of newspapers or several old towels on the floor in front of the refrigerator. Remove all the food from the refrigerator (you can pack it in an ice chest if you want to take your time). Keep a pail or a garbage can handy if your sink's not handy to throw the big chunks of ice in.

Never chip away those ice chunks with an ice pick or any other sharp object that might puncture a line or the compartment lining.

A hand-held hair dryer works super for melting the ice and speeding things up. (Caution: remember that electrical appliances are dangerous if they come in contact with water.) A pan of real hot water set in the freezer compartment helps, too. If your hands get cold, try putting on some rubber gloves.

After you're done with the job, place a couple of layers of waxed paper on the freezer shelf before putting your food back in. Next defrosting time, the ice will just glide off the paper. A light coat of vegetable oil spray around the bottom and walls should also help.

\*　　\*　　\*

Use oven mittens when rearranging or defrosting your freezer to keep from getting "cold" burns on your hands.

\*　　\*　　\*

P       *After I defrost my freezer, the packages stick to the shelves.*

S       If you'll wait just a bit and let the freezer freeze slightly before you put the packages back in, they won't stick.

\*　　\*　　\*

P    *When I defrost my chest-type freezer, I have a prob-*
     *lem getting the water out when the ice melts*

S    Take several thick towels or old bath mats and lay
     them on the bottom of the freezer and then all
     you'll have to do is pick them up and wring them
     out.

\*    \*    \*

P    *I have a chest-type freezer and cannot keep stacks*
     *of food from falling over.*

S    Take heavy grocery bags and label them. For in-
     stance, put vegetables in one, meats in another. It
     will help to keep your frozen food separated and
     the bags will help support the stacks.

\*    \*    \*

P    *The ice in my freezer compartment has an "off"*
     *taste.*

S    This is probably because food in your freezer or
     refrigerator compartment is not sealed airtight. Be
     sure and put onions, as well as other strong foods,
     in foil, plastic wrap or a tightly-sealed jar.

\*    \*    \*

P    *How can I tell if the power was off to my freezer*
     *while I was away on vacation?*

S    Put a few ice cubes in a plastic bag and set the bag
     in your freezer. When you return, if the cubes are
     still shaped the way you left them, no problem. If
     the cubes are misshapen or melted a little, that
     would indicate a power loss or malfunction oc-
     curred while you were away.
     (See also *Refrigerator—Out of Order,* p. 45)

\*    \*    \*

"If you're going away on vacation or an extended trip, store your
valuable papers such as insurance policies, wills, birth certificates,

etc., in the freezer or refrigerator (be sure you put them in a moisture-proof plastic bag).

In case of fire, usually the refrigerator or freezer isn't totally destroyed, and you may save the headaches and time involved in replacing those papers.


*Oven*
*(Also see Stove, p. 45)*

**P**    *What is the best way to clean my oven?*

**S**    My favorite way is to wipe the inside of my oven with plain old ammonia before I go to bed at night. Then the next morning it simply wipes clean as a whistle! Or, you can use a commercial oven cleaner the same way (the oven cleaner works better if your oven is slightly warm).

You can wash all your removable oven parts in your dishwasher. If you don't have a dishwasher, soak those parts in your sink or bathtub with dishwasher detergent (put something down to prevent scratches if you use this method).

\*    \*    \*

**P**    *I simply cannot get the glass on my oven door clean.*

**S**    If you've tried cleaning the grime off with vinegar, ammonia or a window cleaner and that hasn't worked, your problem is probably guck in between the panes. In this case, if you can, unscrew the window panel on your oven door to get to those "inside parts" of the window.

\*    \*    \*

**P**    *The numbers on my oven dial are so worn I can't see them*

**S**    Take a yellow crayon and rub it all over the numbers on the dial. Then gently wipe off the excess crayon. You should have easy-to-read numbers once again. Paint with clear nail polish.

*   *   *

Never line your oven completely with foil—heat simply cannot circulate properly if you do.

*   *   *

Your oven rack makes a great rack to put over the fire for a weiner roast. Take it along next time you go camping!

*   *   *

Always use dishes or cookware with lids in the oven to prevent boil-overs and spills. Aluminum foil can be used for covers. Never fill a dish to capacity.

*   *   *

**P**   *I was told to choose shallow casserole dishes for my microwave. How come?*

**S**   A shallow casserole exposes more food surface to microwave energy. That's why it's preferable to a deep dish.

*   *   *

**P**   *Why do I need straight-sided dishes for microwaving casseroles?*

**S**   It's because food in casseroles with sloping sides can overcook around the edges. Straight-sided casseroles will cook your food more evenly.

*   *   *

Did you know you can cook "heaps" of bacon at one time in a microwave? Just layer bacon on paper towels in a baking dish. Rotate the dish after half the cooking time.

*   *   *

When you barbecue, cook an extra amount, freeze and reheat in your microwave later. Same yummy taste!

### Refrigerator
### (Also see Freezer, p. 36)

Your vegetable bins make super extra bowls for mixing salads for large groups.

\*    \*    \*

Never immerse cold vegetable bins made of glass in warm or hot water. It may crack them. Let them warm up to room temperature before you wash them.

\*    \*    \*

P        *The vegetable bins are always sticking.*
S        Clean thoroughly, wipe dry, and apply a light coating of vegetable oil spray.

\*    \*    \*

Do not block air circulation by lining your refrigerator shelves with aluminum foil or by using mats. Your refrigerator will not cool properly without proper air circulation.

\*    \*    \*

P        *How can I clean under my refrigerator—it seems impossible!*
S        Take heart! Wrap some nylon net or old rags around a yardstick to wipe underneath.

\*    \*    \*

Be sure to vacuum thoroughly underneath your refrigerator at least once a month. Dust on the condenser coils can spell a big repair bill. Also, a vacuum simply won't reach up behind your refrigerator, so it needs to be blown out at least once a year. If you don't have the apparatus to blow it out, call a serviceman to come do this for you.

It may cost, but it's a small price compared to the price of a new refrigerator.

*       *       *

P       *I can't keep fingerprints off my refrigerator door*
S       Try waxing your refrigerator with a kitchen cleaner-wax product made especially for that kind of finish. That should help. But I think your best bet would be to keep a little towel hanging on the door handle. Maybe everybody would grab the handle and the towel at the same time and eliminate prints in the first place. If not, at least you could give it a swipe "in passing" and keep those fingerprints from getting out of hand (no pun intended!).

*       *       *

If you dislike cleaning the dust off the top of your refrigerator, cover it with plastic wrap and just pull it off and toss it away when it becomes dusty (no one will notice the plastic wrap on top). The plastic wrap will adhere better if you just slightly moisten the top of the refrigerator before you put the plastic down.

*       *       *

P       *I have rust streaks on the inside walls of my refrigerator.*
S       Make a little paste of baking soda and water and apply. Most stains will vanish.

*       *       *

P       *I've got ugly brown stains on the glass portion of my refrigerator.*
S       Use full strength hydrogen peroxide to remove them.

*       *       *

P       *The finish on my refrigerator has yellowed.*
S       There are commercial car rubbing compounds

that will lighten the finish on your refrigerator. You may have to make more than one application, but the results are well worth the time and effort!

\*     \*     \*

When moving, or disconnecting your refrigerator, be sure to read your instructions for disconnecting the ice maker (if you're fortunate enough to own one!). Water lines may need to be cut off.

\*     \*     \*

P     *The walls on my refrigerator always have moisture on them.*

S     You need to check the gaskets and the catch to make sure your door is sealing tightly. An easy way to do this is to use a dollar bill or a piece of paper. If it can be inserted between the door of the refrigerator and the refrigerator itself, it means you need to have the gaskets or possibly the catch replaced or fixed (sometimes a good cleaning alone will solve the gasket or catch problem).

\*     \*     \*

P     *I can't get rid of an odor in my refrigerator.*

S     If you're sure the source is not a food or spill,

remove everything from your refrigerator and clean it thoroughly. Be sure to clean every crack and crevice, including cleaning under the gasket.

Some models have a drain tube and you should check the tube and the pan it drains into. Also clean the area underneath the vegetable bins. A cleaning solution of warm soapy water followed by a water and vinegar rinse should eliminate the odor.

If you set a saucer or cup of baking soda or a cup of vinegar in your refrigerator, you will keep it sweet smelling.

\*    \*    \*

*Never, never, never* store an old refrigerator outdoors or in a place where a small child could climb inside. Always remove the door of any junked refrigerator or place the refrigerator with the door flush against a wall when stored. In some cities there are safety organizations which will come pick up discarded refrigerators and dispose of them.

\*    \*    \*

P    *The door won't stay shut.*
S    More than likely, the gasket around the inside of the door needs cleaning. Gently pull the gasket up and you will probably find spills, etc. Use an old toothbrush and some soapy water to clean under the gasket and this problem should disappear. (Also see Refrigerator—Out of Order p. 45)

\*    \*    \*

Make your refrigerator door a message center or an art gallery for your little ones. Magnets in all shapes and sizes will hold your notes or artwork in view.
(See also *Bulletin Board,* p. 23)

## REFRIGERATOR—OUT OF ORDER
Before calling a serviceman, check the following:
1. Is the refrigerator plugged in?

2. Is there a fuse blown or a breaker tripped?

3. Does it need defrosting?

4. Vacuum underneath it and around the back.

5. Check the gaskets to make sure they close tightly.

*       *       *

If your refrigerator goes out, pack your food in an ice chest. For frozen foods, dry ice can be purchased. A fairly small amount of dry ice will keep frozen foods frozen for several days, and there is no mess to clean up such as with ice melting.

If you "ice down" your foods in an extra bathtub or washer not in use, the water will simply drain out and you'll have no mess.

### Stove (Also see Oven, p. 39)

If you're one of those people who automatically go YUCK at the mere mention of the word "stove," join the club! I guess that's the biggest, never-ending job we've got—keeping that critter clean!

However burdensome stove care is, it sure beats cooking Abe Lincoln-style, in a fireplace, or hauling in wood like great-grandma did for the old wood burner! Keep that in mind, and take good care of that feast-fixing family friend.

Whoever said "An ounce of prevention is worth a pound of cure" must have been talking about stovetops and ovens! I'd like to share with you some of the things I've learned (mostly the hard way) about caring for stoves.

Keep some baking soda handy in case of grease fires (a fire extinguisher in the kitchen is your best bet). Be sure to keep the baking soda on the refrigerator or near at hand—never on the back of the stove because you may have to reach across the fire to get to it. Remember, throw a lid on the skillet to smother out the fire; in an oven fire, leave the door closed.

Store matches in your kitchen in a can with a lid. Also, you can toss used matches in an empty soft drink can to prevent wastebasket fires. (Also see Candles, Caution p. 192)

\* \* \*

P How can I get and keep my burner bibs clean?
S Vinegar and baking soda are a few of the household items you can try. Remember that oven cleaners, ammonia or soap pads may pit or scratch chrome burner bibs (and most *are* made of chrome). Once you get them clean, line them with foil to keep them clean.

Also, a nifty trick is to cover burners not in use (especially when you're frying) with a pie tin or plate while using other burners. Spills, boil-overs and splashes will be kept to a minimum on burner bibs if you practice this.

\* \* \*

P The flames don't burn evenly on my gas stove.
S Remove your grates and look at your burners. Clean them well with a toothbrush and make sure they're grease-free. Then take a toothpick and poke it in each little hole. More than likely, the stove has some clogged up holes.

\* \* \*

P My stovetop burners are really grimy.
S Soak them in a little water and dishwasher detergent for an hour or so and scrub well. Then wash them in the dishwasher.

\* \* \*

P Why does the burner on my gas range emit soot?
S This is a sure sign your burner needs adjusting. The utility company in our area usually does this as a free service for customers. Why not check with your local utility company on this?

Some stoves have a drip tray. Pull or remove your stove knobs and lo and behold! There's a little tray that slides out. These trays get covered with glob and gluk—and did you know that cockroaches feast on that mess? So, keep 'em clean!

\*　　\*　　\*

If you'll use a paper towel or napkin to wipe off the grease before you tackle your stove, you'll find it makes an easier and faster job of cleaning it when you take your cloth and soap or whatever to clean it.

\*　　\*　　\*

Covering the electric buttons on your stove with plastic wrap to keep grease from getting in them will save you a heap on a service call later on!

\*　　\*　　\*

If you have the type of stove where you can turn off the pilot light on your gas burners, you can save quite a few pennies by turning it off and using matches each time to light your stove. Also, in the summer your kitchen will stay much cooler without that pilot light on.

\*　　\*　　\*

P　　　*I have a tiny space between my stove and cabinet that catches spills.*

S　　　Put strips of transparent plastic tape along this space. You can also buy an aluminum strip to cover the gap.

\*　　\*　　\*

If you're lucky enough to have a timer on your stove, use it to remind yourself when to take clothes out of the washer, when to leave for appointments, take medicine, make a phone call, etc.

\*　　\*　　\*

P　　　*My new wallpaper behind my stove is getting grease spots on it.*

S         Clean that wallpaper thoroughly and then cover it
with *clear* adhesive-backed paper and it will stay
fresh as a daisy for years to come!

\*    \*    \*

A neat (and best of all, free) splatter guard can be made by tying or
fastening three foil TV dinner trays together and placing them
around your skillet while frying.

\*    \*    \*

The grates of your stove can be placed on a cabinet and are super
for cooling pies and cakes. You won't have to hunt for the old cake
rack.

\*    \*    \*

P         *My vented hood filter is grungy.*
S         If "grungy" means covered with grease, I gotcha!
Just place the whole filter into the dishwasher and
will you be amazed. If you don't have a dishwasher, soak and rinse it in the bathtub or sink in
*dishwasher* detergent and water.

\*    \*    \*

Use red nail polish to mark the "off" position on your stove knobs.
This will conserve energy and money from stoves being left on accidentally.

\*    \*    \*

P         *Keeping my aluminum stovetop clean is difficult.*
S         If hot sudsy water won't do the job, try a paste of
cream of tartar and water, or a commercial aluminum cleaner. Aluminum is easily discolored and
pitted, so be very careful "concocting" home
remedies.

\*    \*    \*

P         *My ceramic stovetop is discolored.*
S         Vinegar to the rescue, again! Just wipe some white

vinegar on, let it sit a minute, and wipe clean. Voila!

\* \* \*

P
S

*My chrome doesn't shine.*
Use vinegar or window cleaner to make your chrome sparkle! I promise once it dries you can't smell a thing.

\* \* \*

P
S

*My coppertone stove looks dingy.*
You probably have a soap film or buildup of some type. Put a little vinegar on a cloth and rub. Or, add one-half cup cornstarch to a gallon of warm water and wipe with this mixture.

\* \* \*

P
S

*The enamel finish on my stove is chipped.*
Porcelain repair kits are now on the market. Colors can be mixed to get just the right shade.

## APPLIANCES, SMALL
**(Also see Utensils, p. 95 and Appliances for the bath p. 102)**

If you know you're going to be on the phone for a long period of time, gather your small appliances near the phone and polish while you talk!

*   *   *

If you plan to use an electric appliance on a dining table, place strong rubber bands on the table legs and thread the cord through. If someone trips on the cord, the cord will come loose from the wall, but the appliance will be more likely to stay on the table.

*   *   *

Why not make pockets in your appliance covers to store cords in? Color-code plugs with squares of plastic tape (blue for toaster, red for mixer, etc.) or paint *T* for toaster, *P* for percolator, etc., on the plug with fingernail polish.

### Blender (Also see Mixer, p. 53)

P       *Is there an easy way to clean my blender?*
S       The easiest way is to add a little soap and water,
        put the top on, turn the blender on and let it clean
        itself. Rinse and dry. A baby's bottle brush will
        reach those hard-to-get-at spots. Of course, never
        immerse the bottom part of your blender in water.

*   *   *

Don't let liquids stand in your blender for long periods of time. Three or four hours won't hurt it, but avoid longer periods of time (it's hard on the gaskets).

*   *   *

P       *My blender leaves marks on my cabinet.*
S       Glue little pieces of felt to the feet of it.

P    *I use my blender for orange juice, and rings of orange pulp are difficult to remove.*

S    Put a little water and some cracked ice in your blender, pop the top on and zap for a few seconds.

\* \* \*

P    *I used a fork to push food down to the blender blades and I ruined my blender. Please warn others of this.*

S    Use a plastic straw to push food down near the blades instead of a metal utensil and you won't have a torn-up blender.

## Can Opener, electric, (Also see Can Opener, p. 96)

P    *How can I clean my electric can opener?*

S    First of all, unplug it before you begin to clean it. Use hot, soapy water and an old toothbrush to get under the teeth of the blade; follow with a hot water rinse. Never immerse an electric can opener in water. You can also use a pipe cleaner to clean under the blades.

   After cleaning, lubricate your can opener using a cotton-tipped swab and cooking oil.

\* \* \*

When your electric can opener doesn't open like it used to, replace the cutting wheel instead of the entire unit.

## Coffee Pot/Maker/Percolator

P    *When I run out of coffee filters, is there a substitute?*

S    In a pinch, make your own filters out of heavy-quality white paper napkins.

\* \* \*

**P**     *My percolator is still good but the glass knob doesn't fit tightly.*

**S**     Wrap a strip or two of aluminum foil around the knob until it fits snugly. By the way, you can get a replacement top for under a dollar at appliance repair shops.

\*    \*    \*

**P**     *The spout on my percolator needs cleaning—I think it's causing a bitter taste in the coffee.*

**S**     Yep, that will do it. Grab a piece of nylon net and push it through the spout with a stick or pipe-cleaner.

\*    \*    \*

**P**     *I have a new automatic drip coffeemaker but my percolator is still good. What can I do with the percolator?*

**S**     You can boil eggs in it, boil weiners or small ears of corn, or keep it full of hot water to make instant tea, coffee or hot chocolate.

\*    \*    \*

**P**     *My coffeepot has stains inside it.*

**S**     Put a couple of tablespoons of automatic dish-washing detergent in it (make sure it's *not* aluminum) and let it perk for a few minutes. Rinse well.

*Crock Pot, see Slow Cooker, p. 62.*

## Disposal

If you don't have a disposal and you don't want vegetable scraps in your trash, liquefy them in your blender and use the liquid for fertilizer around your trees and shrubs. Or, flush the liquid scraps down your commode.

\*    \*    \*

P   *Sometimes my disposal doesn't work.*

S   Many disposals have a restart button that will need to be pushed. It is usually red.

## Knives, electric

Use an electric knife to slice angel food cake—works super!

\*   \*   \*

To avoid accidents, disconnect electric knives immediately after use.

## Mixer (Also see Blender, p. 50)

P   *When I'm mixing, the batter always comes up the beaters to the base of my mixer and makes a mess.*

S   Spray the beaters with a vegetabie nonstick spray before you start mixing.

\*   \*   \*

P   *My mixer bowl slides*

S   Place a damp cloth or towel under it.

\*   \*   \*

P   *My mixer causes splatters all over everything*

S   Use a large brown bag, cut the bottom out and place the bag over the bowl and the mixer. The splatter will go only on the bag. Or, if you place the bowl in your sink, you will only have the sink to rinse out when you're finished.

\*   \*   \*

If you use one certain bowl for mixing, store your beaters and spatula in that bowl—no more hunting.

*Skillet, electric*

You can use your electric skillet to cook corn-on-the-cob, or you can heat rolls in it by placing the rolls on a cake rack in your covered skillet.

\*   \*   \*

Make little foil "bowls" to place different types of leftovers in and heat them in your electric skillet.

\*   \*   \*

P       *What can you do with an old electric skillet that doesn't work anymore?*

S       How about removing the legs from it and using it as a skillet on top of your stove? Or, if it's beyond that (like mine was), it can make a nifty feeding bowl for your pet.

\*   \*   \*

P       *How can I get black carbon off the bottom of my electric skillet?*

S       Dampen the bottom of your skillet, sprinkle automatic dishwashing detergent on it, and then place several damp paper towels over this. Let it sit for a while. Repeat if necessary.

\*   \*   \*

To fry in a practically grease-free way, prop up one leg of your electric skillet slightly. The grease will then drain down to one side.

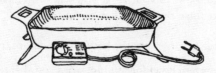

*Slow Cooker*

Keep apple cider hot for a large group, heat it in your slow cooker and then reduce the setting to keep the cider warm.

\* \* \*

Use your slow cooker to keep candy coatings warm (especially good for dipping cherries).

\* \* \*

P      *Help! How do I get dried-on food and goop out of my slow cooker?*

S      Fill the slow cooker with water and dishwashing liquid and let it "cook" for one-half hour or so. It'll be easy as pie to wash then.

\* \* \*

You can cook hot dogs in your slower cooker, too. Cook the weiners for twenty to thirty minutes and then set the buns on top of the weiners for the last ten minutes. Be sure the buns are placed on top of the weiners or they will get wet if they fall in the juices at the bottom of the slow cooker.

\* \* \*

If you have to apply hot packs to an injury, keep the hot pack solution hot in your slow cooker.

\* \* \*

If you're serving food to a large group, borrow four or five slow cookers and put the meat in one, vegetables in another, potatoes in one, rolls in another and so on. The food can be kept at serving temperature while you wash your pots and pans or attend to last-minute details.

\* \* \*

If you need a large strainer, use the basket from your large party-size percolator.

*Toaster*

You can make a toaster cover and two pot holders to match from one valance if you are buying new kitchen curtains and want to put those old ones to good use.

\* \* \*

P *My toaster finish has lost its lustre.*

S Polish it with a little ammonia and water, or white vinegar using a soft cloth.

\* \* \*

P *Is there a way to heat English muffins in a toaster?*

S Stick a toothpick through the top of the muffin and let the toothpick lie across the opening of the toaster. This will allow most of the muffin to drop into the toaster yet remain suspended by the toothpick.

\* \* \*

P *How do I get stuck toast out of a toaster?*

S Use a wooden spatula. Be sure to unplug your toaster before digging with the spatula.

\* \* \*

Did you know that most toasters have a hinged tray on the bottom that catches crumbs? Be sure to keep the crumbs out of your toaster (remember, they attract bugs).

*Waffle Iron*

P *My waffles always seem to stick on my waffle iron.*

S Never leave a waffle iron wet; always clean and dry it thoroughly; then, temper your iron. Waffle irons need to be tempered after each use.

 Clean the iron and then brush the iron with

salad oil. Or, temper the iron by rubbing both sides of a piece of bread with *unsalted* fat, let the bread brown. This will grease the squares.

## CABINETS
**(Also see Medicine Cabinet, p. 106)**

Until someone invents a kitchen cabinet impervious to kids and hubby, I guess we'll have to keep on cleaning kitchen cabinets!

I clean mine whenever they start bothering me (from the looks of them now they haven't bothered me in a long time!)—sometimes it's late at night, sometimes it's when I need to work off a little steam, or sometimes it's on a cold, rainy day.

Sometimes it's just like Christmas, stumbling across things I'd forgotten I'd had! Not being "tall," I can tell you "persactly" what's on the lower two or three shelves. But if Robert Redford were hiding on my top shelf, I'd never find him!

The best way to organize your cabinets is to think YOU! If you're tempted to place your items in the order you saw in the latest home decorating magazine, it probably won't work. Put some newspapers all over your floor and then empty everything onto your floor. If you've got pots and pans and lids in three different places, why not toss them all in an old dishpan or a cardboard box and set them in a handy lower cabinet near your stove.

If you're reaching over that pan you use only to bake fruitcake in during the holidays, move it and others like it to a box and store them on a shelf in your utility room or garage or some other nook. It's better to go fetch them once or twice a year and wash them up than to fret and fume every time you have to move them to get to an item you use daily.

Also, why not keep only the size pans you use every day and store those extra pans and odd-size pans? You only have four burners, so why keep gobs of pans around? You probably use the same ones over and over.

If you have a worn-out chest of drawers or can pick one up cheap at a garage sale, they are super for storing cookie cutters, small utensils, cake decorating kits, etc. A friend of mine with a large accumulation of plastic food-storage containers keeps the lids to them in a drawer. She gave up trying to keep the lids with the bowls (her four kids kept them scattered in every drawer), so she places all of them in a chest drawer and they're easily found. You can set the chest on a back porch or in the garage or utility room if you don't like the looks of it in your kitchen.

If you don't like stooping or it's hard on your back, who says cleaning supplies have to go under the sink? Put them on a shelf you can easily reach and store seldom-used items under your sink. If you have little ones around it's a lot safer to store cleaning supplies up higher anyway. There's some good hints in this chapter on how to secure cabinets from young children, so we'll talk about that in a minute.

I hope that this little section will guide you in organizing your cabinets. Well-organized cabinets will save you time, and make preparing and serving meals a lot easier. It will do wonders for your disposition, too!

### Decorating

P  *I covered my old cabinets with adhesive-backed paper but there are bubbles in it.*

S  Just prick the bubble with a pin or needle and press it down. The pin hole won't show.

### Doors and Drawers
*(Also see Drawers, p. 214 and Childproofing, p. 339)*

P  *How can I keep my baby out of the kitchen cabinets?*

S  Try hooking a dog collar through the handles over knobs, or rubber bands or shower curtain rings (three hooked together) through the handles.

\*    \*    \*

P       *My cabinet doors have magnetic catches that are really hard to open.*

S       Try putting a little piece of transparent tape over the magnetic catches.

\*     \*     \*

P       *The catch on my metal cabinet is broken and an always-open cabinet door is bugging me.*

S       An easy way to solve this is to take a little magnet and glue it where it catches.

\*     \*     \*

Need a little table for a visiting child? Pull out a lower cupboard drawer, lay a cookie sheet on it and close the drawer until the cookie sheet fits snug.

\*     \*     \*

If you're blessed with drawer space, tuck those spice cans away in a small drawer—oh, so handy!

\*     \*     \*

P       *I want my toddler close at hand to keep an eye on him, but his banging pots and pans when I'm in the kitchen is driving me "buggy."*

S       If space will allow, clean out one lower shelf of your kitchen cabinets and put only his toys there. Tell him that this is HIS shelf, but all the rest are YOURS.

        He'll be happier and so will you.

\*     \*     \*

Remember, don't store poisons or cleaning supplies where a baby or child can get to them. If you do have your cleaning supplies under your sink, keep a bicycle lock handy and when children visit, put it between the handles of your sink cabinet.

*Interiors*

**P**     *I have a hard time seeing to the back of my lower cabinets.*

**S**     Its probably because they are dark. If you paint the inside of the cabinets with a coat of bright, white paint, it will really make a difference. Painting just the inside back wall may work. Lining the sides with tin foil to reflect some light also helps.

          *   *   *

**P**     *My pots leave marks on my shelving paper.*

**S**     Just stick a paper plate under each pan when you store it. (You can use the same plate over and over.)

          *   *   *

Write your most-used cookie recipes, cornbread recipe, etc., on 3 × 5-inch cards and tape them to the inside of your cabinet near your flour and sugar. You won't have to drag out your cookbook as often.

          *   *   *

**P**     *My cleaning supplies are always a mess.*

**S**     You can tote your furniture polish, window spray, all your cleaning supplies from room to room in a sturdy plastic tub and then just slide the whole thing under your sink. This is what I do, but I don't have children around who can get into that place.

          *   *   *

Line your shelves with aluminum foil or wax paper. It will protect your shelves and they will be easier to clean next time. Just wad the lining up and throw away.

          *   *   *

If your family is always asking where something is, you can save wear and tear on the old vocal cords by placing a little fruit sticker or magnet on each shelf. Just holler back, "It's behind the banana!" or whatever.

* * *

Store a few spoons, some plastic cereal bowls and plastic juice glasses in your lower cabinets, and even small children can set a breakfast table and prepare cereal.

## Metal Cabinets

**P**     *My metal cabinets look simply awful.*

**S**     Well, of course, sanding them down and repainting them is the best way. But if that sounds like too much work or if you're pinching pennies (and who isn't these days), try covering them with adhesive-backed paper. You get a variety of colors and designs.

* * *

**P**     *I'm replacing my metal cabinets with new wood ones. Any suggestions for using the metal cabinets elsewhere?*

**S**     Would be great to have extra storage for tools in the garage, or how about storing books or magazines in them up in the attic?

## Wood Cabinets

**P**     *How can I get grease spots off my wood cabinets?*

**S**     Wet a cloth with a little water and vinegar and wipe over the spots. Dry with a clean cloth or paper towel.

* * *

**P**   *How can I polish my wood cabinets?*

**S**   One reader suggested using *neutral* shoe polish paste. She said it made her cabinets look as good as new. I would do just a little test spot in an inconspicuous place before I tried any kind of polish or wax on my wood cabinets.

## DISHES AND GLASSWARE

A flat rubber sink stopper placed under a bowl will keep the bowl from slipping. This is especially helpful for a handicapped person.

\* \* \*

Buy white dishes to fill in broken dish sets.

\* \* \*

An old warped hi-fi record covered with plastic wrap makes a cute cake plate for a teen-age party.

\* \* \*

Taking a dish to a covered luncheon or picnic? Make sure you get it back by writing your name and address on a piece of transparent tape with a permanent ink marking pen. Stick the tape to the bottom of the dish; even if it's washed, your name will still be readable.

\* \* \*

Tired of your dishes? Why not swap sets with a neighbor or friend for a few weeks?

\* \* \*

## Chips and Scratches

**P**    *Is there any way to salvage fine china that has nicks and chips?*

**S**    Try gently sanding down the nicks and chips. The fine, wet-looking sandpaper with a cloth backing seems to work best. You can take it to a professional.

\*     \*     \*

**P**    *My ironstone dishes have gray scratch marks.*

**S**    These marks are caused from scratches due to improper storage. To remove the gray marks, rub the dishes with a baking soda and water paste and wipe clean. Store your dishes with circles of felt or paper or paper plates between items. If you can, store the cups on hooks to prevent scratching.

## Cleaning
(Also see Dishwasher, p. 31)

**P**    *How can I remove stains from my plastic dishes?*

**S**    Rub a paste of baking soda and water over the stains. Or, use a very diluted bleach and water solution.
(Caution: too strong a bleach solution may take the glaze off.)

\*     \*     \*

**P**    *I would use my lovely "special dishes" more often if they weren't dusty and didn't require washing for each occasion.*

**S**    If you have storage space in your cabinets, wash your set of dishes and then cover all the glassware with small plastic sandwich bags. Use larger plastic bags to dustproof the serving pieces.

    Or, some folks that don't wash a whole load of dishes in their dishwashers take a few of their "special dishes" and add to the load—that way, you avoid washing the whole set at one time when that "occasion" arises.

\*    \*    \*

Gold-banded or gold-decorated china and glassware should never be washed in an automatic dishwasher.

\*    \*    \*

A thought: Although it certainly is convenient to use disposable dishes when taking food to families of deceased persons, it actually may be better for the families if we used our special china dishes. The bereaved person needs to get out of the house, visit friends, and not totally withdraw. Cleaning and returning the dishes will help the grieved person stay in touch.

\*    \*    \*

Be sure to rotate your dishes. Put the just-washed plates on the bottom of the stack and use the ones off the top of the stack. All of your plates will then stay fresh and dust-free.

\*    \*    \*

P          *I have some beautiful glasses that are stained and discolored.*

S          Drop a tablet sold for cleaning dentures in your glasses with water. Should do the trick!


## FLOORS

On the subject of floor care, a dear gentleman named Bobbs said it all: "When I see a spot on my light color vinyl, it may be only a shadow, so I just eye it for a moment. If it doesn't go away then I clean it up. If it wiggles I step on it!"

I hope there are no more Cinderellas tied down to scrubbing and waxing floors day after day. I think this section will "free" you from the drudgery part and give you time to go to "the ball" or the grocery store or the post office or other exciting places!

## Cleaning and Maintaining

**P**       *I mop my floor, yet it never looks really shiny.*

**S**       You probably have a film left on the floor. Mix one-half cup vinegar with about a gallon of lukewarm or cool water and go over the floor after you've mopped. Be sure your mop is clean.

\*    \*    \*

**P**       *We are moving into a beautiful new home and we want to keep the floors looking like new.*

**S**       I'll be glad to give you a little advice! This is what my mom taught me to do. (1) Dust the floors daily either with a dust mop or a vacuum cleaner so that tracked-in dirt or grit is not ground into the floors. This applies mainly to the traffic areas—it is not necessary to dust under the couch, bed, etc., *every* day. (2) Wipe up any spills immediately. (3) Take time to read the cleaning instructions and recommendations of the manufacturer for your type of floor or carpeting. (4) Always test an unfamiliar product by spot cleaning or treating in an inconspicuous place.

\*    \*    \*

Set your table legs in coasters or rubber casters to keep them from making indentations on your kitchen floor. Moleskin sheets or plasters you buy at the drugstore work well, too.

\*    \*    \*

**P**       *My child got crayon marks on my terrazzo floor.*

**S**       Would you believe a plain old eraser will get them up? An eraser also will sometimes help remove heel marks.

\*    \*    \*

Having trouble dusting your floors in the nooks and crannies? Put on an old pair of wool socks and put those little footsies to work!

Take the socks off and shake them into a trash bag when they've accumulated the dust and then go back to it! You get some exercise, too.

\*    \*    \*

**P**      *How can I pick up small pieces of shattered glass without cutting myself?*

**S**      Pick up the pieces with a dampened cotton ball, or heavy paper towel.

\*    \*    \*

**P**      *How do I get black heel marks off my vinyl floor?*

**S**      First, try a damp cloth and baking soda, or rub a little nongel toothpaste on the mark.

\*    \*    \*

**P**      *How can I get up a gooey spill?*

**S**      Pour salt on most gooey spills and let dry. Then sweep it up and throw the mess away.

\*    \*    \*

**P**      *How do I get the white water spots off my asphalt tile?*

**S**      Rub a little liquid vegetable oil on the spot *only*. It may take more than one application, but it will do the job.

\*    \*    \*

P        *I can't get rid of a squeak in my hardwood floor.*

S        Take a thin bar of soap and rub it down in the crack or "squeak area" as much as you can. Wipe off the excess soap. Or , melt some paraffin in an old pan you can throw out (better still, use an empty coffee can) and add a small amount of light brown shoe polish to match your floors. Gently work the mixture into the crack or squeak.

\*     \*     \*

P        *I have some horrible scratches on my hardwood floor.*

S        Rub walnut or pecan meat into the scratch. You may have to repeat this several times. This really does help.

\*     \*     \*

To keep your favorite rocker from scratching or marring hardwood floors, glue a piece of weather stripping or strips of felt on the bottom of the rocker.

\*     \*     \*

To avoid splashing wax or cleaner on table legs, set each leg in an aluminum square and then fold the square up around the table leg.

\*     \*     \*

P        *My entrance way is a mess in winter. I'm afraid the salt and water tracked in will ruin my floor.*

S        It sure will, luv. Why not put a plastic drop cloth down as a liner, and then a piece of indoor-outdoor carpet right in front of the door?

\*     \*     \*

Out of floor wax? Add one-half cup cornstarch to a gallon of lukewarm water and mop. It will make your floor shine better than the same amount of wax will.

\*     \*     \*

Remember, the more you buff paste-waxed floors, the fewer folks you will have slipping down.

\*    \*    \*

Use nylon net to scrub with when removing wax buildup.

\*    \*    \*

To prevent gumminess and streaks, buff the entire floor before and after applying wax.

\*    \*    \*

If your washer or dryer is in your kitchen area, don't try to wax your floor while they are in operation. The heat they put out can make your floor gummy and it will not dry properly.

### Floor Covering

Bored with a dingy, drab kitchen floor? Buy some adhesive-backed paper with a large flower print. Cut out the flowers and stick them around the floor.

\*    \*    \*

**P**     *How can I remove vinyl tiles?*
**S**     Some of my readers have suggested putting foil
        over the tile and ironing over the tile (wool setting)
        for a few seconds. Then repeat the ironing after a
        bit and lift the tile off with a spatula or pancake
        turner.

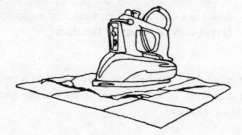

If you want to make a throw rug warm and cozy, place newspapers underneath.

*    *    *

To keep throw rugs from slipping, glue or stitch those foam fabric-softener sheets to the backing, or put a thick foam-rubber pad under the rug.

*    *    *

Avoid discoloring your new kitchen floor—do not use scatter rugs with rubber backings on the new no-wax flooring. The rubber backing will cause discoloration over a period of time.

## FOOD PREPARATION
### (Also see Cooking Out, p. 280)

I just love to open up a magazine and view those luscious foods pictured there. (Honestly, I sometimes think those calories jump right off the page and land in *me!*) It's a joy to create dishes that please our family and friends.

But, as we all know very well, casseroles, salads, soups, whatever, just don't happen! And that's what this section is about—ways to make food preparation easier, more enjoyable, more efficient, and perhaps a little more economical.

*    *    *

Planning a buffet? Write the names of the dishes you're going to serve and put them where you plan to arrange the dishes on the serving table. You won't be as likely to forget any salad or refrigerated dish when you are ready to serve.

*    *    *

When mixing messy things, if you put your bowls in the sink, all the spills go down the drain. No messy countertop cleanup.

*    *    *

Want to save a few pennies on the paper towel bill? Place some newspapers under a couple of paper towels to absorb grease and drain food on.

\* \* \*

P    *I love to experiment with new recipes, but keeping the pages of my cookbook clean and open is a pain.*

S    One way to solve that would be to slide a rubber band across the pages, or take a glass pie plate and place it upside down on your cookbook. An added bonus is that the curved bottom of the pie plate actually magnifies the print!

\* ☉ ✿

A handy and cheap way to have a recipe card holder is simply put the card in the tines of a fork and then put the fork handle in a glass!

\* \* \*

P    *Is there any way to salvage scorched food?*

S    Yes, but you have to act fast. Immediately take the pan to the sink and set it in cool water. Do not scrape the pan. Carefully transfer the food that is not scorched into another pan. The scorched food will stick; the good food will not.

Need to transport a pot of soup or casserole? Place the pan or dish in a large zippered plastic bag and seal. If spills occur, the bag catches them.

\* \* \*

Training a young cook? Hold the spoon backwards when stirring to avoid burns; the splatters will be away from the youngster.

## Bacon

**P**      *What can I do to keep bacon from sticking together in the package?*

**S**      Roll your bacon package in a tube shape and put a rubber band around it before you refrigerate it.

## Bananas, freezing

Got some overripe bananas? Mash them up and put them in a plastic bag. Freeze. Use them later for making banana bread.

## Breads, Buns, and Rolls

Have trouble getting bread to rise in cold weather? If you have a gas oven with a pilot light, just pop in the bread and let it rise. Or, turn the oven to 200°F, let it heat, then turn it off and put the bread in to rise.

\* \* \*

Ever try putting aluminum foil under the napkin in your roll basket to keep them hotter longer? Or, a preheated ceramic tile really does the job.

\* \* \*

**P**      *Does anybody know what to do with leftover hot dog buns after a cookout? They're usually so dry and hard!*

**S**      Just slice 'em into sticks. Butter them, sprinkle a little garlic powder and Parmesan cheese, and then toast them in your oven. They are dandy crumbled over salads. Another favorite of mine is "instant pizza." Spread tomato paste over the bun, put a slice of your favorite "pizza-type" cheese on top, some pepperoni (salami is good, too), other toppings you like, and then bake until the cheese melts. Yummy!

## Brown Sugar

P    *How can I soften hardened brown sugar?*

S    Place the brown sugar in a jar or plastic bag. Put a damp paper towel across the top of the sugar. Redampen the paper towel if necessary; the softening process may take several days. To keep brown sugar soft, always store it in a plastic bag. Or, put a piece of apple with the sugar in the box.

## Butter

To soften butter in a hurry, measure it and then take your potato peeler and shred it.

## Cabbage Odor

P    *I love cabbage but don't like the smell it leaves in my house.*

S    How about adding a little vanilla or cinnamon to a pan of water and let it steam while you're cooking cabbage—it will mask the cabbage smell.

## Cakes

Dislike getting those fingers greasy when greasing a cake pan or casserole? Slip your fingers into a plastic sandwich bag and grease away.

P    *How can I keep cakes from rising up in the middle?*
S    Wrap a strip of wet toweling such as terry cloth around the outside of the cake pan. Reducing the oven temperature also helps. In addition, grease the bottom of the pan only (don't grease the sides); this seems to help.

\*    \*    \*

P    *My chocolate cakes always look tacky because they have the white flour on them that I used to dust the pans with.*
S    If you dust the pans with cocoa instead of flour, you can eliminate that little problem forever!

\*    \*    \*

P    *My mix cakes sometimes seem a little dry and crumbly.*
S    Just add two tablespoons of cooking oil to your mix. It makes your cake more moist and gives it a better texture.

\*    \*    \*

P    *What can I do when the frosting is too thin?*
S    Add a little powdered sugar until you have the desired consistency.

\*    \*    \*

Want picture-perfect cake slices? Freeze your cakes first and then slice.

\* \* \*

Sprinkle some powdered sugar onto your cake plate and your cake won't stick.

### Canned Food

Here's a tip from my college days when living in a dorm with no kitchen. Fill the bathroom sink with the hottest water possible. Place a can of soup, spaghetti or whatever in the sink and shake the can occasionally. Add more hot water every now and then, and you'll have a heated meal.

### Citrus Peels

Lemon or orange peels are easier to grate when frozen.

### Cookies

P How can cookies be kept soft in a cookie jar?
S Put a slice or two of bread in the cookie jar.

\* \* \*

Leftover icing? Spread the icing between two cookies for a delicious treat.

### Corn Silk

P How do I get corn silk off of corn on the cob?
S Get that old faithful kitchen toothbrush and brush downward on the cob.

*Dough*
*(Also see Rolling Pin, p. 99)*

P      *Dough sticks to my rolling pin.*

S      Try placing the rolling pin and the pastry cloth in a plastic bag and keeping it in your freezer until used. An old, clean knee sock makes a good cloth to prevent dough sticking.

*Eggs*

P      *Is there anything at all I can do if I run one egg short right in the middle of making something?*

S      There's nothing more frustrating, right? Well, just grab one teaspoon of that old standby cornstarch *or* one teaspoon vinegar and substitute it for the missing egg. This will squeak you by just fine for *one* missing egg, but of course it won't work for any more. Also, you'll need to increase the liquid in the recipe by three or four tablespoons.

              *     *     *

P      *My egg whites never seem to stay stiff and sometimes never even get stiff—what am I doing wrong?*

S      Your utensils and bowl must be grease-free; absolutely no egg yolk allowed; let your eggs warm to room temperature before you beat them. While beating them, add one teaspoon of cream of tartar to each seven or eight egg whites.

*Fish*

P      *How can I tell if a fish is fresh?*

S      The eyes have it! The eyes should be bright and clear. A fresh fish will have red or pink gills, and its scales will be shiny. Don't buy a fish that has sunken or cloudy eyes.

### Food Coloring

**P**      *I accidentally added too much food coloring to a batter. Could I have fixed it?*

**S**      If you haven't stirred it in, next time grab some paper towels and soak up the excess coloring with the towels.

### Gelatin

**P**      *I love to take molded gelatin salads to luncheon but I can't keep them looking as firm and pretty as they are when I take them out of the refrigerator.*

**S**      This is a problem especially when the weather is a wee bit warm. However, if you'll add a mere teaspoon of white vinegar to your recipe, this will help your gelatins keep firm.

### Gravy

**P**      *What can one do when the gravy turns out too thin?*

**S**      Reheat the gravy. Dissolve a little cornstarch in water and add to the gravy and stir.

### Hamburger shaping

I have several gadgets in my kitchen for shaping perfectly round hamburger patties. But I get in a hurry and just grab this old standby which works just as super! Just take a full No. 2½ can out of your pantry, clean the bottom, press down on the patty and then trim.

### Meatloaf

Need to hurry up that meatloaf for supper? Bake five or six small ones instead of one large loaf.

## Meringue

**P**    *How can I make a really fluffy meringue?*
**S**    Add one-fourth teaspoon of white vinegar to three egg whites. The vinegar really does make a difference!

## Milk

**P**    *My child doesn't like to drink milk.*
**S**    Add a little food coloring or vanilla flavoring to it. It will look and taste better.

## Onions

**P**    *How do I keep onions from making me cry when I'm cutting them?*
**S**    The best thing I've found is to keep those onions refrigerated until you need one. The colder the onion is, the less you'll cry. Other readers have said it helps if you keep your mouth closed tightly, or peel them under cold, running water,

## Parmesan, serving

Baffled as to how to serve Parmesan cheese? A covered bonbon dish is an excellent choice.

## Pie

Want to bake pies up ahead of time for a holiday and don't have enough pie pans? Mix up your pie fillings, line your pie pans with foil, add filling and freeze. When frozen, remove pie-shaped fillings and leave in freezer. This way, you don't tie up your pie pans in your freezer, and you can finish baking your fruit pies when you have the time.

\*    \*    \*

**P**   *How do bakers get that lovely sheen on their pie crusts?*

**S**   Vinegar! Yep, then take that pie crust out of the oven just a few minutes before it's ready, brush the top with a little white vinegar (or cider), and then plop it back in the oven.

### Potatoes

**P**   *How can I keep the skins of my baked potatoes from cracking?*

**S**   The secret to this is to rub butter or shortening over the potatoes before you bake them.

### Salt

**P**   *How can I keep salt flowing freely in the shaker?*
**S**   Add a cracker or a few grains of rice to the shaker. Also, remember to keep the salt in a warm, dry place.

\*     \*     \*

**P**   *How can I keep sugar and salt from getting caked?*
**S**   If you'll put a glass or mixing bowl over the shaker or bowl, you won't have caked sugar or salt.

\*     \*     \*

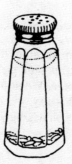

Attach a 2½-inch strip of cellophane tape to make a tab on salt or cereal boxes with the metal spout. Grab the tab to open—no wear and tear on the fingernails.

\*    \*    \*

P    *How can I keep salt and pepper from spilling when I try to fill my shakers that have the filler holes on the bottoms?*

S    Put masking tape over the holes before filling, or put some grains of rice in first and then fill.

\*    \*    \*

P    *The holes on my salt shaker are too large.*

S    Make a bit of paste with flour and water. Put some in a couple of holes, and when it dries the paste works like cement.

\*    \*    \*

P    *What can I do if I run out of salt?*

S    Cut off the top of the cardboard salt container. Under the little metal "funnel" is usually enough salt remaining to get you by.

\*    \*    \*

P    *What's the solution to too-salty food?*

S    If the dish can take it, add a pinch of sugar.

## Spices
(Also see Spice Racks, p. 29)

P    *My herbs and spices don't keep very long, but friends of mine have spices that remain fresh for long periods of time. How come?*

S    The culprit is probably heat. Are you storing your spices next to your stove? Herbs and spices should be stored in a cool, dry place.

\*    \*    \*

If you live alone and like to experiment with different spices, why not buy a spice you'd like to have and give half to a friend and vice versa! Then both of you wouldn't be out the expense or accumulate seldom-used spices.

*   *   *

You'll find it convenient to keep chili powder in a glass shaker jar.

*   *   *

Mix up cinnamon and sugar for cinnamon toast and keep it in a salt shaker.

*   *   *

P   *I goofed and got a dish too spicy; what should I have done to save it?*

S   If you can, make up another batch unseasoned and combine the two. In some instances you can add another can of cooked pinto beans, tomato juice or canned tomatoes. Sometimes adding catsup or a few drops of vinegar helps.

### Strawberries

Don't wash strawberries before refrigerating—they will become mushy. Store them in a colander or plastic woven basket so the air can circulate.

### Syrup

To make syrup or honey easier to pour out of a measuring cup, rinse the cup with hot water before pouring the syrup or honey in to be measured.

## Tea

P    *How can cloudy tea be cleared up?*

S    Refrigeration will cause tea to turn cloudy. Leave it at room temperature until you are ready to serve it. You can clear up cloudy tea by adding a little boiling water.

## Vegetables

P    *Is there a way to keep colors of vegetables from fading out while cooking?*

S    For greener cabbage and redder beets, etc., just add a little vinegar to the water while they are cooking. Did you know this will cut down on cooking odors, too?

## Waffles

P    *I always have too much leftover waffle batter.*

S    Just go ahead and cook the waffles up and freeze them until later. To heat, just drop them in the toaster.

\* \* \*

**P**       *My favorite waffle recipe is 2 cups biscuit mix, 1 egg, ½ cup oil, and 1½ cup club soda. Since this batter will be "bubbly," it will not store well.*

**S**       You should cook it all at once.

## SUBSTITUTIONS

| | |
|---|---|
| **BAKING POWDER:** | 2 tablespoons cream of tartar, 1 tablespoon baking soda, and 1 tablespoon cornstarch |
| **BROWN SUGAR:** | ½ cup granulated sugar, ½ cup molasses, plus ¼ teaspoon baking soda |
| **BUTTER:** | ⅞ cup vegetable shortening or lard |
| **BUTTERMILK:** | 1 tablespoon vinegar or lemon juice plus enough fresh milk to make one cup |
| **CAKE FLOUR:** | All-purpose flour. For one cup measure, level off and remove 2 tablespoons |
| **CORN SYRUP:** | 1 cup sugar and ¼ cup water |
| **EGG: (ONE ONLY)** | 1 teaspoon cornstarch per egg or 1 teaspoon vinegar per egg. Also, increase the liquid in the recipe by 3 or 4 tablespoons. |
| **FLOUR:** | For 1 tablespoon: 1 tablespoon cornstarch OR 1 teaspoon rice starch OR 1 tablespoon arrowroot |
| **FROSTING:** | Top with marshmallows a minute or so before removing pans from oven. |
| **HONEY:** | For 1 cup, use 1¼ cup sugar plus |

¼ cup water (do not use this substitution in delicately balanced recipes).

MILK:

½ cup evaporated milk and ½ cup water to make 1 cup milk. Or, use

1/3 cup instant nonfat milk plus

1 cup water (less 1 tablespoon water).

POWDERED SUGAR:

1 cup granulated sugar and 1 tablespoon cornstarch. Put in blender.

RED FOOD COLORING:

Red-colored sugar (like that used for Christmas baking) or unsweetened powdered soft drink mix

SHORTENING:

Peanut butter for pie crusts

SOUR CREAM:

1 cup evaporated milk plus 1 tablespoon vinegar, OR 1 cup cottage cheese blended with 1 tablespoon of milk and 1 teaspoon lemon juice.

Also, try 1 cup plain yogurt with 1 tablespoon vinegar added.

SUGAR:

Light or dark brown sugar may be used tit for tat. However, there will be a light molasses flavor.

TOMATO JUICE:

½ cup tomato sauce plus ½ cup water

TOMATO SAUCE:

8-ounce can whole tomatoes zapped in the blender

UNSWEETENED CHOCOLATE:

3 tablespoons unsweetened cocoa plus

1 tablespoon shortening or butter

WHIPPED CREAM: Slice a banana or two (to taste) in the WHITE of an egg and just beat until stiff.

No rolling pin? Place dough in a plastic bag and use a large unopened straight-sided beverage bottle as a rolling pin.

## FOOD STORAGE

### Nonrefrigerated Food

To help cut down on pantry clutter, store rice, beans, raisins, etc., in plastic containers.

\* \* \*

P *Please tell me how to get rid of weevils?*
S First, take everything out of your cabinets and destroy every box or bag that is visibly infested with weevils. Check everything including flour, meal, cereals, dried fruits, spices, dry pet food, pasta products, dry beans and peas.

To destroy unhatched eggs, place cartons in which weevils are not visible in the freezer for four days at zero degree temperature or in a 150°F to 160°F oven for thirty minutes.

Next, scrub the shelves with hot, sudsy water using a stiff bristled brush. Then spray the shelves, crevices and cabinet doors with insecticide and leave them closed for three to four hours.

After doing all of the above, put everything into sealable glass jars before returning food to the shelves.

Also, buy small quantities of staples and get into the habit of freezing them before using. Open each package when you bring it home from the store and immediately return any infested item (along with a sales receipt).

*Refrigerated Food*
*(Also see Refrigerator, p. 41)*

| | |
|---|---|
| **P** | *I store foods in bowls with lids but the odors still seem to permeate my refrigerator, and the food does not stay fresh as long as it should.* |
| **S** | A lot of the popular glassware bowls are not sealed tightly by their lids. Place a piece of plastic wrap over the bowl before you place the lid on. |

\*   \*   \*

To store canned pet food that has been opened, so your fridge won't smell, place the can inside a coffee can with a plastic lid and keep in your refrigerator.

\*   \*   \*

| | |
|---|---|
| **P** | *I can't seem to keep vegetables fresh very long in my refrigerator.* |
| **S** | If you line the bottom of your vegetable bin with newspapers covered with paper towels or napkins, you'll find that your lettuce and other veggies and fruits will stay fresher much longer. |

\*   \*   \*

Start a "distress bin"—when vegetables look pretty sad, toss them in that special bin to remind you to use them up right away or to prepare soup.

\*   \*   \*

| | |
|---|---|
| **P** | *How do I prevent ice crystals in ice cream once I've opened it?* |
| **S** | Cover the unused portion with plastic wrap before you put the lid back on and put it in the freezer. |

\*   \*   \*

Check your favorite grocery store and find out which days they receive produce deliveries and which days they put out fresh meat. It does make a difference which day you shop!

## POTS AND PANS

The Food and Drug Administration states that cookware made of aluminum is perfectly safe. The grayish substance sometimes seen on this type of cookware is harmless. Cast-iron pots and pans have been used for generations of homemakers—and the iron absorbed into foods while cooking is actually beneficial. If a cast-iron pot is not kept seasoned, some foods may turn dark and look unappealing, but this will not affect you.

It is safe to use pans with nonstick coatings after the coating have been worn or partially chipped off. The FDA reports that this coating is not dangerous to use under these conditions.

The only precaution I would give would be about using pans or pots galvanized with zinc. Certain foods which are acidic (such as tomatoes) should not be cooked in them, since zinc salts can be formed and can be toxic.

\* \* \*

I can't say this too often—always turn handles toward the rear or side of the stove where a child can't reach up and grab them. Even if you don't have children, it's a good safety habit.

\* \* \*

An old dish drainer makes a great storage container for pan lids.

### Aluminum

P           *My aluminum pans are discolored.*
S           Boil either two tablespoons vinegar or two table-

spoons cream of tartar in the pot for twenty minutes.

*    *    *

P

S

*How do I shine aluminum cookware?*

Cream of tartar works fairly well; however, I would suggest a commercial cleaner made especially for aluminum. DO NOT use any cleaner that contains ammonia—it will pit the aluminum.

## Cast Iron

P

S

*How should I care for my new cast-iron skillet?*

How lucky you are! I have letters from friends who have been using the same skillet for as long as fifty years! Obviously, they have given theirs TLC (Tender Loving Care).

More than likely, your new skillet has been preseasoned and no further seasoning is necessary. Just wash thoroughly (never in the dishwasher), dry and always lightly grease before storing.

If you've acquired a skillet that's discolored or has rust spots, you need to reseason your skillet as follows: First, get all the rust off, using a scouring pad if necessary, then wash and dry. Next, coat the inside of the pan heavily with unsalted grease (preferably suet). Coat the lid also. Place the skillet in the oven for about two hours at the lowest possible temperature. After an hour or so, wipe more grease on the sides of the pan again. After two hours, wash in good soapy suds—your skillet is now ready for use.

After each use, wash in warm, soapy water (don't use scouring powders). Wipe thoroughly, dry and then coat the inside of the pan with oil or shortening or nonstick vegetable spray.

Think DRY when you're thinking of caring for

cast-iron cookware. Wipe dry thoroughly with a cloth or paper towel. Crumple up a paper towel or newspaper and put it in the skillet to absorb moisture. Or, place your skillet back on the stove and heat it until all the moisture is gone and then store it in your cabinet. Be sure and store it in a dry place after use. If you have an oven pilot light, your oven will make an ideal storage place.

## Cleaning

**P**     *Food always sticks to my pots and pans and makes it hard to wash them.*

**S**     Some folks make up hot, sudsy dishwater and wash them as soon as the food is put in bowls. Others fill a pan with water and stick the lid back on it as soon as the pan is emptied. The whole secret to the matter is not to let the food dry out and become crusted on the pan. Let it soak until you find time to wash it.

\*    \*    \*

**P**     *How should a burned pot be cleaned?*

**S**     Dampen the pot and sprinkle baking soda on the burn. Add a little vinegar and let it stand for twenty minutes. Then wash as usual.

\*    \*    \*

Got a pan that needs scrubbing and no scrubber handy? Grab a plastic glass and turn it upside down. Loosen the "goo" with the rim of the glass.

\*    \*    \*

**P**     *My skillet has baked-on grease.*

**S**     Use a piece of nylon net and a little baking soda and water paste. Spray-on oven cleaner can be used. Of course, wash thoroughly.

## Copper

P        *How do I shine copper cookware?*

S        Make a paste of lemon juice, salt and flour, and rub it on. Or, there are very good commercial copper cleaning compounds on the market.

## Nonstick Coating

P        *My skillet is nonstick coated and it keeps getting scratched.*

S        First of all, do not use metal utensils in a skillet with this kind of coating. Secondly, always put a paper towel inside it when you store it so that other pans or articles will not scratch the inside. Also, nylon net makes a perfect scrubber and will not harm the coating.

*    *    *

P        *I love a particular skillet of mine but the coating is shot. Any way I can salvage it?*

S        Sure is! Have hubby or someone with an electric drill with a wire brush attachment grind all the coating off. You'll still have a usable skillet.

## Stainless Steel

P        *How do I shine stainless steel cookware?*

S        Oven cleaner works well to clean baked-on grease, and will help put a shine back on. Ammonia and water can be safely used on stainless steel to clean and shine.

*    *    *

If you have baked-on grease on stainless steel pots and pans, wet a cloth with ammonia and place the cloth and your pot in a plastic bag. Tie the plastic bag tightly and let it sit. This method will even clean around the handles. Caution: do not use this procedure on aluminum pans.

*    *    *

P   *I have water rings on my stainless steel pots. How can I get them off?*

S   Saturate a cotton ball with alcohol and rub.

*Teflon, see Nonstick Coating, p. 89.*


## SINKS
### (Also see Sinks in the bathroom, p. 114)

Kitchen sinks. Boy, oh, boy, they sure do take a lot of abuse sometimes, don't they? From washing the baby, to giving the pet ferret a bath, doing hand laundry and then all the "kitcheny" things like soaking pots and pans and scrubbing the broiler.

Not many of us have ever read an instruction book on the care or wear and tear of a sink, but there really are a few do's and don'ts.

Don't ever, and I mean ever, put hot grease down your sink drain. I know, I know, you always do and have never had any trouble. Well, you are really a lucky one.

My husband is a plumbing contractor and I was told in no uncertain terms, "NO!" When I asked sweetly, "Why not?" I got this explanation. Think, my dear. Where does all that stuff that you suffer the poor little kitchen sink to force down go? The plumbing in your house sometimes looks like a snake.

If you put grease in, even while running hot water, somewhere down the line it will probably congeal and stick to the sides of your pipes. Do this several times, along with the rest of the garbage you put down there and you are asking for trouble.

Before washing out the frying pan, just wipe it out with a paper towel and then proceed to wash and rinse. Don't take chances. Also, to be on the safe side, no coffee grounds or long celery strings should ever grace your drain.

Do run hot water and a little liquid soap once in awhile and a handful of ice with cold water to clean the blades of your disposal.

Don't (again from the professional in my family) use abrasive cleaners on your sinks. Even some of the supposedly mildly abrasive and liquid-type cleaners are still going to take the finish off your sink. You keep using those and you are really going to be in a lot of trouble later on.

Once that glaze is gone, your sink will look like the Fourth Army marched through there and no one bothered to clean their boots.

Do use a spray-on foamy cleaner. You can use baking soda and even sprinkle dishwasher detergent on it and scrub-a-dub without scratching the finish.

The same goes for your bathroom sink and the tub. No abrasive cleaners . . . I know we were all raised to sprinkle that compound and scrub away. If you continue to do this, you will scrub away your nice finish and then be stuck with a tub that no one wants to even sit in. And, honey child, it sure isn't cheap to replace a sink or tub . . . believe me, I know!

## Cleaning

**P**  *How can I get rid of black marks on my sink from pots and pans?*

**S**  They can be bleached out, or use nylon net and baking soda. After you get rid of the marks, prevent them from recurring by putting a plastic place mat in your sink before washing pots and pans.

\* \* \*

**P**  *I like the results of bleach, but I can't stand the smell.*

**S**  After you've rinsed the bleach out of your sink, swish a little fabric softener around in the sink and then down the drain.

\* \* \*

**P**   *We moved into an old apartment and the sink looks horrible—rust stains.*

**S**   Try making a paste of salt and lemon juice or a full-strength solution of hydrogen peroxide. There are some excellent liquid rust stain removers sold comercially that are easy to use.

\* \* \*

**P**   *How do I get stains off sink mats?*

**S**   Put your mats in your sink or your bathtub, spray them with a presoak compound and let them soak clean. Or, try sprinkling a little automatic dishwashing detergent and water on them and letting the mats soak clean. I don't recommend using bleach because bleach is too harsh on the mats and can cause color fading.

*Drains and Stoppers*
*(Also see Drains in the bath area, p. 143)*

**P**   *I have a single sink and the water starts standing because of my dishpan covering the drain.*

**S**   Set your dishpan on a cake rack and this will allow the water to drain. Be sure and protect the sink from being scratched.

\* \* \*

If you drop a small item down the drain, it can be retrieved by bubble gum (chewed, of course!) stuck onto a piece of wire (or a clothes hanger).

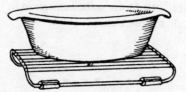

**P**     *I keep losing things because the holes in the drain are too large.*

**S**     Put a piece of nylon net across it or stuff a piece in the drain. Or, cut the top off of a scouring powder can, twist a piece of wire through two of the holes and insert this in your drain. It fits perfectly in most drains..

\*     \*     \*

**P**     *My kitchen sink "clogs" frequently, and I need to learn how to unclog it myself.*

**S**     One way is to pour one cup baking soda and one cup vinegar into the drain. When it foams up, add one pint of boiling water.

Another method is to add about a cup of laundry detergent, followed by a half gallon of boiling water, and then flush with hot tap water.

\*     \*     \*

As a preventive measure in the future, try adding a little vinegar to your dishpan or dishwasher to break up the grease and help keep grease clogs out of your sink.

\*     \*     \*

If your plunger isn't handy try covering the drain with the palm of your hand and making an up-and-down "plunging" motion with your hand.

If that old plug has about had it, slip it into a plastic bag and then insert it in the drain. You'll get a little more life out of it.

*    *    *

If you can't get the drain stopper out by pulling, remember you can work some stoppers loose by a twisting motion.

### Sink and Counter Area

A piece of peg board cut to fit one side of your sink will give you extra counter space when needed. If you cut a hole in the peg board above the opening for your disposal, you can rake the scraps right into the disposal.

*    *    *

Get some carpet padding and a piece of carpet and place it in front of your kitchen sink. When you're standing in front of that sink washing dishes, that carpet feels almost as good as kicking your shoes off!

*    *    *

If you face a blank wall while at your sink, try putting a big mirror on that wall. You can set a pretty flower arrangement where it will be reflected in the mirror, and I guarantee your sink nook will be much cheerier!

*    *    *

P    *I set a hot pan on my laminated countertop, and now I have a very ugly burn spot on it.*

S    One thing you can do is to stick one of those bathtub appliqués over the damaged area and then scatter some more here and there to give the effect of "planned" decor.

*    *    *

No sink top? Cover a board with adhesive-backed paper or paint or stain it; lay the board across the wash basin when needed.

*Stainless Steel Sink*

P *I'm a little nervous about caring for my new stain-less steel sink.*

S Just remember that abrasive cleansers are a no-no. Baking soda, and silver polish are especially good to use for cleaning stainless steel sinks because the main problem with stainless steel seems to be water spots. Vinegar is super for removing water spots.

 To shine stainless steel, rub a little mineral oil over it and buff with a dry cloth.

 Stainless steel will stay looking good if you wipe the sink dry after each use. Keep a towel handy and get in the habit of drying your sink, and I guarantee you'll be proud of your stainless steel sink.

## UTENSILS
**(Also see Appliances, small, p. 50)**

I used to be one of those poor souls who could never find a big stirring spoon or spatula or turning fork—until one day I lumped 'em altogether in an empty coffee can and covered the can with adhesive-backed paper.

 You could hang your utensils by your stove on cup hooks or bend the "branches" on old coffee mug trees to hang them on. Also, you can buy a peg board about two feet by three feet, cover it with adhesive-backed paper if you like, and arrange cup hooks to hold your cooking utensils.

\* \* \*

P *My cooking utensils get tangled together in the drawer and slip around out of place.*

S If you will thumbtack a kitchen towel to the bottom of the drawer and store your utensils upside down, they will not slide around.

## Can Opener
### *(Also see Can Opener, electric, p. 51)*

Protect your nails. Hang a small pair of pliers on the inside of your cupboard door to lift off cocoa lids, baking powder lids, and so on.

*        *        *

**P**        *How can I prevent "beet red juice" or sticky fruit juice from splattering all over when I open a can?*

**S**        Gently make a small opening with a beverage can opener in the can and pour off an inch of juice and then open as usual.

*        *        *

Put a napkin on the palm of your hand and under the bottom of the can to prevent spills on the floor when using a wall can opener.

*        *        *

**P**        *I get frustrated because I have to dig through the drawer to find my can opener.*

**S**        Several solutions to this nuisance—tie a ribbon or yarn on the opener to spot it easily or attach it to a magnetic hook on your refrigerator.

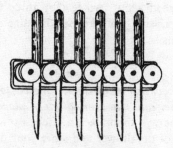

*Knives*

P        *How can I store sharp knives?*
S        Fill a coffee can or plastic container about three-fourths full with uncooked rice and store the knives blade down in the can.

\*    \*    \*

Make it a habit to place all sharp knives on the drainboard to be washed by hand instead of slipping them into the dishwater.

\*    \*    \*

P        *How can I make an inexpensive rack for holding my knives?*
S        One neat way is to glue thread spools together on a board as closely as possible. The blades will drop between the spools but the handles won't.

\*    \*    \*

P        *I have a beautiful set of knives with handles made of ebonite (looks like hard plastic). They have become whitish and dull with hard water deposit.*
S        Get a soap-filled pad or fine steel wool. Do NOT wet them. Scour with the grain of the handle, rubbing vigorously. This will remove soap film. Then pour vegetable oil on a tissue and rub hard on the handles.

\*    \*    \*

Scrape a serrated steak knife across cheese spread on crackers or cream cheese sandwiches to make a pretty shell design.

*Knives, electric*
   *(See p. 53)*

*Measuring*

P       *I always have to fumble around in the morning looking for the coffee measure.*

S       Slip a heavy rubber band around the can or jar and stick the measuring spoon under it.

\*     \*     \*

Before using containers as substitute measuring cups, be sure they are a "true" measure; for instance, a quart mayonnaise jar sometimes holds more than four cups liquid.

\*     \*     \*

Did you know that the cap off certain small bottles of vanilla measures one teaspoon, and off some larger bottles measures one tablespoon?

\*     \*     \*

If you save yogurt cups, they measure exactly eight ounces and they are throwaways, no cups to clean up!

\*     \*     \*

Cut a measuring chart out of an old cookbook and tape it to the inside of your cubpard near your staples. Sure comes in handy!

\*     \*     \*

P       *I have a hard time reading the numbers on my measuring cup.*

S       Make those marks stand out by going over them with waterproof felt-tipped markers or red nail polish. Also, remember to hold the glass cup up and look across to the other side to read the numbers.

\*     \*     \*

Fasten hooks on the underside of a cupboard to hang measuring cups. Pick up an extra set of measuring cups at a garage sale and store them in your canisters.

Buy a couple of inexpensive sets of measuring spoons and keep them in your flour and sugar canisters. A set stored in your mixing bowl is handy.

*       *       *

P          *My measuring spoons get separated or all tangled*
           *in the drawer.*
S          One solution is to hang or tie them together on a
           key chain.

## Rolling Pin
### (Also see Dough, p. 75)

Heaven help a duck! Did you know that you can fill a hollow, plastic rolling pin with a beverage, freeze it, and then you have a nice cold drink to carry along? Hubby could even tote one along in his golf bag!

*       *       *

P          *I was told not to wash my rolling pin.*
S          Some folks never wash them, just shake them off
           and place in a plastic bag to store. I wash mine by
           hand with warm sudsy water and dry thoroughly.
           Of course, we're talking about the wooden kind.
           No problem caring for the hollow, plastic kind.

## Spatula

Use a putty knife (buy one at any hardware store) to remove pieces of fudge, brownie squares, etc. You'll wonder how you ever got along without one!

## Spoons

P          *We at the office have tried everything to keep the*
           *sugar and creamer spoons clean and dry at the*
           *coffee area. Nothing seems to work!*
S          Spell out "cream," "sugar," and "stir" with plastic
           tape in raised letters. Use red tape or a bright

color. Stick the tape words on the handles of the spoons.

\*     \*     \*

**P**    *What can I use my seldom-used grapefruit spoons for?*

**S**    They really do come in handy when you want to core tomatoes and apples.

\*     \*     \*

**P**    *Do wooden spoons need to be seasoned?*

**S**    Sure do! Scrub your spoons clean and place them in hot water for a minute or so. Towel dry. Let 'em dry thoroughly (several hours). Then heat some cooking oil to medium hot and dip the spoons in the hot oil. Let them cool and then wipe dry. Seasoning keeps the spoons from absorbing cooking odors.

### Stainless Steel Flatware

**P**    *How can I get my stainless flatware to shine?*

**S**    Soak the flatware in hot water and a little ammonia; rinse and dry. Soaking in vinegar and water does a super job, too.

### Strainer

Instead of a conventional metal strainer, purchase a fish net strainer (the kind you use with an aquarium). It stores flat, is rustproof.

\*     \*     \*

If you don't have a strainer, clip nylon net around a bowl with clothespins.

\*     \*     \*

A tea strainer works well as a flour shaker or sifter.

# 2

## *Your Bath*

Problems in the bath area seem to be more centered on things like storage, taking care of the tub and shower, making bathroom accessories like shower curtains, carpets and rugs last longer, and most difficult, keeping it in order.

The bathroom doesn't have to be a mess and always in need of cleaning. Everyone and anyone who uses it should be responsible for keeping it neat and clean.

When I got married, one of the things that David and I agreed on was separate bathrooms. We were lucky enough to be building our house, so we could do this, and let me tell you it has saved many a fight. I can't complain about shoes or socks on the floor, he can't complain about fighting his way through hanging pantyhose or the sink filled with hand washing.

If you do share a bathroom, there are things you can do to make it easier for all concerned. This is where good old common courtesy comes in. No one likes to find hair all over the sink, or the top always off the toothpaste . . . so think about those who have to follow you. Pretend you are a guest at someone's home—and always pick up after yourself!

There are some good hints on how to recycle, repair and make last longer all those little items in the bath that add up to money. Hints on how to save a shower curtain, help save a bath mat, and even how to use the hundreds of soap slivers you end up with will help you save many dollars.

At the end of the chapter is a really nifty substitutions list that just might save a shopping trip sometime when you are out of just one thing. In fact, you can use some of these substitutions all the time, and again those saved pennies will start to pile up.

## APPLIANCES
**(Also see Appliances, small for the kitchen, p. 50)**

*Curlers and Curling Iron*

| | |
|---|---|
| **Problem** | *My electric curlers create so much heat when I use them in the bath.* |
| **Solution** | Cover them with a hand towel before and after using, to help reduce the heat. Be sure there is no chance of fire. |

\* \* \*

| | |
|---|---|
| **P** | *The cord to my electric curlers drives me crazy.* |
| **S** | Save a toilet paper cardboard roll, fold the cord up |

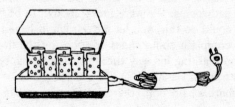

and stuff it inside so you have just enough slack to
plug it in.

\*     \*     \*

**P**      *My electric curlers don't work anymore. Any*
       *suggestions on what I can do?*

**S**      Heat your curlers in boiling water. Then use as
       usual.

\*     \*     \*

Need to press a hair ribbon in a hurry? Why not grab that curling
iron!

### Electric Toothbrush
### (Also see Toothbrush, p. 112)

An electric toothbrush with a spare brush can be used to clean
rings and to clean around faucets.

### Hair Dryer

Use your hair dryer to dry water spots on clothing.

\*     \*     \*

Some hair dryers will fit nicely into the tumbler hole in toothbrush
holders. A convenient stand!

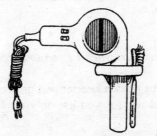

## BATH AREA

*Bathtub, cleaning*
*(Also see Shower Stall and Shower Head, p. 108)*

Supervising a child at bathtime? Why not clean the bath while you have to be in there anyway?

* * *

P   *How do I get a yellow ring off my procelain enamel tub?*

S   Even though it is not a rust stain, liquid rust remover will probably get it off.

* * *

P   *How do I get a rust stain off my bathtub?*

S   First, try lemon and salt, then, if that doesn't work, use a liquid rust remover, rinse and dry. Never leave the rust remover on very long. Also, DO NOT use liquid rust remover on a fiber glass tub.

* * *

An old nylon stocking is perfect to scour your tub with. When finished, just toss in the trash.

* * *

If bending over or kneeling is too hard on your back, buy a child's mop or extra toilet bowl brush or long-handled car wash brush to scrub your tub with.

* * *

P   *My knees hurt when I kneel to clean out the bathtub.*

S   Use your garden kneeler pad or keep two sponges to kneel on that you use only for this purpose.

* * *

P      *What is good for removing stains from fiber glass tubs?*

S      A paste made of baking soda and water left on the stain overnight will usually remove the stain. Use a damp cloth and scrub. Never use anything abrasive.

## Bathtub Mat

P      *I hate a soggy bathtub mat.*

S      Most nonslip mats will stick on the tile wall by themselves and dry. Or, cut off the top of a bleach bottle, poke some drain holes in it, roll the mat up, place it in the container and stand it in the corner of your tub to drain.

## Decor

The bath area is ideal for some plants that need steam and moisture—and they add to the decor as well.

\*     \*     \*

P      *What will remove decals from tubs?*

S      A prewash spray works well if you let it sit a while. Then, gently try to pull up the edges. Applying extreme heat, as from a hair dryer, will help loosen the glue.

\*     \*     \*

P      *I removed some decals from my porcelain enamel tub, but there are stains remaining.*

S      Scrub the stain with automatic dishwashing compound and hot water.

\*     \*     \*

If your bathtub really looks shot—no more glaze or lustre, but is otherwise still in good condition—why not consider having it professionally resurfaced or reglazed? Let me tell you, chickadees, it's sure cheaper than a new tub!

### Drains
*(Also see Drains and Stoppers, p. 121)*

P    *I can't clean under the drains in my tub or sink.*

S    Take a steel crochet hook to pull out hair, etc., from a drain where you can't remove the strainer.

\*    \*    \*

P    *The drain is sluggish.*

S    Is there some hair or gook under the strainer? Clean it out. (Some strainers pull up, some twist up.) Also, pour one cup baking soda down the drain. Wait a minute or so and then pour one cup of vinegar down the drain; follow with one-half gallon of *boiling* water.

\*    \*    \*

Drains smell? Pour baking soda and hot water down the drains once a month.

### Medicine Cabinet
*(Also see Cabinets in the Kitchen, p. 57)*

P    *I use several different shades of lipstick and they really mess up my medicine cabinet when they fall over.*

S    Use the plastic top from any spray can to hold two or three lipsticks.

\*    \*    \*

P    *I always knock over at least four bottles trying to get something in the back of the bathroom cabinet.*

S    Put your bottles, small boxes, etc., on a lazy Susan

and all you have to do is twirl it around to get the bottle that you want.

### Mirrors

Got a bunch of girls hogging the mirror? Why not hang a full-length mirror horizontally in the bathroom!

\* \* \*

P      *I hate foggy mirrors.*
S      Use your hair dryer to defog them; hang a towel over the mirror before beginning your shower; or keep a small windshield wiper blade handy to wipe the glass.

\* \* \*

Can't see the back of your head when blow-drying your hair? Mount a mirror on the wall behind you in addition to the mirror in front of you!

\* \* \*

Use your soap slivers to leave messages on your bathroom mirror. That's one way to get it clean!

\* \* \*

P          *What can I use in place of mirror cleaner that I'm*
           *buying at the store?*

S          Ammonia and water works well. Newspapers are
           super to wipe with—won't cost you a penny, ei-
           ther.

### Shower Stall and Shower Head
### (Also see Bathtub, Cleaning, p. 104)

To mend holes in a shower curtain, repair them with strapping tape
(not masking tape).

\*     \*     \*

Place extra shower curtain hooks on the inside of the curtain between
folds. Use the hooks to hang small things and hose on to dry. When
the curtain is pulled, the drying garments don't show.

\*     \*     \*

P          *I hate a yucky, damp washcloth sitting in the cor-*
           *ner of the bathtub.*

S          Use the corner tag on the washcloth and hang it
           on a shower curtain hook. If your shower hooks
           are closed, open one or two just for this purpose.

\*     \*     \*

P          *My shower curtain "hovers" around me.*
S          Wet it on the side next to the tub, plaster it to the
           tub and it will stay put. Or, attach magnets or

fishing weights to the hem to make it hang straight down.

\* \* \*

P   *I have mildew on my plastic shower curtain; how can I get it off?*

S   Machine launder the curtain in one-half cup bleach and your usual laundry detergent. Throw in a couple of light-colored towels at the same time for "rubbing" action. If you stretch your shower curtain open the full length of the tub to dry each time, you will be less apt to have a mildew problem. Also, you can cut the mildewed bottom off a curtain and still have a usable curtain.

\* \* \*

P   *I like to wash my shower curtain but how do I keep the plastic from wrinkling so?*

S   Always remove the curtain from your washer after the rinse; never spin one dry. To get the wrinkles out, put the curtain in the dryer on very low heat for just a couple of minutes and then rehang immediately.

\* \* \*

Tired of an old shower curtain but can't afford a new fancy one? Buy some nylon net, fold several thicknesses, punch holes for the rings using your old curtain as a guide, and you'll have a pretty new curtain for a fraction of the cost! Use a plain plastic shower curtain as a liner.

\* \* \*

Save old shower curtains for painting or remodeling. Cut in squares to protect carpeting in bad weather, or save for a mattress protector for visiting children. Throw an old curtain over the spare tire to keep suitcases from being scuffed in the trunk of your car.

\* \* \*

P    *We live in an older apartment and it is impossible to lower the curtain rod. Consequently, all shower curtains are too short.*

S    Instead of one set of rings use three sets forming a chain effect at the top; or, replace the curtain with plastic draperies that are available in longer lengths.

\* \* \*

P    *My shower curtain won't slide on the rod.*

S    Rub a bar of soap or baby oil on the rod.

\* \* \*

Some shower curtains can be tinted. Also, felt-tipped permanent ink pens can be used to color white or light areas of the outside of a shower curtain for a color scheme change.

\* \* \*

Tarnished rods or unsightly shelving poles can be covered with plastic slip-on covers.

\* \* \*

P    *I have a dark-colored curtain that always has water spots and soap film.*

S    In between washings, try spraying the inside of it with prewash spray, let it sit awhile and rinse.

\* \* \*

P    *How do I get black off an aluminum shower frame?*

S    An automobile rubbing compound works well.

\* \* \*

P    *I can't unclog lime deposit buildup in the shower head.*

S    Unscrew the head and soak it in vinegar; then, use an old toothbrush to scrub it clean. You may have to use a toothpick to poke through the holes.

For a slippery shower with no mat, place a terry-type hand towel on the shower floor.

\* \* \*

P   *How can I get a straight flow from my shower spray?*

S   If it won't adjust to straight, secure a plastic sandwich bag tightly over the head and cut one corner off. Be sure water flow is low-medium.

\* \* \*

P   *The shower track needs cleaning—how can I do it?*

S   Use full-strength hydrogen peroxide, saturate cotton balls and pull them along the track with a tweezer.

\* \* \*

A tiered wire or plastic basket hung in the corner of the shower will provide storage for quite a few bath items and drains well.

\* \* \*

P   *The wall side of our tub is wallpaper and is not protected from the spray of the shower.*

S   Using a tension rod, hang a clear plastic liner over the wallpaper. When the shower is not being used, open the curtain to display the wallpaper.

# BRUSHES

### Hairbrushes

P    *Any quick way to clean my hair brushes?*
S    A little hot water and a dab of hair shampoo works
     great, rinse well.
         Putting hair brushes in that old standby of am-
     monia and water in a glass jar does wonders.
         For plastic-type hair brushes, you can put them
     in a sock, tie a knot in the ankle part and drop in
     your washing machine along with a load of laun-
     dry.

### Toothbrush
*(Also see Electric Toothbrush, p. 103)*

Why not keep sets of toothbrushes for everyone in each bath in
your home? This might make things less hectic at busy rush
times.

\*    \*    \*

Buy a few extra toothbrushes on sale and keep them on hand for
guests.

## CARPETING, CLEANING AND MAINTAINING
(Also see Carpet, p. 195)

P    *How can spots on the carpet around the toilet bowl
     be removed?*
S    More than likely, those spots are bleached out and
     can't be removed. However, take a crayon the
     color of your carpet and color over the spot. Then
     put your iron on low setting, place wax paper over
     the spot and apply heat until the crayon is
     melted.

Be sure that cleanser from the toilet bowl brush is not dripping and causing the spotting.

\* \* \*

P    *I washed my bath carpet and it shrunk.*

S    You can salvage the rug by sewing fringe around the edges, wide enough to make it the original size.

\* \* \*

Two or three old bath towels sewn together make a nice bath mat that is easily washed.

\* \* \*

P    *I bought a fur-type rug and it looks matted and tangled.*

S    Brush that "critter" with an old stiff hair brush. A little fabric softener in the rinse cycle will help with those things.

\* \* \*

**P**          *The edges of my bath carpet ravel.*

**S**          Spray the underside edges with hairspray or apply
               clear glue to the edges.

*     *     *

**P**          *The throw rugs on my tile bath floor slide.*

**S**          Sewing some used foam fabric-softener sheets on
               the backing will help keep it in place.

*     *     *

**P**          *The small rug that fits around the base of the toilet
               will not stay in place.*

**S**          Sew elastic loops on the rug and hook the elastic
               loops over the bolts at the base of the toilet.

## SINKS
**(Also see Sinks in the Kitchen, p. 90)**

SINKS AND BATHTUBS—NO ABRASIVE CLEANERS,
PLEASE. This is the same story as enamel kitchen sinks . . . use
spray-on foamy-type cleansers or liquids. Once you scratch and mar
the finish, you will be cleaning and cleaning and never get the surface
clean and shiny.

*     *     *

**P**          *Why can't toilet bowl cleaners be used on tubs and
               basins?*

**S**          Because that's talking apples and oranges! Toilet
               bowls are usually vitreous china; tubs and basins
               are cast iron or steel with bonded porcelain finish.
               Don't take a chance on ruining the finish on your
               fixtures. Carefully follow instructions on all clean-
               ing products. Remember, cleansers are carefully
               formulated for different finishes.

*     *     *

P        *How can I repair porcelain chips on my sinks?*

S        Buy a porcelain repair kit; the oil paint can be tinted to match your porcelain to a "T."

\*    \*    \*

Attach your old "scrubber" toothbrush to your cleanser can with a rubber band and have it always handy.

## STORAGE
**(Also see Storage Space for odds and ends, p. 213)**

Only one bathroom and several people who want to keep their things in the drawers? Use sturdy shoe boxes. They can be put under the sink or wherever. Just slide them out, use what you need and put the whole thing back.

\*    \*    \*

P        *I don't have enough shelf space in my bathroom to store all the cans of hairspray, etc.*

S        Hang a see-through shoe bag on the back of the door or even on the wall behind the door. Everything slips right in. You can see what you need; if

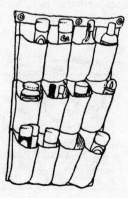

there are a lot of people in the family they can each
have a row of pockets.

\* \* \*

Do you sometimes put your rings on the bathroom or sink counter
and then walk off and leave them and worry about them? Then you
should use one of your seldom-used little dainty bowls, or a small
pretty ash tray to hold all your pieces of jewelry when you need to
take them off for washing dishes, doing laundry, painting, etc.

\* \* \*

P *My makeup brushes are always rolling around in
the drawer.*

S I use a pretty little vase or an extra wine glass to
hold them, right out on the counter.

\* \* \*

Avoid spilling or breaking bottles of shampoo by transferring your
shampoo to clean, empty, plastic detergent bottles. Label them properly, of course.

\* \* \*

P *Where can I keep that extra roll of toilet tissue so
I don't have to crawl under the bathroom basin?*

S Use a boutique tissue box, cut the bottom out and
slip in one roll of tissue. This can sit on the back

of the commode or in any convenient place and looks attractive.

\*    \*    \*

P      *Our bath does not have a toothbrush holder.*
S      How about a glass "frog" that's used for flower arrangements, or put up cup hooks for your brushes that have holes in the handles.

\*    \*    \*

P      *I don't have enough shelf space in my bathroom.*
S      Small wicker baskets look cute hung on the bathroom wall, and sure do hide clutter. Each member of the family can have his or her own.

\*    \*    \*

A wooden case for soda pop bottles mounted diagonally on the wall is a handy nook to store small personal items. Paint it, of course, to match your bathroom colors.

## TILES

P    *How can I get grout clean between my ceramic tile?*

S    Make a paste of bleach and scouring powder (luv, remember that bleach and ammonia DO NOT mix, so check the powder to make sure it contains no ammonia) and scrub with an old toothbrush or fine-grade dry steel wool pad on dry ceramic tile. Then rinse well.

Dingy grout can also be painted with latex paint.

\* \* \*

P    *My ceramic tile shower walls are covered with scum.*

S    Make a paste of bleach and scouring cleaner (use a cleanser that has NO ammonia), then scour with nylon net and rinse well. You can use a prewash spray, let sit and wipe clean. (No fiber glass, please.)

After you have the wall clean, if you'll simply get in the habit of wiping down the wall with a towel after each bath, the walls will stay scum-free. Also, switching from regular soap to a detergent soap will help immensely!

## TOILET BOWLS AND TANKS

### Brushes

P    *Where can I dry the toilet bowl brush?*

S    Place the brush under the commode seat hanging over the bowl and let it air dry.

\* \* \*

To protect the finish on your bowl, don't use a worn toilet brush. The metal can scratch or destroy the finish.

＊     ＊     ＊

Don't have a brush holder? How about an old flower pot or an empty bleach bottle with the top cut off.

＊     ＊     ＊

To keep the brush holder from getting rust, line the holder with a plastic bag.

## Cleaning

P     *How is a ring around the toilet bowl removed?*

S     Pour two to three cups of household bleach OR vinegar (don't mix—use only one product at a time) in the bowl and let it sit overnight. Liquid rust remover will sometimes remove the ring.

It may be that the clean water tank on the toilet may be the cause of the ring. Be sure that the tank is kept sediment-free to insure that clean water is going into the bowl. Liquid rust remover may also be used to clean the tank.

＊     ＊     ＊

To prevent rust on the screws on the toilet seat, paint the screws with clear fingernail polish.

＊     ＊     ＊

P     *I hate to clean the top of the water cabinet in the back of the commode. It gets covered with dust and powder so quickly.*

S     Cover the top with a hand towel or cut an old

place mat in half and use that. Just flip it over
when needed and wash it once in awhile.

*Water Flow*
*(Also see Water Conservation, p. 127)*

Find out where the main water valve cutoff is for your home *before*
an emergency situation arises.

\*    \*    \*

P    *How can I stop a toilet from overflowing?*

S    First, open the tank lid and pull up on the rod or
arm that goes to the float. This will stop the flow
of water. Keep a piece of wire handy to hang over
the side to suspend this arm in the "Up" position.
Then determine what the stoppage is and clear the
bowl with a plumber's helper. Also, there is a valve
on the base of the toilet that will shut the water
off.

\*    \*    \*

P    *How can I displace water in the toilet tank to conserve water?*

S    Put an open glass jar (like a medium-size mayonnaise jar) upright in the tank.

\*    \*    \*

P    *The toilet doesn't seem to have as much water flow
as it used to.*

S    Check under the rim. It could be that the holes are
clogged with lime deposit and water simply can't
surge through. You can carefully poke into the
holes with a paper clip. Use a hand mirror so you
won't have to stand on your head!

\*    \*    \*

Unsightly or missing knobs over the bolts at the base of the toilet? Some rounded deodorant bottle caps will fit.

\*　　\*　　\*

**P**　　*I want to clean stains out of the bowl. How do I lower the water level?*

**S**　　Use a quick up-and-down motion with a brush or mop, or better yet, from as high as possible pour a bucket of water quickly into the commode. The water level should lower and stay that way since you are not flushing the toilet thereby letting more water out of the tank.

\*　　\*　　\*

**P**　　*What do I do when the toilet won't flush?*

**S**　　Remove the top from the water tank. Check the floating "ball" that operates the valve that fills the tank with water. Check the wires and arms which hold the float. Bent coat hangers and paper clips can be used as temporary spare parts in a pinch.

The usual cause of not flushing is that the lift wire has come loose from the flush ball or the trip arm. The flush ball is the stopper that regulates the flow of water into and out of the bowl.

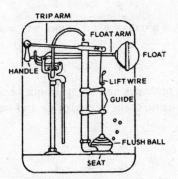

## TOILETRIES
(Also see Wise Shopping, p. 127)

Bothered with perspiration on your wrist from your watch? Rub your skin with a roll-on antiperspirant and let dry before putting on your watch.

\*    \*    \*

P        *What can I use if I run out of deodorant?*
S        Plain old baking soda is a terrific underarm de-
         odorant. Just pat on with an extra powder puff.

\*    \*    \*

Out of eyebrow pencil? Use a soft lead pencil in a pinch, but only on brows. *Don't* get near your eyes.

\*    \*    \*

P        *I don't have an eyebrow brush.*
S        Those old toothbrushes come in handy for making
         beautiful eyes. I use a stiff one to separate my
         eyelashes (it's ten years old and still going strong).

\*    \*    \*

Brown eyeshadow can be used to contour; if it is a little dark, mix with powder.

\*    \*    \*

Lipstick mixed with a dab of hand lotion, will work great as rouge.

\*    \*    \*

Don't leave your perfumes and colognes out in the direct sunlight . . . sunlight will cause them to evaporate and maybe even change the fragrance.

\*    \*    \*

**P** *I love the bath powder that goes along with the perfume I buy, but both cost so much.*

**S** Mix a box of the "expensive stuff" half and half with plain baby powder or baking soda, or spray a little of the good perfume on some baby powder, close tightly and let dry. It will do the trick.

\* \* \*

**P** *I love dusting powder, but besides dusting me, the floor sure gets a workout.*

**S** Stand in the tub and you can just rinse away whatever misses your body.

\* \* \*

Old bathpowder puffs are great to throw in your lingerie drawer to add a little extra fresh, beautiful fragrance.

\* \* \*

**P** *What can I use to scrub my face with?*

**S** Oatmeal is the old standby. Also, a little salt with a drop of oil is very abrasive and can be used, but be careful not to overdo it.

\* \* \*

**P** *My little ones have such a hard time with the big bars of soap, so they don't wash their hands as well as they should.*

**S** Cut the larger bars in small hand sizes so your little ones feel that they were made "especially" for them. They will be more likely to use the soap since "it's mine." Also, save the little soap slivers just for them. They don't have any excuses when they have their "own" soap!

\* \* \*

**P** *What's the difference between a soap bar and a detergent bar?*

**S** Soaps are made by the action of alkali or fat and

fatty acids; detergents are synthesized chemically
from materials derived from petroleum.

\* \* \*

Don't throw away the wrappers from bars of soap . . . slip them in
between your linens or, if you have a guest room that isn't used often,
place these wrappers on the pillow until the day your guests arrive.
When your company pulls back their sheets, they will smell a lively
fragrance rather than mustiness.

\* \* \*

**P**     *I hate fighting with the last few squirts of shampoo*
    *in the bottom of the little plastic tube.*

**S**     Hang the tube from the bottom end with a clip-
    type clothespin that has that little hanger on it.
    Hook it on your shower curtain rod. All the sham-
    poo will be right at the top end the next time you
    use it.

\* \* \*

To keep hair from "souring" between shampoos, rinse the hair with a mixture of one-fourth cup apple cider vinegar and three-fourth cup water after your shampoo.

\* \* \*

P       *What can I use as a hair conditioner?*
S       Mayonnaise—works wonders! Rub it in, let it sit, and then wash. Or, beat one whole egg and rub it into your hair. Let it sit for five or so minutes and rinse out well . . . added protein.

\* \* \*

P       *We go through a box of tissues a day when a member of the family is sick—and the tissue costs so much.*
S       Use a boutique tissue box, cut the bottom out and after taking the cardboard roll out of the toilet tissue, put the roll inside. You have easy pop-up tissues, very cheap, and they can be carried about if you travel from room to room.

\* \* \*

P       *Toothpaste costs so much—what can I use instead?*
S       The recipe is 1-½ cup salt, 1 pound baking soda, and ⅛ ounce bottle of oil of wintergreen (or your favorite flavor). Simply blend well.

\* \* \*

Want to get the last of the toothpaste out of a tube? Put the cap on tightly, place it on the floor, and step on it. Or, put a pencil at the end and roll up the tube all the way to the opening. . . . You will be surprised how much more paste comes out.

\* \* \*

Disinfect toothbrushes and holders with alcohol when colds are going around.

\* \* \*

Did you know that toothpaste will get marking pen ink off skin, get rid of onion and garlic odor on skin, and also take skid marks off of some vinyl floors?

*    *    *

Don't forget to brush your tongue once in a while to help have a fresh breath.

*    *    *

P    *My safety razor needs a thorough cleaning.*
S    Put a denture cleanser tablet in a pint container with water; put your razor in there and let it soak clean. Scrub with an old toothbrush and your razor will look like new.

*    *    *

Hot water bottle sprung a leak? A temporary solution is a piece of adhesive tape over the leak; apply a tire inner-tube patch to mend it permanently.

## TOWELS

Remember, towels are used to dry off clean bodies and hands, so save yourself time and money by not washing them after each use.

*    *    *

P    *We never have enough towel racks to hang towels on when company comes.*
S    Give each a coat hanger marked with their name or color-coded and then you can hang several of these on one towel rack.

*    *    *

Want a pretty way to set out guest hand towels? Roll them up and put them in a pretty wicker basket or flower pot set out on the counter.

*    *    *

Pretty, heavy-duty paper towels folded and placed in napkins rings make nice guest towels.

\* \* \*

If you find that the washcloths on your matched towel sets wear out faster than the towels, purchase two washcloths per set.

\* \* \*

P      *How can I get my family to use a towel more than once?*

S      Assign each person a certain color, or a different pattern and assign each person a towel rack or hook.

\* \* \*

For guests, use colored plastic tape to mark their towels.

## WATER CONSERVATION
(Also see Waterflow for the toilet, p. 120)

P      *Which uses the most water—a bath or a shower?*

S      A shower takes five to fifteen gallons per minute; a full tub bath, thirty to fifty gallons to fill the tub. A shower lasting five or six minutes would use more water. The moral is: take a short shower and a half tub bath.

## WISE SHOPPING
(Also see Toiletries, p. 122)

It seems like every time you go to the store, the prices are never the same. They are a few pennies higher than the last time. The price increase of things may slow down a bit, but you can be pretty sure that they aren't going to go back down.

What really got to me one day was looking at the price on a can of tuna and being shocked that it was the same as two weeks before! Now, that's unusual!

We all know that you should shop sales, use coupons and comparative-shop. Sometimes I don't have the time or want to waste the gas to go to three different stores to get their specials. You need to ask yourself if it's worth saving a nickel on a roll of toilet tissue when you have to drive ten miles to another store.

I think the best way to save money is to buy in bulk. If you have the space to store paper products and things that will keep six months to a year—and you can afford it—by all means buy a lot.

I wait until things like paper towels, napkins, toilet paper and tissues are on sale; then I buy twenty or thirty packs of toilet paper and ten boxes of tissues. Yes, I might look silly rolling up to the checkout counter with a basket full of nothing but toilet paper, but I guarantee that we have never run out. You know that the next time you go into the store it's going to cost more, so why not?

Buying in quantity like this may not be practical for you if you don't have a place to put it. Have you ever thought of stuffing toilet paper, paper towels, etc., under a bed? No one will see it, it's not going to go bad, and so what if it gets a little dusty—it's all wrapped up anyway! Think about it.

## SUBSTITUTIONS

| | |
|---|---|
| AIR FRESHENER: | Strike matches |
| BOWL CLEANER: | Full-strength bleach OR |
| | vinegar (not together) |
| COLD CREAM: | All-vegetable shortening |
| CREME RINSE: | Fabric softener diluted with water (use with caution) |
| DENTAL FLOSS: | Coarse thread |

| | |
|---|---|
| DEODORANT: | Baking soda |
| FACIAL MASK: | Shaving cream |
| GLASS CLEANER: | Alcohol, ammonia or vinegar |
| PUMICE STONE: | Nylon net |
| SHAMPOO: | Mild liquid dishwashing detergent diluted with water |
| SHAVING CREAM: | Baby oil |
| TALCUM POWDER: | Cornstarch, or cornstarch and baby powder |
| TOOTHPASTE: | Baking soda plus salt and flavoring |

*3*

# *The Laundry*

Wash day blues! As far as I'm concerned, it should be wash day whites!

Laundry problems seem to be the questions most often asked. It seems that the same problems bug most everyone. "How do I get ball-point ink out?" "How can I get my things white?" or "What about smelly tennis shoes?" The answers are in this chapter!

After living in an apartment all my life and having to use the apartment washing machines or drag everything to the laundromat, it is a real luxury to have a washer and dryer at home.

Laundry day for me was always a pain. I don't know why, but pulling all those wet clothes out of the washer and then lugging them across the laundry room into the dryer was just really hateful. The worst part of doing laundry was the folding and putting away. I hated it—and I lived alone and had only *my* laundry to do.

WELL, I am now married and live in a house with my own washer and dryer and it is hog heaven. I do my laundry and David does his own—that way there are no complaints about lint on the socks or "You lost my favorite T-shirt" or "Why is this white shirt gray?" I still hate folding and putting everything away, but the satisfaction of seeing the bottom of the laundry basket makes it bearable.

My personal philosophy on getting the dreaded deed done is to do it a little at a time, or as needed. For some people I know that's not practical, but if you have the facility in your own home or close by it's worth it. It's like cleaning an oven to me—if you do it a little at a time then it isn't hard to clean, but if you wait and wait and let the gunk build up, boy, oh, boy, do you have a chore ahead of you!

There is a very useful spot and stain listing in this chapter with some really good information. You will probably get tired of hearing me say, "Use prewash spray" or "Grab the box of dishwasher detergent" (I don't own any stock in any company—have never gotten a free box or can) but the stuff is great! I tried to give you home remedies, things that you have on hand, that you can use since few of us keep cleaning solvents or things like that around.

If the answer to your problem isn't here, let me know and I will be sure to include it in the next book or print it in the column.

Good luck! Because sometimes that's what it takes to get the laundry done, have everything match up, not fade, and be lint free. AMEN!

## COLORFASTNESS

If the tag on clothes, linens, etc., says "colorfast," that means the colors are set and should not run. If it doesn't say anything about it, you have to be careful when laundering.

Always read the care instructions on the labels of all garments you plan to buy. If it says "dry-clean only," think if you want to spend the time and money to always get it dry-cleaned. Be sure you are prepared for it to run, if the label doesn't say colorfast.

✳   ✳   ✳

**Problem**     *I bought a new T-shirt and the color ran.*

**Solution**     It's painful (and expensive) to learn from experience, isn't it? Next time soak your new shirt in cold water and white vinegar before washing. The vinegar and cold water "set" the color.

*  *  *

**P**     *How do I test for colorfastness?*

**S**     Soak a small portion of the garment for two minutes in a light suds at the temperature you will be using for regular washing. Look for traces of dye. If the dye does bleed, wash that item alone.

*  *  *

A very simple way to test for colorfastness when you get a garment home is to wring out a wet washcloth or rag and rub over an inside seam. If color comes off you can bet it's gonna bleed when you wash it.

*  *  *

**P**     *My new colored towels are almost too pretty to use —how can I keep them looking new?*

**S**     Always wash them in warm water with detergent and tumble dry them. You should wash dark colors separately. Because the dyes in vibrant colors may be sensitive to bleach. I do not suggest bleaching colored towels.

## DETERGENTS, FABRIC SOFTENERS AND BLEACH

Always check the unit price when buying laundry detergent and the likes—bigger is not always cheaper. It pays to check.

*  *  *

A metal grapefruit spoon is great to open detergent boxes with—sure beats breaking a fingernail.

*  *  *

Never, never, never use liquid dishwashing detergent in your clothes washing machine—you will end up with enough bubbles to float you to the moon!

\* \* \*

**P**   *I am tired of lugging a measuring cup to and from the laundromat. Plus I have lost several.*

**S**   The plastic type 8-ounce yogurt or sour cream cartons are perfect. Measure and mark if you use less than eight ounces. If it gets left behind, big deal, and it sure is lightweight!

\* \* \*

**P**   *I use the very concentrated liquid detergent, and I feel I'm wasting so much that is left in the cup.*

**S**   If you will use a soft plastic cup, you can throw it in the wash and get every last drop used . . . no money wasted here.

\* \* \*

**P**   *I hate measuring detergent. It is such a chore to look at the measuring cup and figure out how much half a cup is.*

**S**   Use the plastic tops from cans, or even sturdy frozen juice cardboard cans; measure one-half cup

or whatever you want and cut off the juice can
. . . most large tops are one-half cup.

\*   \*   \*

P   *I ran out of laundry detergent at midnight and
really didn't want to go to the store.*

S   In a real pinch, I have used one-fourth cup powdered dishwasher detergent BUT only on clothes
that can stand a little bleach. This is for an emergency situation—don't use it all the time.

\*   \*   \*

P   *I ran out of fabric softener in the middle of doing
my laundry.*

S   You can use the creme rinse that you rinse your
hair with. Mix one or two capfuls to a quart of
water and pour in the machine on the rinse
cycle.

\*   \*   \*

P   *What can I do if I forget to put liquid fabric softener in the wash at the right time?*

S   Put just a dash of the liquid fabric softener on a
washcloth and toss it in your dryer; you have your
own homemade fabric softener sheet!

\*   \*   \*

P   *My towels don't absorb moisture as they used to.*

S   It may be that you're using fabric softener too
frequently on your towels. Stop using fabric softener for a few washes and that should help. Then
use maybe every other time.

\*   \*   \*

Out of household bleach . . . hydrogen peroxide can be used on many
things to remove stains. Always first test a spot that doesn't
show.

## DRYING

*Indoor Drying*

P        *I do hand laundry in my tiny apartment. Where
         can I hang all the things I have to dry. I have no
         balcony.*

S        If you have a lot of things to hang up to dry, put
         them on coat hangers, and you can hang a lot of
         hangers over your bathtub shower rod. You can
         put several bras and slips on just one hanger. If
         you worry about dripping, use your old plastic
         shower curtain to drape over the floor.

*        *        *

Putting up extra towel racks is worth the cost of having the space
to hang dry items.

*        *        *

P        *I hang my clothes in the basement to dry and it
         takes forever.*

S        Turn on a fan to circulate the air and they will dry
         much quicker.

*        *        *

P        *I always run out of pants hangers and hate to go
         buy some. The pants legs crease when hung on a
         regular wire hanger.*

S        Use two hangers at a time and place a magazine
         over the bottom, then cover with plastic bags over
         them and staple or tape 'em together. (I like this
         way.) If you have time, you can tie old pantyhose
         around them.

*        *        *

P        *I have several garments that say "dry flat" and I
         really don't have any place to do that.*

S       If you can, spread them out on some plastic or paper on the hood or trunk of a full-size car, in the garage, natch. When the bathtub is not in use, it makes a marvey place to lay things out to dry. It's out of the way, and you can shut the curtain and not even have to see the laundry.

\*    \*    \*

For extra strength in wire hangers, put two together and tape them at the neck; they will hold most heavy garments.

\*    \*    \*

If you have dresses that have little spaghetti straps or a large neckline and always fall off the hangers while drying, just fold them over the hanger at the waistline—no wrinkles and they won't fall off.

## Machine Drying

P       *When I dry my laundry at the laundromat, I hate having to run three different dryers (which cost money) just because I have things which need different temperature settings.*

S       Put all your things in one dryer and stop it after a few minutes to take out those quick-drying things. Then a few minutes later, pull out the things that are dry and finally leave the heavy-duty things in the longest.

\*    \*    \*

P       *My clothes come out really wrinkled even after going through the dryer.*

S       You might be overloading your washer and dryer. Things need room to move around. If you pack the washer tight, natch they are going to twist and wrinkle. Also, the dryer should never be stuffed— or else, Wrinkle City!

\*    \*    \*

If you remove permanent press fabrics immediately from the dryer, give them a shake, and place them on hangers, they will usually remain wrinkle-free. Sometimes just a light touch-up with a warm iron is all that's needed.

\*   \*   \*

P       *I hate having to use my hand to clean the lint filter
        on my dryer.*
S       Don't throw the fabric softener sheets away when
        you are finished with them; just grab a used one
        and wipe that lint away.

\*   \*   \*

Never place "rubberized" items such as girdles, bras, etc. in a dryer on high heat. If you do, they will ruin. Always use low heat or air-dry setting to dry them.

## Outdoor Drying
*(Also see Blankets, p. 153 and Drying Carpet, p. 197)*

P       *Can I dry blankets outside?*
S       Yes, if you avoid drying them on very windy days
        or in bright, direct sunlight. High wind may
        stretch a wet blanket and bright sun could fade
        some colors. If possible, hang them lengthwise
        over two or more lines to keep the blanket's shape
        and to speed drying time.

\*   \*   \*

P       *I live in an apartment and do a lot of hand wash-
        ing to save money, but I've run out of places to
        hang things to dry.*
S       If you have a balcony or area that gets sunlight
        and is secluded from public view, garden chairs
        turned upside down make super little clothes-
        lines.

\*   \*   \*

Short of line space? You can place lightweight things over some of the clothes or sheets that have already been hung.

\*   \*   \*

P   *My hands get cold when I hang my laundry in chilly weather.*

S   Fill a hot water bottle with hot water and put it in your laundry basket; every time you pick up something to hang, hold the bottle for a second to warm up those hands. Or, you can wear rubber gloves.

\*   \*   \*

Wash towels and work clothes first because it takes longer for them to dry on the line.

\*   \*   \*

P   *I have so much laundry to hang on the lines that there is never enough space to hang it, and I have to do it in shifts.*

S   Honey child, you are going to love this one and it is so simple you are going to say, "Why didn't I think of that?" Hang the clothes crosswise on the lines, from one line to the other, instead of length-

wise. You can hang a lot of laundry on just two lines.

## Ironing
*(Also see Post-washing, p. 156)*

Sprinkled some ironing and can't get to it? Put it in a plastic bag in the refrigerator and it will keep for several days. Or, stuff it in your freezer. But don't forget!

\* \* \*

**P**    *I have a tiny apartment and really hate putting up the ironing board for just one shirt.*

**S**    Can I help you? I can iron on the floor better than most people using an ironing board! Just put a thick towel down, sit yourself on the floor and iron away.

A more conventional way is to put a few magazines or newspapers on the kitchen counter, cover with a towel, and use your counter for a hurry-up ironing board.

The dadgum easiest and quickest way is to throw a towel over the corner of the bed, and you even have a curved edge for the shoulder seams.

\* \* \*

**P**    *I have to iron long tablecloths for a church banquet—how can I keep them from dragging on the floor?*

**S**    First of all, if you can iron them at the banquet hall and put them directly on the table, they will not wrinkle. Also, put a card table by your ironing board to drape the tablecloth over—it won't drag on the floor.

\* \* \*

**P**    *I hate ironing handkerchiefs and little things like that.*

**S**    Place the light things on top of each other, iron, turn over and iron again. You get double-duty!

\*     \*     \*

**P**    *It seems that my ironing is more wrinkled when I pull it out of the basket than when I put it in.*

**S**    For those things that you have to iron, don't throw them in the basket and pile things on top of them. Hang them loosely on hangers or lay them out flat somewhere. The less wrinkles to contend with, the better.

\*     \*     \*

**P**    *I hate walking back and forth to each closet to hang up the clothes when I am ironing.*

**S**    Put one of the metal hooks that slips over the front of the door and gives you a place to hang clothes on the back on the closest door to you. Do all your ironing at once, then grab the clothes that go to each room and make only one trip.

\*     \*     \*

**P**    *My iron has a buildup of starch.*

**S**    If it is a light buildup, you can scrub the cool iron with some nylon net, or an old toothbrush and a

little baking soda. If you have a nonstick coating
on the iron, never use anything abrasive. If the
buildup is rather heavy and has been on there a
long time, most home remedies don't work well.

\*   \*   \*

Buy a tube of iron cleaner (you can find it in fabric stores); it is as
easy as pie to use and you will have a slick-bottomed iron in nothing
flat. It costs only about a dollar and lasts well over a year.

\*   \*   \*

**P**        *My steam iron is clogged.*
**S**        Pour white vinegar into the iron and let it steam
             for about five minutes. Then unplug the iron and
             let it cool for awhile. Empty the vinegar out and
             rinse the iron thoroughly by pouring water in and
             out.


**HAMPERS**
(Also see Sorting, p. 156)

**P**        *I am always forgetting to wash something that I
             didn't put in the hamper, like a bathrobe or blan-
             ket.*

S    As soon as you think about it, write yourself a note
and throw it in the hamper. When you see it, you
will know right where to go and nothing will escape getting washed.

\*    \*    \*

P    *So many times things to be cleaned are not that
soiled, and I hate crunching them up and putting
them in the hamper.*

S    Hang the item wrong side out in your laundry or
closet. Then on laundry day you know at a glance
what needs to be washed, and they are hardly
wrinkled.

\*    \*    \*

P    *Getting the heavy, overstuffed laundry basket from
the bathroom to the laundry room is almost impossible.*

S    Loop a dog leash or something sturdy through a
handle and drag the beast. Much easier than lifting
and carrying.

\*    \*    \*

P    *My clothes hamper smells mildewy sometimes.*

S    Be sure that there is no dampness in there. Always
air-dry things before throwing them in the hamper. This is a great place to throw those small soap
slivers. They will keep things smelling fresh in
most cases.

I am not a miracle worker—if you run a gym,
nothing is going to keep that hamper from stinking
—short of putting all gym clothes in a plastic bag
(and I am not going to be responsible for what
happens when you open it up!).

\*    \*    \*

P    *My laundry hamper smells worse than my son's
tennis shoes.*

S   That's pretty bad, but one sure way is to do the laundry as often as is needed. But if you can't get those things out in a hurry, sprinkling a handful of baking soda in the hamper every now and then will sure help. It won't hurt your clothes at all; just shake it to the bottom of the hamper when you pull the things out to wash.

*  *  *

P   *My family just won't clean their pockets before putting things in the hamper.*

S   Finder's keepers is the rule—if its money it's yours, if it's a frog they can have it back! Place a large clean coffee can or catchall in the spot where the laundry is done. If they don't sort through the pockets, then it's all yours.

    You can place a can or note in each hamper as a reminder.

## HAND WASHING
### (Also see Detergents, p. 132)

Soaking items in the bathroom? Place them in a clean plastic bucket or trash basket with water and soap and put it in the tub or shower.

If anyone needs to take a bath, they can simply remove the container and replace it afterwards.

\* \* \*

P     *I hate hand washing lingerie.*
S     Wash it in your machine using a gentle or delicate
      cycle. Or, using mild detergent and cool water,
      place the articles in the bathtub and rub-a-dub-
      dub using a plumber's helper with a rubber suction
      (clean, of course!). Drain the water, refill and
      rinse. Do not put nylon lingerie or delicate fabrics
      in a dryer.

\* \* \*

P     *I hate hand washing my underwire bras.*
S     I put mine in a pillow slip, or laundry bag, close
      the end and run them through the washing ma-
      chine on gentle cycle. It's better to air-dry but
      depending on the fabric content it might go in the
      dryer. Always check the label.

\* \* \*

When hand washing small items in the sink, you can use a tiny plastic glass, like a juice glass, as a plunger. Just "squash" the glass up and down and make your own washing machine cycle.

\* \* \*

P     *Can I hand wash a silk blouse?*
S     Yes, I do mine using a mild liquid detergent and
      cool water (a gentle, swishing action)—no twisting
      or wringing—rolling it in a towel first, then hang-
      ing it up to dry, out of direct sunlight. Remember
      though, if you try to remove a spot yourself on
      silk, it will circle. So, leave spot removal on silks
      to professionals. Iron on the wrong side with a
      pressing cloth—be sure to use low setting.

\* \* \*

P       *How do I launder sweaters?*

S       Wool or part wool sweaters can be washed by hand in a mild detergent. Dissolve soap or detergent in lukewarm water, and squeeze suds through the sweater. Rinse gently and thoroughly. Gently squeeze (don't wring) out as much water as possible. Roll the sweater up in a thick towel and squeeze gently to remove excess moisture. Lay the sweater out flat to dry ( be sure and shape it).

\*     \*     \*

P       *I have some dingy clothes which need whitening.*

S       This has got to be the greatest! Especially for kids' white socks and baby clothes. Pour one gallon of hot water into a *plastic* container. Add one-half cup of automatic dishwashing compound and one-fourth cup of bleach. Stir well. If clothes can't stand hot water, let it cool first. Let the clothes soak for thirty minutes, then wash as usual. Use one-half cup vinegar in the rinse water.

## JEANS AND SNEAKERS
### (Also see Patching, p. 178)

P       *My kids' jeans have "white spots" on them.*

S       If the white spots are caused from bleach or faded, or if the white spots are threads of the material showing through, this tip will work. Pick a crayon the color closest to the jeans and gently rub it across the faded area. When you've reached the wanted shade, put a piece of waxed paper over the area and press with a warm iron. The heat will set the color to keep it from washing out for awhile. The color will eventually wash out, but just repeat the application.

\*     \*     \*

P *I have a lovely jeans outfit that's only a few months old, and the vest and blazer are so much darker than the pants.*

S You should always wash matching pieces, or multi-piece outfits together. If there is any fading or color change, they will all change at the same time. You could wash the two darker pieces a few times and see if they fade to match the pants.

\*  \*  \*

P *I hate stiff new jeans.*

S I use a plastic laundry tub (you could use a clean plastic trash can) and cold water, plus a cup or so of fabric softener, add my jeans and let them soak overnight.

 Just pop them in the washer the next day; using the fabric softener, water and wash as usual. Sometimes it still takes a few washings to get them comfy—but this helps wonderfully for that first wearing.

\*  \*  \*

P *I want to keep my new jeans dark blue as long as possible.*

S Before you put your jeans in the wash, turn them inside out. Also, dry and iron them (if you do) inside out. Washing your jeans in cool water helps. If you are line drying, it helps to hang the jeans in a shady spot to prevent fading.

\*  \*  \*

P *I hate washing shoe laces—I always lose them.*

S Untie them from the tennies and either sprinkle with detergent and scrub with a toothbrush or tie the laces through a shirt button hole and run them through the wash.

\*  \*  \*

After washing your tennis shoes, use a spray-type soil repellent to give them a good going-over on the outside. It will help keep dirt from grinding in and they are much easier to get clean the next time.

## LABEL DEFINITIONS

P        *Sometimes I find the cleaning instructions on the labels in clothing confusing.*

S        I didn't realize one could come across so many different labels. Natch, these labels are put in clothes by the manufacturer for a purpose so it pays to "read and heed." Hope the following list will help you understand those labels a little bit better!

BLOCK TO DRY:                   Shape the garment to its correct size and shape while drying.

COLD WASH—COLD RINSE:           Use cold water from faucet or cold temperature setting on the washing machine.

COOL IRON:                      Iron item at lowest setting.

DAMP WIPE:                      Just wipe with a damp cloth or sponge with a little mild detergent. Surface clean only; do not soak or get item wet.

DELICATE CYCLE—GENTLE
  CYCLE:                        Can be washed in the machine that has this setting; if not, wash by hand.

DO NOT IRON:                    Do not iron or press using heat.

DRY-CLEAN ONLY: The article can be dry-cleaned professionally or you can clean it in a self-service dry-cleaning machine.

DRY FLAT: Lay garment on flat surface to dry.

DURABLE PRESS CYCLE—
PERMANENT PRESS CYCLE: Use appropriate machine setting. Or, use warm wash, cold rinse and short spin cycle.

HAND WASH: Launder by hand only with mild liquid detergent in lukewarm or cool water. Item may usually be dry-cleaned.

HAND WASH ONLY: Launder by hand only in mild liquid detergent in lukewarm or cool water. No machine washing or dry cleaning.

HAND WASH SEPARATELY: Hand wash alone or with same colors.

HOME LAUNDER ONLY: Do not use commercial laundry (temperatures are too hot).

HOT IRON: Iron at hot setting.

IRON DAMP: Dampen the article before ironing.

LINE DRY: Hang damp and allow to dry.

MACHINE WASH: You can wash and dry the article by your usual washing method.

NO BLEACH: No kind, no how!

NO DRY-CLEAN: Do not dry-clean. Follow label instructions for cleaning.

NO SPIN: Remove garment before final machine spin cycle.

NO WRING—NO TWIST: Line dry, drip dry or flat dry. Wringing or twisting of garment may cause wrinkles or loss of shape of garment.

PROFESSIONALLY DRY-CLEAN
  ONLY: Do not use a self-service machine. Have garment cleaned only by professional cleaners.

STEAM IRON: Iron or press with steam.

TUMBLE DRY: Can be tumbled in dryer at recommended heat on label.

TUMBLE DRY, REMOVE
  PROMPTLY: Can be tumble dried in a dryer at recommended heat but if your machine doesn't have a cool-down cycle, remove the article at once when tumbling stops.

WARM WASH—WARM RINSE: Use warm water from faucet or warm machine setting.

MACHINE WASH SEPARATE: Machine wash alone or with same colors only.

## MACHINE WASHING
**(Also see Pretreatment, p. 158-160)**

### *Machine Washing Procedures*

If your washer or dryer doesn't work, these hints may save you an expensive service call. For either one, check to be sure it is plugged in and if a fuse is blown or a circuit breaker tripped. For the separate appliances, check the following:

WASHING MACHINE

1. Are the water faucets turned on?

2. Is there a kink in the hose?

3. Is the selector button pushed in all the way?

4. Is the load of clothes balanced? Some washers turn off automatically if the load of clothes becomes "lop-sided." Rearrange the clothes and push the button to start the machine again.

5. Is the lid closing tightly? There's a button under the lid that cuts the machine off when the lid is raised.

DRYER

1. If gas, is the striker working properly or is the pilot light on?

2. Does the lint trap or filter need cleaning?

3. Is the exhaust vent blocked?

4. Is the door closing tightly?

\*    \*    \*

Even your washing machine needs cleaning now and then. Fill the machine with hot water and pour one quart of vinegar in. Run the machine through the entire cycle. There can be a residue left by detergents and minerals in hard water areas, but the vinegar wash will clean it.

* * *

P    *I think I have hard water.*

S    Here's an easy way to see if you have hard water problems: Add one-fourth teaspoon powdered laundry detergent to one pint of warm water. Shake. If there are no suds or if the suds don't stay "sudsy," the water is probably hard. Increase the amount of detergent you use and give clothes an extra rinse, using a little vinegar.

* * *

P    *Long-sleeve shirts always tangle in the washer, and it's like pulling eye teeth to get them undone sometimes.*

S    Simply button the sleeves to the front of the shirt- (button one or two buttons of the shirt) and no more problem.

* * *

P      *Help! I was doing the laundry and the machine looked like Mt. St. Helens with all the suds.*

S      You can sprinkle them with salt, and then rinse well; it won't hurt the fabric. Running a bar of soap through detergent suds will kill those little devils instantly . . . this is good to know when washing dishes.

\*    \*    \*

P      *With everyone in our house doing their own laundry, keeping up with washing instructions can be a problem.*

S      Post the general laundry instructions in a place where all can read easily at a glance what temperature, how much detergent, etc.

\*    \*    \*

P      *Is it necessary to rinse clothes in hot water?*

S      No! The disinfecting and cleansing of the detergent has already taken place. You're merely rinsing out water from clean clothes, and cold water works just as well as hot. Plus, we all need to conserve energy any way we can!

\*    \*    \*

Add about a cup of white vinegar to your rinse water. The vinegar dissolves all the "gook" and soap film residues and gets your wash cleaner. Don't worry about hurting your clothes—one cup of vinegar is too mild to harm fabrics.

\*    \*    \*

Give your clothes an extra spin in the washer after they have gone through the usual cycles. You will be amazed at the extra water left in garments. They will dry faster in the dryer, and line dry quicker, too.

**Blankets**
*(Also see Outdoor Drying, p. 137)*

P      *My blankets don't come out soft and fluffy after
       they're washed.*

S      Rinse them in two cups of white vinegar to a
       washer full of water. The vinegar will help restore
       their softness and fluffiness, and they'll smell fresh,
       too!

                    *      *      *

P      *My blankets need cleaning but it costs so much to
       take them all to the cleaners—dare I try to wash
       them myself?*

S      No problem, if you follow a few basics. Check the
       label on your blanket to see if it is washable. Then
       fill your washer with detergent and water. Make
       sure the detergent is *completely dissolved* in the
       water before adding the blanket. Put the blanket
       evenly around in the water and let it soak fifteen
       to twenty minutes. Then start the washer and let
       the blanket agitate on gentle for about three min-
       utes.

       Rinse them in two cups of white vinegar to a
       washer full of water. The vinegar will help restore
       their softness and fluffiness, and they'll smell fresh,
       too!

**Delicates**
*(See Hand Washing, p. 143)*

Delicate fabrics such as knits, sheers, etc., should be washed separately and require gentle agitation or hand washing.

*Diapers*

Never use ammonia to disinfect diapers. Your baby will wind up with an A-1 case of diaper rash if you do. Wring the diapers out and wash them in your washer using hot water and detergent. Rinse thoroughly (two rinses are preferable for diapers), adding one-half cup vinegar in the final rinse.

*Items, heavy*

P       *My rubber-backed bath mat peels and comes off in the washer—a mess.*

S       Wash and dry it in a pillow case; if a pillow case is too small, make one out of an old sheet.

*Small Items*

P       *I always lose my baby's tiny socks when I put them in the washing machine.*

S       Those lovely little socks can be troublesome, but if you will simply safety pin them to a towel or large piece of clothing they will never be lost again.

*Laundromat*

If you have to do your laundry in a laundromat or in your apartment laundry room, you know how frustrating it is when you want to do your laundry and you don't have the "correct change, please!" Always keep a cookie jar (even if it's only a mayo jar) with extra quarters, dimes and nickels . . . you will then be assured of always having the correct change for the laundry. If you need mad money, it's there—at least enough for a pizza!

\*　　\*　　\*

If you take your wash to a laundromat or you can't hear the timer on your washing machine or dryer, carry a little egg timer with you

. . . it sure saves on leaving your things in too long, which can cause unnecessary wrinkles in permanent press things.

*    *    *

If you use a laundromat, it's worth the time at home to sort your laundry into the loads that you will have to do. If you get there and there are only two machines available and you have three loads, it is a simple matter to at least get two done without much hassle.

### Lint

**P**    *My clothes end up with lint all over them.*

**S**    Turn the garments inside out before washing. If you do your wash at a laundromat, wipe the inside of the machine out first with wet paper towels before using.

### Pretreatment
### *(Also see Stains and Spots, p. 157)*

Part of the reason that pretreats and presoak cleaners work so well is that you put them directly on the offending spot. Keep a squeeze bottle (clearly marked) that you have filled with liquid dishwashing detergent handy . . . give those nasty spots a quick squirt, a little rub, and toss in the machine—you might be surprised!

*    *    *

**P**    *I always forget which clothes need extra treatment when it is laundry time.*

**S**    As soon as you take an item off and you know that it needs to be spot-treated or whatever, pin the spot with a safety pin or put a clothespin on it to draw your attention to it on laundry day.

*Post-washing*
*(Also see Ironing, p. 139)*

P          *After wearing a dress only once, sometimes it is still clean enough for me to wear it again, but I hate to hang it in my closet with the newly laundered clothes.*

S          If you will hang a garment up immediately after taking it off, your body heat will make most wrinkles fall right out. Let the item air well before putting it in your closet and it will be ready for your next wearing without a fuss.

*Silk*
*(see p. 144)*

*Sweaters*
*(see p. 145)*

**SORTING**
**(Also see Hampers, p. 141)**

P          *Sorting clothes—there are so many people in my family that just putting the clothes away after washing is a major chore.*

S          Sort them all in one place and divide them so that each person has their own pile. Then let them put their own things away.

\*    \*    \*

P          *Finding the right size sheet to match the pillow cases is a really hunt-and-seek chore in my house.*

S          If you have different size beds, mark the size of each sheet on one edge with a permanent marker . . . twin, king, etc. Then you can see which sheet it is without having to pull out and unfold.

If you will make a package when folding the laundry, you won't ever have to search for the lost sheet again. One top, one bottom, and the pillow cases (all the same size and pattern) all folded together. Pull the whole kit and kaboodle out and no more looking for the lost pillow case.

\* \* \*

**P**    *Turning socks right side out drives me up the wall —my boys just won't listen.*

**S**    Wash them the way they throw them in the hamper; if it doesn't bother them to wear them inside out, it shouldn't bother you. Look at it this way— they will be right side out every other wash time!

\* \* \*

**P**    *Matching up socks is the world's worse chore when laundry day comes.*

**S**    Tie them together loosely at the tops, or pin them together; or, buy all one color and never have to worry again!

\* \* \*

**P**    *I can never tell which socks are my son's and which are my husband's—they both wear the same size now.*

**S**    Code them: Use blue thread for one and red for the other. Whip a few stitches in the top of each sock.

## STAINS AND SPOTS

It seems the whole world is one big spot. I don't know if we are just a messy lot, or it's a fact of nature that very few things remain stain-free for a lifetime.

This section on stain removal should help you through the irritating times at home when you get a "spot" on something and want to know how to get it out.

A lot of the solutions to these problems are simple things you have around your house because I have tried to make it as easy for you as possible.

The first and foremost rule to stain removal is to get to it ASAP (as soon as possible), if not quicker. The general rule is: Flush with cold water then proceed to do your magic.

Always consider what the stain is, how long it has been there and what kind of material you are working on.

I wouldn't touch velvet or silk with a magic wand. When in doubt, *don't*. If you have something that is very expensive or very special, it is worth the money to take it to a professional cleaner. They know what they are doing. Always tell them what the stain is, and don't be embarrassed to tell them if you have done anything to it to try to get the stain out. If you aren't honest, when they put their cleaning chemical on it, there might be a reaction that you won't like.

For home care, the simplest is the best. Following all instructions both on the garment and on the bottle of whatever you are using is very important. If one thing doesn't work, be sure to rinse well before going on to the next or you might end up with a hole in the fabric.

When removing a spot, work from the back of the material first; you don't want to push that stain in even more. Always blot from the outside of the stain in; otherwise, you will end up with a larger spot than you began with.

Prewash sprays are great, but remember, most of them need to be rinsed in warm water to work well. Also, just spraying on and tossing into the machine sometimes isn't enough. A little elbow grease, or wrist action, is required first to work at the spot.

Read instructions and information *before* starting to spot treat something instead of afterwards when you have already ruined your favorite shirt or blouse.

\*    \*    \*

| | |
|---|---|
| **P** | *My clothes are gray.* |
| **S** | Check your water supply. If it's cloudy or has sediment in it, naturally your clothes are going to look that way, too. Maybe the water is too hard |

and you need to use an extra amount of detergent and also a fabric softener. You might be overloading your washer; clothes need to agitate freely.

\*   \*   \*

**P**   *Ring around the collar—I hate it and I know it's not my fault. I only do the wash!*

**S**   You are right, honey child. Ring around the collar is not the fault of the person doing the wash, but the person who wears the shirt. I am not saying that the person who wears the shirt doesn't bathe, it's just a basic fact of nature that no matter how well you scrub the back of your neck there are oil glands back there that really do get a workout.

If you will have the wearer of the shirt take a piece of white facial tissue or a white washcloth, put some rubbing alcohol on it and rub over the back of his neck, he will see the result and know it's not your fault.

There are several things that you can do to prevent this. Be sure the neck is clean by rubbing it with alcohol before putting on the shirt. If it is really bad, one can put an antiperspirant on the back of the neck providing there are no allergies . . . it really helps.

If shirts do have ring around the collar, you can rub chalk into the "ring" to absorb the oil prior to laundering his shirts. Also, you can use prewash spray on it. Another good way to get rid of it is to rub in some hair shampoo before your usual washing. This is where that old extra toothbrush comes in handy, too. Just give a little scrub-a-dub-dub and no more yuck!

\*   \*   \*

For spit-up stains on baby clothes, make a paste of unseasoned meat tenderizer and water, rub it on the stain, and wash as usual, rinsing in vinegar and water.

\*     \*     \*

P       *I have tried several things but can't get a stain out —what can I try now?*

S       Some folks have good luck with the hot sun and lemon treatment; it depends on the stain but it's worth a try. Wet the stain with lemon juice and spread the garment out flat so the sun's rays will get to it full strength. Leave the garment out all day.

\*     \*     \*

P       *What are some common stain removers?*

S       A list of common stain removers are:

1. *Chlorine Bleach:* Don't use bleach full strength. One part bleach to four parts water is about right. Always read the bottle instructions.

2. *Detergent Paste:* Mix enough detergent granules with water to make a paste. Test materials for light bleaching.

3. *Hydrogen Peroxide:* The three percent solution can be used straight out of the bottle (you can buy this at a drugstore).

4. *Vinegar:* Use only white vinegar (cider or wine vinegar might spot light fabrics). One part white vinegar to four parts water.

HELOISE'S GUIDE FOR STAIN REMOVAL

ALCOHOL:       Rinse hurriedly in a cold water and vinegar solution. If the alcohol is spilled on the carpet, sponge up the alcohol spot quickly with a water and vinegar solution and then dry with paper towels. If the color has "bled," the damage can't be undone.

ANTIPERSPIRANT:
Blot the spot with a paper towel moistened with a solution of vinegar or baking soda. Soaking may be required. Wash in the hottest water safe for fabric.

BALL-POINT INK:
Hair spray works well on most inks. Spray and blot the stain with a clean cloth.

Fingernail polish remover (if safe for fabric) and prewash sprays will work on some ink stains.

BEVERAGES, FRUIT JUICES, COCKTAILS:
Do not use soap. Remove spot with liquid detergent or hydrogen peroxide bleach.

BLOOD:
Flush with cold water first and use a liquid detergent next. Dampen and sprinkle unflavored meat tenderizer and let sit. Hydrogen peroxide is another very good home remedy if fabric can take light bleaching. Just pour on and let bubble away, then rinse out in cold water.

CANDLE WAX:
Flick off as much of the hard wax as possible with your fingernail or a plastic credit card. Place paper towels on either side of the material where the wax stain is and iron on a low to medium setting, depending on the fabric. If any stain remains, go over it with liquid detergent and water, and then rinse or wash as usual.

CANDY:
Rub a little detergent on the stain with cold water and rinse; for stubborn red stains, soak the item in strong laundry detergent and a little bleach (if material will take it), or treat with prewash spray.

CATSUP:

Blot up as much as possible. Rinse or soak in cold water. Spray with prewash product. Liquid detergent works sometimes.

CHEWING GUM:

Place an ice cube on the gum to harden it. Then scrape it off with a spoon. Go over the back of the stain with a prewash spray and wash as usual. You can also put the garment in the freezer to harden the gum and then scrape it off.

CHOCOLATE:

Always use cold water. Use a prewash spray, ammonia, or sometimes hydrogen peroxide. Work into fabric and let set. Rinse out in cold water.

COFFEE:

First rinse in cold water, then bleach if safe for the fabric, or use nonchlorine bleach (powdered). This is an exception to the "don't use hot water" rule: After spot treating wash in the hottest water safe for the fabric.

COSMETICS:

Grab that bar of soap and wet the stain a little and rub-a-dub-dub! If the stain remains, use straight liquid detergent, work into the spot and launder as usual.

CRAYON:

See "Candle Wax." Use same method.

FRUIT:

The sooner you get to the fruit stain the better. Flood the stain with cold water and then treat with a prewash spray. If the stain has dried, soak it in cool water. Then work some detergent in the stain and rinse. Use a color-safe bleach when laundering.

GRASS:

If material is bleach-safe, use bleach according to bottle directions. If not, use hydrogen peroxide to soak in, then launder as usual.

GREASE:

Treat with commercial degreaser product. Or place the stain face down on paper towels and go over the back with dry cleaning solvent, working from the outside in. Always use a clean white cloth. Then, dampen the stain with water and go over it with a bar of soap or liquid detergent. Hair shampoo will break down some types of grease.

LIPSTICK:

Treat with prewash spray and rub the spot with a clean paper towel. Keep applying the spray and keep changing the paper towel. Finally, dampen the stain and rub a bar of soap over it. Wash as usual.

MILDEW:

Lemon juice and salt, or white vinegar and salt will kill the mildew. Place in sun. Wash as usual. Always wash separately—you don't want to spread that stuff.

MILK:

Soak in warm water using an enzyme presoak product.

MUSTARD:

Use peroxide or white vinegar to get it out. Don't use ammonia. Wash as usual.

TEA:

See "Coffee."

URINE: (carpet)

Absorb as much of the liquid as possible with paper towels. Then go over the area from the outside in with a solution of white vinegar and water. Keep blotting with paper towels until no wetness comes through. If a stain remains, a mild solution of liquid detergent and water should do the trick, being sure to rinse well. You can sprinkle with baking soda or salt to absorb any extra moisture, and it helps deodorize.

If you use salt, be sure and empty the vacuum after picking up.

URINE: (clothing)

Soak the stain in an enzyme presoak product with a little bleach. Wash as usual. Sponging with diluted white vinegar or perborate bleach may help restore the original color. NOTE: Do NOT use ammonia on diapers.

WINE:

I have great luck with pouring club soda on the stain, then rinsing in cool water. If the material is bleach-safe, go to it (natch, according to bottle instructions). Dishwasher detergent does wonders on stubborn stains like wine. Make a paste with a little water and scrub with an old toothbrush. Wash in the hottest water possible for the material after first spot treating.

# 4

## *Sewing*

Sew! If you think this chapter is going to tell you how to make a suit or whip up some new slip covers for your sofa, I hate to disappoint you, but that's not the kind of information most of you ask Heloise. What this chapter will help you with are some of the problems that we fimble-(no, not nimble-) fingered people face.

I, for one, can fix almost any garment with a few safety pins, some glue or tape, and a lot of luck. I won't guarantee that my kind of mending will last forever, or is really the "proper" way, but it will hold me through most any day, and then some.

The problems you face and feel frustrated about are the problems that we all encounter one time or another. So, don't feel alone when the bobbin runs out and you have just sewn the straightest seam in your life, or the button you sewed on yesterday falls off right in the middle of lunch.

I hope you never know sheer panic such as I did at a dinner party in a very fancy restaurant with a pretty new dress on, when the nylon thread from the hem caught on something and unraveled all the way to the restroom.

That's when what I like to call my "Heloise ingenuity" comes to the rescue. Well, it was either come up with some way to fix it, or start a new style for the messy, raveled look. Tape to the rescue! I popped over to the front desk, explained my plight and the desk clerk gave me an entire roll of tape (bless his sweet soul). It worked beautifully.

I know some people who hem all their blue jeans with silver duct tape. They swear that it holds through washing after washing, and nary a stitch sewn. All power to you if that's what you can live with. Remember, it's you that has to live with it. If tape and safety pins don't bother you, then by all means do your best. The most important consideration is how it looks on the outside . . . if safety pins show through, then I suggest you look at yourself the way others will see you.

If you can't mend a garment back to its original look, and it just can't be worn, don't give up. We all need lounging-around clothes or grubbies to wear while washing the car and potting plants.

Do you know that industrial shops like plumbers, mechanics, etc., pay for a box of rags (at last check it was seventeen dollars here in San Antonio) . . . you just might have a gold mine in your sewing hamper. Put all your scraps, unmendables, etc., to good use. Give them to the grease monkey in your family, or use them to wipe up spills or really greasy messes, and then have no guilt about throwing them away.

Get out that needle and thread and save a shirt today . . . it may turn out to be your favorite. I am still wearing my father's military shirts that are over fifteen years old and my very favorites.


## BUTTONS

Cut buttons for doll clothes out of a plastic lid using a paper punch, then poke holes for the thread with a hot needle (only adults should handle a hot needle).

| | |
|---|---|
| **Problem** | *Keeping those teensy little buttons in place when making garments for a wee one is so hard.* |
| **Solution** | Roll a small piece of regular tape in a circle, sticky side out. Stick the tape onto the back of the button, then position the button on the fabric. It will stay in place while you stitch; then cut away the tape using small, curved cuticle scissors. |

\* \* \*

| | |
|---|---|
| **P** | *I hate having to use several strands of thread when sewing on buttons that get a lot of wear and tear.* |
| **S** | Nylon fishing line, or dental floss, is very strong and will hold through most any rough treatment. |

\* \* \*

Having trouble sewing on a coat or suit button? Slip a round toothpick or tines of a fork between the button and the fabric. Sew the button on over the toothpick or tine. Remove the toothpick (or tine) and wrap the remaining thread around the thread holding the button, forming a post. This creates some "play" in the button and it won't pop off.

\* \* \*

To keep matching buttons together, stick them to a strip of cellophane tape. Cover with a second strip of tape. Snip off buttons as needed.

**P**      *Buttons, buttons, buttons—they're all over my sewing basket.*

**S**      Use those nifty twisties from bread or plastic bags. Slip them on and you can even color-code.

*        *        *

A real quick way to keep buttons together is to slip them on a large safety pin and pin it closed.

## MACHINE SEWING

*Bobbins*

**P**      *I don't have enough bobbins.*

**S**      In a jam, transfer the thread left on one bobbin onto a three inch piece of plastic straw. Now you have an empty bobbin to use. The straw will fit back on the spindle of my machine to use as the top thread. Why don't you try it on yours?

*        *        *

P      *I always run out of bobbin thread right in the middle of a project. It drives me batty.*

S      Fill two or three empty bobbins with the various colors you need . . . no more frustration. Bonus: you can use the thread for hand stitching. A few extra bobbins are worth the investment.

\*     \*     \*

P      *I have the hardest time remembering how to wind my bobbin and put on the zipper foot on my machine. I know it's silly, but . . .*

S      Always keep the instruction booklet nearby. If you have a permanent sewing area, place those pages in easy sight, or tape them to the back of the machine.

     You can also tape the threading diagram right on the machine.

## Height Adjustment

P      *I'm a shortie and I cannot find a table low enough for my portable sewing machine.*

S      Try using a typing table (used ones can be found very reasonably priced).

     To keep down vibration, put a sheet of one-inch foam rubber under the machine. The height of the table, even for a "shortie," should be perfect.

\*     \*     \*

Your sewing machine table makes a wonderful extra display, or serving table when not in use. Just cover with a pretty tablecloth or printed sheet.

## Needles

P      *Changing needles in my sewing machine is a major chore. I seem to be all thumbs.*

S         Slip a needle threader into the eye of the sewing machine needle. You can hold the needle steady while inserting it into the correct position, yet your fingers will be back out of the way.

## Oiling

P         *I am always having to have my machine cleaned and oiled.*

S         A sewing machine is like any other electric appliance that moves; you should keep it as dust-free as possible. Always cover it when not in use; it will save you money in the long run.

\*     \*     \*

P         *I oil my machine but I got oil on the fabric as soon as I started sewing.*

S         Stitch through a blotter (or paper towels) to catch any excess oil, or stitch through a layer or two of scrap fabric first.

## Pedals

P         *The foot control of my sewing machine "wanders" and I'm forever chasing it.*

S         Glue a piece of foam rubber or self-gripping tape on the bottom of the control. It will stay put.

\*     \*     \*

P         *The foot pedal on my machine gets unbelievably dusty and dirty, even though I consider myself a good housekeeper. I know this will cause damage eventually.*

S         Cover the pedal with a plastic bag and place a twistie around it to close it. It will keep it clean and dust-free, and this is important, considering replacement costs. You can use it as long as it

doesn't slip around. If it does, place it on a piece
of foam rubber.

\*   \*   \*

P     *I have always used a sewing machine with a knee
      pedal. My new one has a foot pedal, but I prefer my
      old knee one.*

S     Place the foot pedal at the correct height and tape
      it to the leg or pedestal, etc., of your sewing ma-
      chine with masking tape.

## Seams

Save yourself time from getting up to go iron each seam one at a
time. Sew all small pieces at once, then iron them all at the same time.

## Static

P     *I'll be sewing along and suddenly my machine
      starts acting cantankerously.*

S     Some of the fabrics we sew on today cause a
      buildup on the needle and machine that you are
      unable to see. Also, hair spray, grease in the air,
      etc., cause buildup. Clean the needle, the bottom
      of the pressure foot, and also the tension discs
      often with plain old rubbing alcohol and a cotton
      ball, or cotton swab.

## Supplies, machine
(*Also see Machine sewing, p. 168*)

P     *My sewing machine has no drawers for holding
      sewing paraphernalia and other drawer space is
      already at a premium in our house.*

S     Make a small (or as large as desired) shoebag-type
      holder and hang it over or near your sewing ma-
      chine. It will keep all those little odds and ends

such as a tape measure, seam ripper, scissors, etc., together in one place.

\*    \*    \*

Hang a calendar towel on the wall behind your sewing machine so you can see it at a glance.

Besides making an attractive wall hanging, you will have something to pin your guide sheet to when sewing, without damaging the walls.

\*    \*    \*

Put a double band of stretch or knit fabric around the neck of the sewing machine to put the pins in as you sew. They are right there and always handy.

\*    \*    \*

P    *How can I mend a loosely knit sweater or fabric without the pressure foot catching in the loops?*

S    Use the reverse stitch and sew backwards. The rounded edges on the back of the pressure foot will glide over the loose weave with nary a snag.

\*    \*    \*

P    *How can I tell when the tension on my machine needs adjusting?*

S    Put a dark spool of thread on the top spindle, white thread on the bobbin; then, stitch on a neutral color material. If the top tension is too loose or tight, it will easily show up. The same with the bobbin. Adjust until you have a perfect stitch.

\*    \*    \*

P    *I am a novice seamstress with a new sewing machine and keep forgetting how to thread it properly.*

S    Cut the thread off at the spool when you want to rethread with another color, etc., but leave it in all the stations. Put on the spool with your new color.

Tie the new color onto the old one with a double

knot and *gently* pull it through all the tension stations, and if the knot is not too large, through the eye of the needle.

You'll be ready to continue sewing in a jiffy.

\* \* \*

P   *I can't thread elastic through a casing easily.*

S   Stitch down the seams that will be inside the casing (before making it, of course); then afterwards, the elastic should glide right through.

\* \* \*

P   *How can I topstitch when my machine has only one spindle to hold the spool of thread? One thickness of thread doesn't seem to do the job.*

S   Try using a piece of heavy plastic drinking straw as a post extender. The more narrow paper straw would probably work best since the holes in a spool of thread sometimes aren't very large.

\* \* \*

P   *I sew a lot and find it difficult to thread my sewing machine needle because the polyester threads fray so badly.*

S   Tape a small piece of soap to the top of your sewing machine. (If you are afraid it might harm the finish, fold a piece of foil or a piece of plastic and place it under the soap).

When ready to thread the needle, dampen the thread and roll it on the soap with your finger.

This seems to seal and stiffen the thread so it will go through the needle easier.

\* \* \*

When threading your sewing machine, put the pressure foot in the down position onto the pressure plate.

This will give your fingers more room to get at that ornery small needle hole with the thread.

If you cannot see well enough to thread your sewing machine needle while it's in the machine, remove it, thread it, then reinsert it in its proper groove.

## PATTERNS AND CUTTING

Taking care of a pattern is really worth the effort. If you find a pattern that you like and one that fits, etc., you can use it over and over.

Finding the perfect pattern, or one that you really like may take some time. The hardest part is that you really have to be honest with yourself. When the pattern says thirty-six inches around the hips, if you are thirty-nine or forty, honey child, that isn't gonna cut it. I know we all like to fit into a size smaller, but when you get home, no one knows but you ... so by all means, be realistic.

If you can't seem to get all those pieces back into that tiny paper envelope, there really is a simple solution. Place the smaller pieces all on top of the larger ones, press lightly with a warm iron and fold to fit.

If you have a lot of patterns to store, roll them up, place each one in a brown paper lunch bag, and cut off the picture and all the outside information (amount of material, accessories needed, etc.) and tape them to the outside. It's all there and easy to locate. You can even make little notes to yourself such as, "like this pattern," or "was easy to sew," or "only needs one zipper."

Take care of those patterns and they will take care of you ...

*　　*　　*

P　　*Sewing saves so much money, but, oh! how I hate to cut out the garment when I'm really in the mood to just start sewing.*

S　　Besides having to cut out the garment, many times you can't find matching thread or may have even misplaced the pattern.

　　You can solve all these problems by cutting out two or three items at once, then placing each one in a separate box, along with needed sewing notions and instructions.

Then, on the day you are in the mood to sew, you won't take a chance of getting "out of the mood" as everything will be at your fingertips.

\*    \*    \*

P    *How can I cut fabric in a perfectly straight line?*
S    As you know, the sales people who work in fabric stores use a grooved table to measure and cut. You can do the same thing by pulling an extendable table apart slightly and using the center opening to guide your cutting. Keep fabric taut as you cut.

\*    \*    \*

Before cutting a pattern out, be sure to measure yourself (or whomever you are sewing for) and the pattern to be sure you have the same measurements. . . . sometimes a size twelve can be a ten or even a fourteen. . . .

\*    \*    \*

P    *I don't have a cutting table, and I'm unable to get down on the floor to cut fabric.*
S    Use the dining room (or any long) table extended as far as possible. If you have a protective pad, turn it slick-side down, to protect the table from pins. If you find the dining room table too low, ask for help and set the table on four cans of equal height. Canned goods out of your pantry work fine.

\*    \*    \*

P    *How can I lengthen a pattern without having to cut the piece apart?*
S    Merely pin down the length of the pattern to the "adjusting line," be it the waist-, hip- or hemline. Place a pin directly across the cutting line at this point so when you come to it you will naturally stop. At this point, unpin your pattern, and slide it down, adding the extra length needed. Repin and continue cutting.

P       *When I use tape for my pattern it always tears the pattern or leaves gunk on the material.*

S       Pink hair tape is perfect and is especially good for materials like leather and Ultrasuede that really shouldn't be pinned.

\*       \*       \*

P       *What can I use if I don't have a tracing wheel?*

S       A pizza cutter works just like a tracing wheel.

## Hand Sewing and Mending

Place a small pillow in your lap when doing hand sewing. You won't have to lean over so far to see what you are doing.

It gives you a smooth, soft surface on which to work and is a wonderful backsaver. Especially nice when embroidering.

\*       \*       \*

P       *My eyesight is poor and I can't sew well on dark fabric when doing hand sewing.*

S       Use a white thread, along with a dark one through the needle. The white thread will enable you to see where you have stitched. When you're finished, remove the white thread.

\*       \*       \*

P       *The hem came out of my dress and there was no way to repair it at the moment.*

S       Tape the hem carefully with clean adhesive-backed tape, or even double-sided sticky tape.

\*       \*       \*

P       *When I let a hem down, the crease mark shows.*

S       Dampen the crease with white vinegar. Place a press cloth over the material, then press with a moderately hot iron.

\*       \*       \*

P      *I discovered a hole in my pants pocket at work and didn't have a needle and thread to sew the tear.*

S      Either pull the pocket out, or work from the inside and wrap a rubberband tightly around the hole. It will keep you from losing your belongings until you have time to mend it properly.

*   *   *

Going to the doctor's and have to wait, or have a long-winded friend? This is the time to do that mending. Just take one or two small pieces at a time. My, how the work flies!

### Learning to Sew

P      *I want my little girl to learn to sew, but I'm not sure of a good way to begin to teach her.*

S      To start her off, cut up scraps of material you have left and let her make a patchwork quilt for her doll's bed.

     She will learn how to put the colors and pieces together and how to sew them.

     What's more, she will have the special pleasure of using something which she has made all by herself.

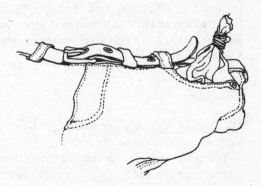

*Marking*

Use a leftover sliver of soap for marking seams, hems, etc. The mark will disappear after a hot iron hits it. Better than tailor's chalk.

\*   \*   \*

P   *I use a lead pencil to mark darts, etc., but I have a terrible time getting it off.*

S   Don't use a pencil. Use a sliver of soap instead. It will wash right out.

\*   \*   \*

P   *Tracing darts always tear the patterns after a few uses. Now what?*

S   When the pattern is new, make holes in the pattern where the darts should be and stick on little round paper reinforcements like those you use on note-book paper. Each time you mark your pattern, use a piece of chalk through the reinforced holes.

*Organizing*

P   *I am really messy when I sew and I hate to clean up after myself.*

S   Tape a large grocery or shopping bag to your sewing machine or cutting table and toss those tiny fabric scraps and bits of thread in it. Once you get into the habit, I promise your sewing area will be a mess no more.

*Patching*

P   *My sons get holes in their jeans even before I can wash them twice (or so it seems).*

S   When patching holes in jeans, especially in the knees, since you are doing it anyway, put a patch on the inside as well as the out. Double protection.

Prevention is the answer, though. Start out by putting patching on the inside. No one will see them and it will save you a lot of work later.

\*     \*     \*

P    *Those iron-on patches don't seem to stay put very long. The edges curl.*

S    If that is the case, it's worth the extra time to just run a line of stitching around the edges.

\*     \*     \*

P    *I hate sewing on patches! And I have three boys in scouting!*

S    First, use a fabric glue to hold the patch in place. Just a dab—then when it dries, stitch the patch on in jig time! No slipping or sliding.

## Professional Touches

P    *I get so tired of the same old look. Seems as if you can spot my homemade clothes a mile away.*

S    Check mail order catalogs and fashion magazines to keep up with the latest looks and colors. You'll get lots of ideas from them. Sometimes adding an extra pocket here, a little trim there, will jazz up your clothes.

## SCISSORS

A quick way to "oil" your scissors is to carefully rub them in between your fingers and thumb. There is usually enough natural oil to lubricate the blades without a lot of drip or fear of too much oil on your scissors.

Be sure to give your scissors a good cleaning and oiling every once in a while, as they will get a slight buildup of threads and grime from the material you cut. (Always wipe well and cut some scraps first before using to be sure no oil is left).

\*　　\*　　\*

P　　*My sewing scissors are always missing, and it's not me that moves them from my sewing area.*

S　　Little hands do seem to spirit them away, don't they? Tie your scissors to your machine, or sewing table, with a long piece of yarn (if you want it to look pretty), or twine, etc. They won't go very far.

\*　　\*　　\*

P　　*I hate running back and forth to snip little threads when I am pressing things. And sometimes I don't get around to doing it later.*

S　　Attach an extra pair of small scissors to the end of your ironing board with enough slack so you can use them. (Caution: if you have little ones around, be sure they don't think this is a play toy).

\*　　\*　　\*

P　　*Any way to quickly sharpen my scissors?*

S　　For everyday scissors, cutting sandpaper or a steel wool pad helps sharpen them enough. If you have special sewing scissors that you paid a few bucks for, take them to a professional.

\*　　\*　　\*

P　　*I always stab myself reaching into my sewing basket to locate my scissors.*

S　　Stick the pointed end of your scissors into a piece of cork, and no more worries.

## SEWING POINTERS AND SUPPLIES
### (Also see Organizing Your Sewing Box, p. 185)

*Basting*

**P**    *I could cry when the gathering is nearly perfect—and nearly finished—then the basting stitch breaks.*

**S**    Never trust just one row of basting stitch. Take the extra time to stitch three gathering rows about three-eighths inch apart, leaving long strands on each end to work with. If one thread breaks, you will still have two to hold on to. Always pull the bobbin threads from each end, working toward the center.

*Bedspreads*

**P**    *I want to make a ruffled bedspread for my little girl's bed, but panic at the thought of keeping all those gathers intact until I can stitch them in place.*

**S**    "Steal" a spool of monofilament fishing line from your husband's tackle box. Lay the fishing line (don't cut it off the spool) on the ruffle just above the seam line. Zigzag *over* the line, but don't catch the fishing line in the stitching. Continue all around the ruffle.

When finished, the line will slide easily through the material. If you knot the line first, you can gather it up some as you go, if you like. Stitch the ruffle onto the spread, being careful not to catch the fishing line. Pull it through and rewind.

## Belts

**P**    *I can't make belt loops that look neat.*

**S**    The easiest way I've found is to use about six strands of sewing thread, six inches long. Slide the strands under the pressure foot and use a zigzag stitch catching all six strands. Neatest and quickest belt loop you ever saw!

\*  \*  \*

**P**    *Turning belts, straps and suspenders of new garments is such a struggle.*

**S**    After sewing your belt inside out, attach a safety pin of appropriate size to the closed end of the belt and just push it through (large end first) to turn it right side out. The pin glides easily through the material and you can feel where it is as you work it along. No chance of losing it.

## Collars

**P**    *I can't get collar points to look tailor-made*

**S**    After trimming the collar seam close to the points, turn the collar right side out. Thread a needle and tie a rather large knot in the end. Insert the needle through the stitches at the collar point and pull it through. Cut the thread off close to the fabric and you have a "professional" pointed collar.

## Equipment

**P**    *I'm told using the proper tools helps to give home sewing a more professional look, but after pricing hams, sleeve rolls, etc., my budget says, "wait awhile."*

**S**    No need to . . . make your own! A roll of toilet tissue covered with foil, then with terry cloth or any fabric which will withstand the heat of an iron, makes an excellent pressing ham. Or, use an old wig form as a pressing ham, covering it per above. Great!

A half-used roll of paper towels, covered as suggested above, can be used as a sleeve roll, and a small pressing board to fit inside a pants leg, or whatever, can be made from an empty cardboard tube that fabric stores use to roll bolts of material.

Pick one up the next time you're buying fabric. (Or just go in and ask for one. Most stores just throw them away.) Pad it somewhat, then cover it with any desired fabric. This board can even be used as a seam board for pressing straight seams. Just stand it on its side.

This equipment is so handy and lightweight, you can keep it right at your sewing machine.

And, you surely can't beat the price!

\*    \*    \*

Use a magnet to pick up spilled pins and needles off the floor.

\*    \*    \*

P       *My seam ripper is always missing.*

S       Glue a small magnet to your sewing machine head. The metal part of the seam ripper will quickly adhere and hang on. Just remember to always put it there after each use.

### Fabrics, difficult

P       *Single knit T-shirt material always curls on the edges.*

S       Lightly spray starch the cut edges and let dry. You will give it just enough stiffness to make it easier to work with.

\*    \*    \*

Sewing velvet and need to press some pieces? Place them right side down on top of a heavy terry or turkish towel, and press gently.

\* \* \*

P      *I sew a lot of heavy fabric and the needle sticks.*

S      Lightly rub a bar of soap across the seam line and it will help the needle go in easily.

\* \* \*

P      *When I sew the new sheer fabrics, the seams always pucker.*

S      Try using strips of tissue paper under each seam as you stitch. It will help keep the fabric in place, thus causing less pulling and tugging, and it tears right off.

## Fasteners (hooks, etc.)

P      *I can't match up snaps when sewing them on a garment.*

S      Sew the small part of the snap on first. Rub a piece of chalk over the little point, then carefully place the top piece of fabric over the snap in the proper position and rub the back with your finger. The chalk will mark the spot for the top part of the snap.

\* \* \*

P      *The eye part of my hook & eye came off and I couldn't get to a sewing box.*

S      A small safety pin on the wrong side of the fabric works as an eye in a pinch.

## Fitting

P      *I would love to sew for my grandchildren but I don't live close to them so fitting is a problem.*

S        Ask their mother to draw the outline of the child on a piece of butcher paper, or something similar. Include waist measurement, height, arm length, etc., on the drawing. Fitting will then be a cinch. They will enjoy doing it, too. What a wonderful record of growth later on.

### Leftover Fabrics

Cutting off a pair of jeans? Save the legs to make a "ditty" bag for a catchall for the kids, or a clothespin bag.

### Organizing Your Sewing Box
### (Also see Sewing Pointers and Supplies, p. 181)

P        *My sewing box looks as if a tornado hit it . . . always*

S        A small metal or plastic tool box is good. Also, the small plastic boxes with lots of little drawers in it can store many different items, and you can see what is in each drawer.

*   *   *

P        *I always stick myself on loose needles in my sewing box.*

S        Drop them in a clear plastic pill bottle and snap on the top. Tape an adhesive bandage on the out-

side and just slide your threaded needle through the padded part of the bandage after using, like a little pin cushion. Wrap the extra thread around the bottle.

\*    \*    \*

P      *Spools of thread in my sewing box become un-wound and the ends get so tangled I have to cut them to get the spools apart.*

S      Once you get them apart, tape the ends of the thread to the spool with a smidgen of clear adhesive tape. The thread won't come unwound, and it's a simple matter to remove the tape when the thread is to be used. Save the tape and reuse it later on the same spool.

     This is a good rainy day project for the kids. They love it!

     Another idea which works well is to put the spools of thread of like colors in a clear plastic bag. Close the bag with a twistie, then place them in a drawer of your box. The colors can be easily seen for quick selection and the tangling problem is solved.

\*    \*    \*

An empty adhesive tape spool makes a handy holder for a tape measure.

\*    \*    \*

P      *My knitting needles get scattered to the four winds.*
S      Save an aluminum foil box to store those needles in.

### Retrieving Needles

     Before discarding a pin cushion, cut the covering with your scissors.

Hold it over a pan or pie plate, etc., and carefully check the sawdust inside for pins and needles. Amazing, sometimes, how many are buried inside.

*    *    *

Put a pin cushion in the guest bedroom, along with several needles threaded in different colors of thread. Stick a few safety pins of assorted sizes in the pin cushion, also.

Your guests can sew on a button, etc., without asking you for assistance and will appreciate your thoughtfulness, even if the items are not needed.

### Rickrack

**P**     *For the life of me I can't sew narrow rickrack in a straight line.*

**S**     First tape it in place with transparent tape. Stitch right through the tape, then the tape is easily pulled off afterwards.

### Sleeves

**P**     *Putting in sleeves frustrates me!*

**S**     One of the simplest ways I know to put in a sleeve is to stitch it in before sewing up the side seams. It's easier to ease in the fullness and then the entire side seam can be sewn in at one time.

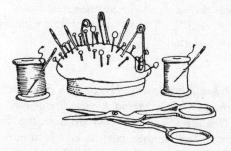

*Zippers*

P  *When I put a zipper in a garment, it puckers after*
   *laundering.*

S  This is due to the zipper shrinking. Zippers, as well
   as seam tape, hem tape, lace, etc.,—even the fabric, if it is washable—should be preshrunk before
   sewing into a garment. Nonwashable fabric, such
   as woolens, should be professionally blocked.

\*  \*  \*

P  *My zipper always sticks and I have a heck of a time*
   *getting it up.*

S  Use a lead pencil. The graphite in the lead helps,
   but don't use too much and get it on your garment.

## THREAD HANDLING AND STORING

P  *I can never find the color of thread I want without*
   *digging through the maze of thread stored in a*
   *drawer.*

S  Drive headless nails at an angle into a peg board,
   or the right size board for you. Hang the board
   over your sewing machine and you will be able to
   select the color needed quickly and easily, without
   having to hunt and seek.

\*  \*  \*

As I never seem to have the right color thread when I need it, I find
that clear nylon thread can be used instead.

It's a little more difficult to use when doing hand sewing, but it
will match any material.

\*  \*  \*

P  *When hand sewing, I can't get a nice little knot in*
   *the end of the thread for the life of me.*

S  Don't fret, 'cuz I have a hard time, too. First, wet
   your fingers, then put the end of the thread between your forefinger and thumb, then wrap the

thread around your forefinger once, and kinda roll the thread to the end of your fingers so that it catches on itself, and slowly pull to form a knot. Got that? If all else fails, sew a few stitches and tie a knot then.

\* \* \*

P   *My thread always curls up when I am hand sewing.*

S   Starting at the needle end, run your fingers all the way down the thread to the knot to untwist it and you can also slowly draw the thread between a warm iron and the ironing board to untwist it.

\* \* \*

P   *The thread always frays and I never can get it through the eye of the needle easily.*

S   A squirt of spray starch or hair spray to the rescue! Press it between your fingers, let dry and it will go right through.

\* \* \*

When using polyester thread for sewing by hand, it's prone to snarl and twist in a most aggravating way.

To overcome this, get into the habit of giving your needle a counterclockwise quarter turn each time you pull the thread through the material.

\* \* \*

P   *Static electricity causes polyester thread to knot so badly it makes hand sewing difficult.*

S   Rub a fabric softener sheet or a candle over the entire length of thread in your needle. You'll have no more tangles.

\* \* \*

P   *You wouldn't believe how tangled embroidery thread becomes when I work with it!*

S   Use one of those sponge hair rollers. Just wrap the thread around the curler, then close the fastener.

* * *

To hold a lot of spools of thread, use a plastic foam wig stand.

Insert sturdy toothpicks about one inch apart—all over the "head"—then put a spool on each one. A matching bobbin can also be placed on the toothpick.

Looks very colorful placed in your sewing room with the different shades of each color grouped together. Easy to grab the one you want.

## SUBSTITUTIONS

A dollar bill is one eighth of an inch more than six inches. Knowing this can be handy if there is nothing else to measure with.

* * *

An old, clean lipstick case makes a super portable sewing kit. It holds needles and safety pins. Great to tuck in your purse or travel kit.

* * *

| | |
|---|---|
| P | *I don't sew often and hate to buy a pin cushion.* |
| S | Use a big sponge. An old cloth-type powder puff works well and smells nice, too. |

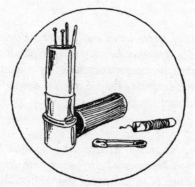

# Odds and Ends

Sometimes it's hard to put things in the right place, so this is the answer to all of those "where does this go?" questions.

This chapter will help you with problems from carpets and candles to closets. You'll find answers to insect troubles, furniture and painting questions and storage dilemmas.

Carpet care is something I'm constantly asked about—particularly the removing of spots and stains. I want to stress that if you have a major problem with your carpet, by all means call a professional. It's worth the money to have the problem taken care of by an expert if you aren't sure what to do. Beyond that, home carpet care has a few basic rules. You should vacuum often, clean up spots and stains as soon as possible and give your rugs a complete cleaning at least every eighteen months.

If an entire carpet doesn't need cleaning, you can have just the traffic pattern cleaned at much less cost.

Other sections in this chapter will give you some good tips on caring for candles and what to do if you have a problem with candle wax. Closets are a world of their own, and the problems with them are very easy to solve.

So if you have a problem that you can't find the solution to anywhere else, look through these odds and ends.

## CANDLES

Candles are so romantic, aren't they! I just love to eat dinner by candlelight, and they make such a nice touch when decorating.

One of my favorite hints about candles is an idea that is super. If you have a fireplace, you know how dull they look in the summertime when you are not using them. Candles to the rescue. Fill your empty fireplace with a few candles, light them at night, and you can enjoy a warm glow all summer.

\* \* \*

Never go off and leave candles burning. Even if they are in votive holders they can be a hazard.

\* \* \*

**Problem**     *I have so many bits and pieces of candles left over —I hate to throw them away.*

**Solution**     Use a coffee can and carefully melt all of your little scraps together, add a wick, and you can make your own "leftover" candle.

\* \* \*

**P**     *My candelabra holds ten candles, and they always sell them by the dozen.*

**S**     Always buy the same color, or wait until you have ten different colors and have a rainbow of colors.

\* \* \*

Putting a candle in front of a mirror will reflect the light more.

P  *Lighting candles is a chore—I always burn my fingers*

S  Use a piece of spaghetti to light your candles. It's very long and you can get down into the holders when the candle has burned down.

*  *  *

P  *I always scorch my hand when lighting candles on a birthday cake.*

S  Remember to start from the inside first, or work from the top of the cake down. Use a long fireplace match.

*  *  *

Always burn your candles a few seconds, blow out and then trim the wicks before your dinner party. Then they will all burn evenly and light easily.

*  *  *

P  *My candles just don't burn very long and they drip, drip, drip.*

S  If you will keep your candles in the freezer, they will burn longer and hardly drip at all. Don't ask me why, but it sure works at my house!

*  *  *

P  *My 12-inch candle broke right before my company arrived.*

S  Hold it under hot running water to soften the wax, then press together with your fingers.

*  *  *

P  *My candles never stand upright.*

S  You can wrap tape around the bottom to get a snug fit, or put some clay in the holder and press the candle down.

*  *  *

P    *How can I remove candle wax from my candle holder?*

S    If the holder can stand hot water, just soak it in the sink and most of the wax will rub right off. Never scrape at the wax if your holder scratches easily.

\*    \*    \*

Make your own candle holder. Use a drinking glass or jelly jar, fill it with salt or sand and put your candle down in this. Safe and also attractive!

\*    \*    \*

P    *I hate blowing candles out—I usually get wax everywhere.*

S    Why not cup your hand behind the flame while you blow? This keeps the wax from splattering.

\*    \*    \*

P    *I use candles for decoration—how can I clean them to keep them looking fresh?*

S    Use a soft cloth dampened with rubbing alcohol.

**CARPET**
**(Also see Carpet, cleaning and maintaining, p. 112) and Scraps,**
**p. 199**

When you put carpeting in your home, there are a few questions you have to ask yourself before you start looking:

1.  How much do I want to spend?

2.  How much traffic wear and tear will the carpeting have to stand?

3.  Do I want this to last twenty years, or just a few years?

4.  How much time will I have to spend taking care of it?

When you answer these questions you will then have a good idea of what to buy.

If you have children and your carpet is going to get a lot of wear and tear, people running in and out all day long, then you need something that will hold up well. If it's for an area that doesn't get much traffic, you can buy something that isn't as sturdy.

Be honest with yourself about how long you want to keep it. I don't know about you, but after five or so years, I am ready for a change. If you pay twenty dollars a yard, you are not going to want to pull it out in just a few years. I personally would rather buy less expensive carpet and replace it more often than live for twenty years with expensive carpet that I'm tired of.

The padding underneath will make cheap carpets feel like the good stuff. Put more money into thick padding, and when you walk on it, it will feel like the thick carpet.

If you are going to vacuum every day (which you should) then you can put down short, cut pile. But if you know that you aren't going to pull out the vacuum except on Saturday, then don't get a carpet that will show dirt, foot marks, and all the things that end up on the floor.

*Cleaning*
*(Also see Stain removal, urine, p. 163 and Carpeting for the bath area, p 112.)*

P       *I have deep shag carpeting and find it difficult to care for.*

S       Pick up litter and crumbs before they have a chance to settle deep into the rug. There are special rakes to keep the pile upright. Be careful when using rug shampoo machines. Rotating brushes tangle and untwist individual yarns.

\*   \*   \*

Put a plastic bag under furniture legs after shampooing to prevent rust marks on the carpet.

\*   \*   \*

P       *I want to shampoo my carpet but it will be impossible not to walk on it until dry.*

S       It won't hurt to walk on it if you put down brown paper bags over the traffic area.

\*   \*   \*

P       *Dirt and animal hair seem to cling to my carpet near the baseboards and is difficult to vacuum.*

S       Dampen a sponge and wipe the carpet, or buy an extra toilet bowl brush just for brushing up next to the baseboards.

\*   \*   \*

P       *Candle wax dripped on my new carpet.*

S       Scrape off as much of the wax as you can with a dull knife. Cover the remaining wax with paper towels or napkins. With your iron on synthetic setting, place the iron over the napkins. As soon as the napkin shows wax, replace the napkins and "iron" again. Repeat until all the wax is removed.

P  *Is vacuuming really all that important?*

S  You bet your carpet! The more often you vacuum, the longer your carpet will last.

You should do it every day lightly to remove dirt, etc., and then *really* good once a week. If you don't, the longer the dirt and debris sits on the carpet, the deeper it gets ground in and the harder to remove.

Don't just run over it quickly, either. When you are vacuuming for real, go over the area slowly and crisscross to be sure you give the vacuum a chance to really get all the dirt up.

## Drying
*(Also see Drying clothes, p. 135)*

P  *Any way to dry a damp spot quickly?*

S  After you have blotted up as much moisture as possible with paper towels, you can use your hand-held hair dryer to dry the area.

\*  \*  \*

P  *Our carpeting got soaked when the window was left open and it rained.*

S  If it is a large area, and it really soaked through, you should call a professional to come out and extract the water. If the carpet is just surface-wet, you can dry it out yourself; but if it got down into the padding, you must pull up the carpet and let that dry out. If you don't, Mildew City.

## Indentations

P  *I moved some furniture and now I have indentations in the carpet that I can't get rid of?*

S  Moisture from a steam iron and brushing the nap of the carpet will get your carpet to straighten up.

Of course, you don't want to place the steam iron directly on the carpet—just hold it above to let the steam get on the carpet, and then brush the carpet with your hand or an old hairbrush.

\*　　\*　　\*

P　　*I can't get rid of deep pile indentations in my deep shag carpet.*

S　　Take a hairpin to pry up the matted areas. Put the hairpin through the loop and pull gently.

## Petproofing
*(Also see Stain Removal, urine, p. 163-164 and Insect Problems, p. 209)*

P　　*How can I get rid of fleas in my carpet?*

S　　Since fleas that result from developing larvae can live several weeks without food, you have to be sure you get to the source of the problem—namely, the eggs.

　　Carpets, rugs, upholstered furniture and the pet's bed have to be thoroughly vacuumed. Then apply an insecticide. Be sure the product doesn't stain before you spray or sprinkle your carpets and upholstered furniture. You must reapply in a few days.

\*　　\*　　\*

P　　*How can I get pet urine stains out of my carpet?*

S　　The only way to avoid a color change or dye loss in your carpet is to act quickly. The first thing to do is grab some paper napkins or paper towels and blot up as much of the urine as possible. Throw down a handful at a time. Keep removing the paper towels and adding more until you see no more moisture. By stepping on the paper covering the wet area, your weight will help the absorption of the urine into the paper.

　　Next, take one teaspoon of nonalkaline detergent (such as used for laundering fine washables) and mix it with one-half pint of lukewarm water. Blot, don't rub or brush, this mixture into the stain. Work from the outside edge to the center of the stain. Put a little solution on the stain and blot, then rinse with tap water.

A mixture of one-third cup white vinegar and two-thirds cup lukewarm water will help deodorize. Repeat the blotting process. Remember, keep blotting until there is no more moisture on the towel or napkin. After getting up all you can, sprinkle salt or baking soda on the spot to help absorb whatever moisture is left and to deodorize. Finally, put down a half-inch layer of paper towels or napkins and weight them down with a heavy book and allow about six hours for it to dry.

## Repairing

**P**      *Cigarette burns in carpet!!!*
**S**      Trim the burned yarns off with scissors. Get some "fuzz" from around the baseboards or clip a few yarns here and there in inconspicuous places. Place some household glue into the hole and glue the yarns in the hole. Place paper towels over, weight down with books and leave for twenty-four hours.

*    *    *

For a surface scorch from a cigarette on your carpet, rub a silver dollar or a fifty-cent piece on the scorch. The burned part should flick right off.

## Scraps

There are a whole slew of things you can do with carpet scraps and what a way to save money! You can pick a handful up at your carpet dealer for very little. Watch for sales for carpet remnants, too—it's an ideal way to really get your money's worth. Below are just a few ideas for you.

1.  To soundproof and deaden noise in some rooms, install carpet scraps on the ceiling, and walls, if you can.

2.  Cut down on noise in the kitchen area or where there is no carpeting on the floor. Glue carpet scraps on bottoms of tables and chairs to absorb noise.

3.  Great to put under sewing machines and typewriters to keep them from scooting around and to absorb noise.

4.  Wonderful for lining windowsills, etc., where you put your plants to sun. No drips or rust spots.

\* \* \*

P   *I was told not to use leftover carpet scraps as throw rugs in the heavily traveled areas.*

S   Yep, that's true. Feel the back of a piece of carpet and you'll notice it is somewhat abrasive. Anything abrasive on top of your new carpet will cause premature wear. If you want to use the leftover pieces, glue some sheeting on the backing first.

*Static Electricity*

**P**         *I am plagued by static electricity from our carpet.*
**S**         Sometimes putting a little moisture in the room
              such as filling a vase with water or using a vapo-
              rizer will solve the problem.

                  Or, spray a little antistatic spray on the soles of
              your shoes (never directly on the carpet).

## CLOSETS

Do you hate to clean out a closet? Do you have a hard time finding
what you want in your closet? Do you dread opening the door for
fear of what's there?

This section will help you arrange, rearrange, clean, and fix your
closet!

Before going any further, I want to give you Heloise's never-fail
method for getting a closet in tip-top shape.

You have to be dedicated and ready to really clean your closet out.
Not just going through to see what you don't want, but attacking full
force.

Start at one end and work your way through each piece of clothing. If there is the slightest question, take it out and throw it on the
bed. Ask yourself honestly: "Have I worn it in a year?" "Does it still
fit?" And this is real honesty!—"Is there really any hope?"

Now that you have a pile of clothes and shoes on the bed, go
through them again. If you put something back, remember it the next
time you clean out. If it turns up twice, it should be a candidate for
the out box.

It will make it easier to "get rid of" if you know that whatever you
don't keep is going to a charity, or church, etc.

*Doors*

**P**         *I have noisy sliding closet doors.*
**S**         Buy some rubber buttons (the kind made to go
              underneath toilet seats or on each side of a shower
              door). Tap them into the door jamb at each side

of your door frames to prevent the doors from banging.

\*     \*     \*

Make sure closet doors can be opened from the INSIDE to prevent small children from becoming panicky or perhaps suffocating. Also see p. 339

\*     \*     \*

Be sure to keep closet doors shut most of the time, especially on walk-ins. It's like heating or cooling an extra room.

### Linen Closet

When putting your fresh linens away, always rotate them. Put the newly washed towels and sheets on the bottom and then always work from the top. You should rotate clothes, too. Be sure and inform your family of the system.

Don't be like the man who read the hint and started taking his shirts off the bottom of the stack without saying anything to his wife. She was putting the fresh ones on the bottom of the stack, not saying anything to him. He couldn't understand why it seemed like he was always wearing the same two or three shirts.

\*     \*     \*

If you have closet space, or an extra shelf in your bedroom, put the sheets you use on that bed in there. Saves you a few steps going back and forth.

\*     \*     \*

Linen cabinet too cramped? Fold your towels in half and then roll them—they will take up less space.

\*     \*     \*

P         *I love satin sheets—my husband hates them.*
S         Use the satin bottom with a cotton top that matches the pattern, or a cotton bottom and satin top.

Mix and match sheets for something a little different. A brown solid with a brown and white stripe.

### Odor

P      *My closets are always damp.*

S      A temporary solution would be to use your vacuum cleaner to put in warm, dry air, or a room dehumidifier would help. (Leave a small light on.)

\*    \*    \*

P      *My closets are musty.*

S      Be sure they are well ventilated. Open closet doors a few hours each day or night and let them air out. Never put dirty clothes back in the closet.

\*    \*    \*

P      *Frankly, my closets just smell.*

S      Be sure you follow the above advice. To keep a "sweet smelling" closet, I sprinkle baking soda on the floor and in shoes; I make my own deodorizer by using a small jar—punch holes in the lid and drop in a few cotton balls with oil of wintergreen (or your favorite fragrance.).

\*    \*    \*

P      *When I store my clothes away in a bag, even though they are clean they still smell musty when I take them out.*

S      Slip a used fabric softener sheet or the wrapper from your bar of soap in the bag.

### Organizing

P      *I can never find anything in my closet.*

S      Arrange your closet by putting all blouses together, pants, skirts, etc. Then hang them by color within each category. If you want to, you can mark the section to make it easier. Group all shoes together by color, too. If you want a blue blouse and a pair of pants, you know just where to find them.

\* \* \*

P  *I have to share a closet with a roommate.*
S  Divide the closet evenly and either put up a marker in the middle, or, to add a little decoration, paint each half a different color.

\* \* \*

Make your closet do double-duty. To make more space in a crowded closet, put two poles on one side. Hang skirts and blouses on the higher one and shirts and trousers on the lower one.

\* \* \*

P  *My kids can't reach the clothes rod in their closets.*
S  Attach a piece of wire or strong cord to each end of the pole, forming a loop in the part hanging down. Run a second rod through the loops.

Bookcases can easily be made by removing sliding closet doors and adding shelves if you are converting an unused bedroom into a den.

* * *

If you have clothes that hang in the closet and don't get worn much, it is a good idea to vacuum them once in a while to get rid of dust, etc. If you can, always store them in light plastic cleaner bags to keep the dust off. Don't ever put real leather or leather-type garments in plastic; they must breathe to stay healthy. Same goes for furs.

### Poles

**P**       *My hangers won't slide on the wooden poles in the closet.*

**S**       Rub furniture polish on the poles or place shower curtain rod plastic covers over them.

## FURNITURE

### Arranging
### *(Also see Floors, p. 80)*

Need to balance a piece of furniture? Use a garden hose washer instead of a piece of paper—works better and won't show.

* * *

**P**       *I'm having a hard time deciding how to arrange my furniture—and it's hard work moving it around.*

**S**       Make a scale drawing of your room. Cut out pieces of paper for your furniture to scale, and move the furniture around on the paper until you decide how you like it best. No backache for you!

* * *

**P**       *How can I move heavy furniture without scratching the floor?*

S    Put flattened-out milk cartons, magazines or pot holders under the legs, and just slide.

*   *   *

P    *Our sectional sofa is always sliding.*

S    Cut small pieces of foam rubber or sponges to fit under the legs of the furniture.

## Dusting and Polishing

A baby's brush or a thin paint brush are super for dusting ornately carved furniture or bric-a-brac shelves.

*   *   *

P    *Furniture polish costs so much—surely you have a goodie!*

S    How's this! Mix one-third cup each of boiled linseed oil, turpentine and vinegar. Don't try to boil your own linseed oil—you can buy it at a paint or hardware store. Mix the ingredients together and shake well before using. Pour on a soft cloth to apply and wipe completely dry with another clean, soft cloth.

*   *   *

P  *I love lemon oil polish but I always seem to get blobs on my rag—and that means too much oil on my furniture.*

S  Fill an empty window cleaner bottle with lemon oil. Spray the polish on the dust rag—no more blobs!

## Repairing

P  *My child stuck some adhesive-backed pictures on my furniture.*

S  Rub vegetable oil or mayonnaise on the stuck paper, leave it awhile, and it should come right off without damaging the furniture.

\* \* \*

P  *I'm just sick—I now have a cigarette burn on my table.*

S  Dip a cotton swab in clear fingernail polish *remover* and rub over the burn very carefully. If the burn remains, scrape the burn gently with a dull knife until the discoloration is removed. Fill the depression that is left with clear fingernail *polish*. Apply a thin layer, let it dry, apply another layer, let it dry, and so on until the hole is filled up. Then cover with regular furniture polish.

\* \* \*

P  *I want to repair some holes in unpainted wood furniture with patch plaster but can't match the light brown shade of the wood.*

S  Mix instant coffee into a little plaster until you get the right shade.

\* \* \*

P  *I have some leather-topped furniture and someone spilled alcohol on it.*

S      Alcohol will bleach the leather white, so get some saddle soap and clean the entire top of the table. After it is thoroughly dry, apply a scuff-type liquid polish to the area (use a color that matches as closely as possible) and don't use too much polish. Test a spot. If it stains the leather too dark, pour the polish on a clean cloth and very lightly coat the entire top of the table to even the color.

\*     \*     \*

P      *I'm just at a loss what to do—I have a scratch on my new dining room table.*

S      Rub the scratch with the meat of a pecan or walnut. Or, take a crayon of the same color of the table (or an eyebrow pencil) and fill in the scratch. But try the pecan meat trick—it really works super!

\*     \*     \*

P      *How can I remove a water stain from my furniture?*

S      If it is a fresh water ring, blot and buff with a soft cloth. Use mayonnaise and cigarette ashes mixed together. Rub it in well; let it stand for a while.

## Upholstery

P      *I have dark-colored upholstered furniture that collects lint.*

S      Since constantly vacuuming it isn't much fun, use an old clean nylon stocking or pantyhose to wipe it down. It will pick up the lint.

\*     \*     \*

P      *I need new furniture throws but they are so expensive.*

S      Shop around for a sale on bedspreads. A spread can be used instead of a throw and is usually a lot cheaper (good choice of colors, too!).

Recovering your living room furniture in a luxurious fabric that won't stand the wear and tear of your darling grandkids—why not save the old washable slipcovers. Everyone will be more at ease when they come to visit.

## INSECT PROBLEMS
**(Also see Petproofing carpet, p. 198)**

P   *How can I keep ants off a picnic table?*

S   Fill tin cans with water and set each table leg in a can. On permanent concrete tables, saturate strips of cloth with insect repellent and wrap around each table leg.

\*   \*   \*

P   *Flying insects in my bedroom at night drive me crazy.*

S   Sheer frustration, right? Try this. Keep lights off in your room, but open the door to the bath or another room and turn on the lights there. The bug will fly towards the light in that room and you can close the door and shut the bug out of your room.

\*   \*   \*

To preserve an insect in a jar for a child's observation for a few hours, cover the jar with a nylon stocking held secure by a rubber band. Water can be dripped through the nylon without drowning the creature.

\*   \*   \*

P   *I'm allergic to insect spray.*

S   When there's a stinging critter you'd like to get rid of, use hair spray or spray starch to zap 'em in their tracks. Some deodorant sprays will also do the trick.

P   *How can roach infestation be prevented?*

S   First of all, roaches come inside primarily for food and water. Remove those two sources and half the battle is won. (Don't forget the pet feeding dish.)

The second thing to do—and this positively has to be done well and done often—is to destroy any and all eggs. Roach eggs, or sacs, are brownish in color, about the size of a grain of rice, or larger. Any dark place is a haven for roaches. Thoroughly vacuum areas such as the motor under the refrigerator, under all furniture (turn chairs upside down and look under the seats), pipes under the sink, under the dishwasher, under stove burners, behind the water closet at the back of the toilet, under the washing machine, back of the piano, folds and headings of draperies, behind bookcases, behind dressers, etc. After the eggs have been vacuumed up, get rid of the bag and apply a good roach spray.

\*   \*   \*

P   *Any home remedy for roaches? It costs so much for a professional.*

S   Yep. Here's a favorite that does work, although not as fast as a commercial spray. Place a mixture of boric acid and sugar in cupboards and other places where roaches are. CAUTION: This mixture is poisonous, so be sure children and pets cannot get to it. Also, remember if there's any food, water or garbage left out, the roaches won't be as likely to feed on this poison.

## PAINTING

After opening a new can of paint, using a hammer and a large nail, punch five or six holes in the lid retaining groove. Of course, be careful not to slop paint around. When you dip the brush in the paint and then wipe it against the side of the can rim, the paint fills the groove as it always does. But with the holes, it runs right back into the can.

\* \* \*

Write the date, brand and color of paint used under the light switch for a handy reference.

\* \* \*

A skateboard makes a nifty scoot-along seat when painting baseboards.

### Paint Splatters

Flattened-out corrugated boxes are good to cover floors with when painting.

\* \* \*

Glue a large plastic-coated paper plate to the bottom of open paint cans to avoid splatters and spills.

\* \* \*

Ever caught in the midst of painting and have to drop everything? Put the roller or brush in a plastic bag; make sure the bag is airtight. Your brush or roller will remain moist for a while.

Keep a small bottle of paint handy for touch-ups (a nail polish bottle and brush is terrific for this).

\*   \*   \*

P          *How can I keep paint from running down my arm?*
S          Slit a paper plate in the middle and push the brush handle through it.

\*   \*   \*

Baby oil will remove most paint spots from skin.

\*   \*   \*

When painting baseboards, use a window blind slat or piece of cardboard to put along the floor edge—no paint on the floor or carpet.

\*   \*   \*

Painting a bathroom? Wet some newspapers and place over the bottom and sides of the tub—they'll cling, and no paint drips on the tub.

\*   \*   \*

Wrap hardware in foil before painting. This means metal parts like door knobs, hinges, pulls, etc.

## Steps

Paint the lowest step white for safety.

\*   \*   \*

P          *How can I keep everyone off the steps long enough for me to repaint?*
S          Why not paint every other step, let them dry, and then paint the remaining ones.

## STORAGE SPACE
### (Also see Storage in the bath area, p. 115)

The secret to solving storage problems is to utilize every nook and cranny to the best advantage. Boxes can be stored under beds, and small items such as children's toys can be combined into an old canister set. Think DOUBLE-DUTY! Used lozenge boxes can be used to store hair pins. Cancelled checks can be stored in the cardboard boxes cheese comes in; packets of salad dressing mixes, soft drink mixes, or even baby's socks can be stored in boutique facial tissue boxes.

It's a lot of trouble, face it, to make a place for everything and keep everything in its place. But once you organize your storage space to the fullest advantage, it's downhill and shady the rest of the way!

\* \* \*

*Blankets*

P     *I have no room at all for storing blankets.*
S     Lay them out flat between your mattress and bed-springs.

*Cedar Chests*

P     *I need to mothproof some clothing but I don't have a cedar chest.*
S     Line a drawer with heavy-duty foil; wrap the contents securely in heavy-duty foil and then scatter moth crystals or balls throughout the drawer.

\* \* \*

P     *The cedar aroma has disappeared from my cedar chest.*
S     Using fine sandpaper, rub *with* the grain lightly to restore the scent. Vacuum to remove the dust. If

this doesn't restore the cedar scent, purchase some oil of cedar and wipe the *inside lid* of the chest only. Lay a strip of plastic or foil on top of clothes so the oil will not get on clothes.

*　　*　　*

Remember, a cedar chest can be dangerous to a small child. Keep it locked or better yet, remove the lock so a small child cannot be trapped inside.

### Drawers
*(Also see Doors and Drawers, p. 58)*

**P**  *I need more drawer space for my baby's things.*

**S**  Use see-through closet bags with shelves (the kind made for shoes or sweaters) to store baby's blankets, sheets, sweaters, etc.

### Garage
*(Also see Garage and auto care, p. 248-252)*

**P**  *We have room in our garage to store lots of boxes, but it's hard to locate the box we need without rummaging through everything.*

**S**  Use a clipboard and make a note of everything you put in a box. Label the filled box "A," "B," "C," etc. Keep the master list in the house and you can locate the desired item pronto!

### Out-of-Season Storage

**P**  *I have no place to store seldom-worn or out-of-season clothes.*

**S**  Pack them away in large flat boxes and store them under your bed. Or, use heavy-duty plastic trash

can liner bags (make sure they're closed tightly) or
store things in empty suitcases.

\*   \*   \*

Store seasonal items such as heaters or fans in plastic garbage bags.
They'll be dust-free and ready to go when you need 'em (they'll last
longer, too).

# PART TWO

# Outside the House

## Introduction

So much more goes on in our lives besides doing the laundry and cleaning the kitchen. Thank heavens!

This second part of the book, "Outside the House," is about those things that come up around our home—and away from it.

Chapter six, "Things that Grow," is about plants, flowers and gardens. Whether you live in a house or in an apartment, you probably have at least one growing green thing (and no, I don't count mildew in the shower!). There are all kinds of technical books around about the do's and don'ts and the how-to's of plant care, so this chapter follows the Heloise school of thought. That means let's do it the easiest and quickest way.

The problems in Chapter six are the simple ones that you and I face every day. A lot of the solutions are homey-type things that a plant "expert" may never have heard of. But I know these things work for me and have worked for my readers for over twenty years. I think you'll find them helpful when it comes to taking care of those delightful companions that don't talk back and don't ask questions!

"Auto Care" (Chapter seven) is another of the very important things we sometimes need help with. We have become such an auto-mobile society and depend so much on our cars that it's a must to keep our cars in tip-top running shape. With the cost of cars today, buying a new one can be almost as big an investment as the down payment on a home used to be.

In the auto care chapter, I'll tell you the little things that you can do for yourself, from how to help your car smell good to how to solve potentially serious problems with some very, very simple solutions.

If you're like me, the very mechanical things are better left to a professional but the easy things like washing, waxing, and making spiffy, you can do all by yourself. To start with a dirty, depressed-looking car, to wash it, clean the inside, polish all the chrome and then be able to stand back and view the finished product feels great!

Car care doesn't have to be difficult. If you start out with the right attitude, you will make things very *easy* for yourself later on. As with cleaning a kitchen, if you do things a little at a time, as they're needed, it's not hard to have a clean car.

"On the Move"—Chapter nine—could be an entire book just about moving and traveling.

Moving can be traumatic when we have established roots and friendships and have invested a good part of our life in one place. But there's a plus side. Moving can be a new start; we get to see new things. As much as I disliked leaving my friends, I always was excited about meeting new ones at the other end. And you know, the friends I "left behind" are still my friends. Distance needn't destroy a friendship.

I learned from many, many moves as a military brat, and a lot of traveling for business that the key to making things easy—or shall we say as painless as possible—is to PLAN. Preparation is essential. Don't wait until the last minute to find out that the movers are only movers and not packers, or that they won't take your grandmother's rocking chair because it's an antique. Call, ask questions, write things down.

Moving and traveling sometimes go hand in hand. For the traveler who leaves home with a suitcase and a plane ticket, the most important rule is still to PLAN. I never go anywhere without writing out my itinerary and checking all reservations ahead of time.

Learning the art of packing is not so hard if you decide first what you are going to take. Lay it all out on the bed, stand back and ask yourself whether you really need all of those clothes. Probably not. Then, pack your suitcase. After it is packed and closed, pick it up and heft it for a moment. How heavy is it? You are probably the one who is going to have to carry it. Can you leave anything else at home?

Traveling, camping, gardening and even moving should be enjoyable experiences. I hope you don't get into problems, but if you do, the chapters in Part Two will help you out!

—Hugs, Heloise

# *Things that Grow*

Things that grow! Let's see: children grow, pets grow, the cost of things keeps growing, and we all grow older, don't we?

Some of the really nice things that grow are green, smell nice and really look pretty. Namely, plants, flowers and that nifty garden of yours.

Flowers bring so much joy, are so simple to arrange and can make a sad or rainy day perk up. Flowers can bring sunshine when there is none, can say, "I'm sorry," "I love you," or "I miss you."

I love flowers because it's the way I say, "Thank you for being so nice." Don't you feel special when you receive some flowers? I know I do.

Next best thing to fresh flowers are indoors' plants that make a dreary apartment come alive, or a dull office look a little more comfortable. When you put pretty green plants in an area, it helps make it more comfortable and homey. Remember, too, that you don't have to go and buy expensive plants. Part of the fun is getting a little bitty thing for eighty-nine cents and watching it grow into a big beautiful addition to your house, apartment or room.

## FLOWER ARRANGING
**(Also see Indoor Plants, p. 237)**

Need some greenery for an arrangement in a hurry and none to be had? Carrot tops are a good substitute. Or, go into your yard and snip a few branches of leaves from your shrubs.

\*　　\*　　\*

| | |
|---|---|
| Problem | *When I make an arrangement, the side I work from looks great, but the back looks terrible—and I want it to look pretty from all sides.* |
| Solution | Work in front of a mirror, and you can see what you are doing all the way around. |

\*　　\*　　\*

| | |
|---|---|
| P | *I crush the flowers laying them on the sink while making an arrangement.* |
| S | Use your dish drainer and place it over a sink full of water. The flower stems can stay in water and the blossoms will be held apart. |

\*　　\*　　\*

| | |
|---|---|
| P | *I have trouble keeping flowers arranged in a large, wide-mouth flower vase.* |
| S | Cut a circle of plastic foam to fit into the top of the vase and punch holes for the stems to go through. Or, you could crisscross transparent tape across the top of the vase and just stick the stems through the open squares made by the strips of tape. |

\*　　\*　　\*

No florist frog? Children's dough compound or a piece of plastic foam works well.

\*　　\*　　\*

Stems too small to fit firmly in the holes of the frog? Cut green drinking straws in short lengths. Insert the stems in the straws and the straws into the frog.

\*   \*   \*

P        *I like to make arrangements with roses but the blooms never open all at once.*

S        Go ahead and cut your roses in the bud stage. They won't open if you keep them in the refrigerator. Leave the buds in the fridge until you have enough for an arrangement. They should all open at about the same time when you take them out.

\*   \*   \*

P        *I always end up scarred when I try to arrange roses with thorny stems.*

S        It will help if you will wear gloves, but also using a clothespin or kitchen tongs will keep you away from the thorns.

### Dyeing

P        *I know shasta daisies can be dyed, but I don't know how to do it.*

S        Cut the stems at an angle. Mix one-half cup water with one small bottle of food coloring. Stand the

stems in the coloring for several hours to dye the flowers. The solution can be reused. This also works on other flowers.

## Maintaining Freshness

**P**      *Fresh flowers are so lovely, but sometimes so sad when the entire group seems to die at the same time.*

**S**      Silk flowers are really nice and you don't have to water them. They don't die on you, but they don't smell pretty and you do need to dust them.

     Well, you can have your fresh flowers and silk, too. I saw the loveliest arrangement that was part silk flowers and part fresh ones, and it was really difficult to tell which was which.

     After asking around, I found out that this was a continual bouquet. They pull out the fresh flowers when they look bad and add new ones when needed. To keep the live flowers watered, they wrapped the stems in a wet tissue and put 'em in a plastic bag held in place by a rubber band and then placed them in the container. You could buy some orchid tubs to put them in. Isn't that a nifty idea!

\*    \*    \*

When you have fresh flowers or a loose arrangement, you should cut the stem off a little each day, and when you do trim them, be sure that you cut at an angle so there is more stem exposed to drink up as much fresh water as possible.

\*    \*    \*

**P**      *A beautiful arrangement of flowers was delivered and they died the next day.*

**S**      You should check the water in arrangements immediately. The florist can't send them out with water in them, so the first thing to do is give those beauts a drink of water.

\*    \*    \*

If you receive flowers or a potted plant as a gift and they die the next day or are really in bad shape (natch, you have watered them and not abused them), call the florist who delivered them and tell him. Nine times out of ten he will be more than happy to replace them.

Sometimes there are conditions beyond the florist's control that have caused the flowers to expire before their time, and if this is the case don't hesitate to let him know. If you don't tell him, he will have no way of knowing that something was wrong.

* * *

P   *I got some fresh cut flowers that really looked rather droopy . . . Should I have sent them back?*

S   Flowers need a little TLC (Tender Loving Care), too. Remember, they go from the florist cool storage, to the truck or car, and then into your home —and every one of these places has a different temperature. Pop them in the fridge for an hour or so and see if they perk up.

* * *

P   *Any way I can salvage a cut arrangement? Some of the flowers look good though a few have had it.*

S   Pick out the flowers that have fallen by the wayside and add some greenery or new flowers—go to your garden and snip a little. They will look lots better!

* * *

P   *The stems of most flowers are always too short to arrange in my favorite tall vase.*

S   Put some pretty marbles or colored pebbles in the vase to the point where the stems reach; not only will it help hold the flowers, it is really very attractive.

* * *

P   *Does it hurt to leave flowers out all night?*

S   You really should put them someplace cool for the nighttime, even if it means moving them to the floor. Be sure to watch out for pets because some flowers are poisonous.

\* \* \*

The ideal temperature for flowers is between 40°F and 50°F. Always place your flowers someplace that is cool. You can put them in the fridge at night to make them last. Remember, florists keep flowers refrigerated, and usually at a temperature somewhere around 40°F. So, pop them in the fridge.

\* \* \*

**P**     *I had a flower arrangement for a dinner party and the stems drooped, making the arrangement look terrible.*

**S**     If the stems are small enough, insert them in plastic straws. Also, a great way to extend stems.

\* \* \*

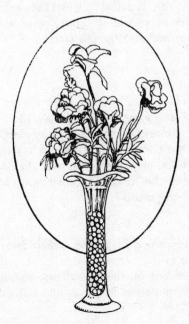

P      *Does it hurt flowers to clean the stems off?*

S      Not in the least; one of my sources even uses a vegetable brush to lightly brush the stems to clean them. This helps keep the water clean, too.

\*    \*    \*

P      *My fresh cut flowers don't stay fresh.*

S      Cut flowers last longer if all leaves are removed from the stem part that is under water.

\*    \*    \*

When you get flowers, snip one-fourth inch off the bottom of the stem while holding the stem under water; the stem seems to absorb water faster that way.

### Money-savers

P      *I like to take flowers to friends in the hospital but I can't afford arrangements.*

S      Buy a special coffee mug and then arrange a single flower or two in it. Your friend will enjoy the flower and also the gift later.

### Transporting

P      *My child loves to carry fresh flowers to school— how can he get them there safely?*

S      Cut a little of the top off a 2-liter plastic bottle and put some water in it. Then put in the flowers and some foil or plastic wrap over the neck.

     Send the flowers on their way, and have no crushed petals.

\*    \*    \*

P      *I never can get cut flowers to their destination with-out a spill.*

S      Depending on the size of the vase and arrange-ment, put them in one of the soft drink cartons made for 32-ounce bottles, or set them in a cardboard box or grocery paper sack weighted down with an old catalog or magazines.

*Water Tips*

**P**    *Do I have to change the water every day in my flower arrangement?*

**S**    You really should change the water as often as possible, and every day is best.

\* \* \*

Don't put fresh flowers on top of the TV to display them. The heat will make the water evaporate very quickly and your flowers will not last long at all.

\* \* \*

**P**    *My mother always told me to add a teaspoon of sugar to the water when I put cut flowers in a vase.*

**S**    It's an old wives' tale, but who knows! It surely can't hurt. I sometimes add a little soft drink in the

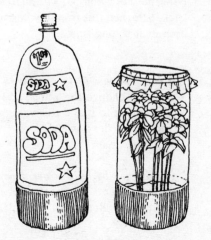

hopes that it's like a shot of glucose . . . seems to help.

*    *    *

**P**    *I would like to use a clear vase that I have but the water looks yukky.*

**S**    To keep the water from clouding up, add one tablespoon of bleach to one quart of water. Change often.

*    *    *

**P**    *I want to change the water in my flower arrangement but it is so large that I just hate taking the whole bunch out of the vase.*

**S**    Use a turkey baster to remove the old water and add the new without ever disturbing the arrangement.

*    *    *

**P**    *I add fresh water to my flowers and they still look pretty sad.*

**S**    When you add or change the water for flowers, use warm water and they will draw it in much faster. Now, not hot water but warm tap water will do the trick. I learned this from my florist Ed, and he has been at it a long time.

*    *    *

**P**    *The water always looks terrible in my flower vase.*
**S**    When you change the water, add a few drops of food coloring to it and the water will be as pretty to look at as the flowers!

*    *    *

**P**    *I am plagued by hard water deposits in vases.*
**S**    Take heart! Let the vase soak in a solution of vinegar and water. Then wipe clean with a bit of nylon net.

| P | *Quite frankly, my flower arrangement stinks.* |
| S | The stench from the flower stems is the culprit. Add a few drops of bleach in the water next time. |

## GARDENING

Gardens! How wonderful if you are lucky enough to have a yard or an area where you can grow big beautiful plants.

Gardening to me really means starting with earth and an idea. If it's flowers and plants, beautiful. Or, even better yet, a vegetable garden! How wonderful to plant those seeds, tend your garden through the weeks or months, and then, like raising a child, see and enjoy the finished product.

With more and more of us trying to save money, one sure-fire way is to have a vegetable garden. In this section on gardens, I have given you some tips that should make it a little easier on you to get that job done.

❊    ❊    ❊

An old garbage can with the bottom rotted out is an excellent container to start a compost pile in. Just toss in fruit peels, vegetable scraps and the like, and pop on the lid. When the compost is ready to put on your garden, just pull off the can and start spreading.

### Personal Protection

| P | *I can't work around the shrubs in my garden without getting stuck with thorns and branches.* |
| S | Cut the arms off an old heavy sweatshirt and slip them on when you're working around thorns. |

❊    ❊    ❊

Save soap slivers and drop them into an old nylon stocking. Tie the stocking around an outside faucet for a quick cleanup when you are through gardening.

❊    ❊    ❊

**P**      *My roses "attack" me when I'm trying to cut them or work on my bushes.*

**S**      Wear long oven mitts and it makes the task less painful.

\*   \*   \*

**P**      *My fingernails are a mess after gardening.*

**S**      Run your fingernails along a bar of soap before you start digging in the dirt and they'll be easier to scrub clean.

\*   \*   \*

**P**      *I absolutely kill my hands carrying dirt and rocks to my garden in my pail.*

**S**      Use a piece of old garden hose or a small rubber tire and slip the piece around the wire handle. When you carry the bucket it won't cut into your hand.

\*   \*   \*

Pin a hand towel onto your waistband to wipe the sweat off your forehead and out of your eyes while working in the garden on hot days.

\*   \*   \*

**P**      *How can I beat the heat while working in my garden?*

**S**      Wet a large handkerchief, wring it out and put it on your head, then put on a wide-brimmed straw hat. Let the handkerchief hang back on your neck almost touching your shoulder. You may look like a sheik, but you stay cool!

\*   \*   \*

**P**      *My knees kill me when I'm gardening.*

**S**      If you're a gal, wear an old nylon stocking and stuff the knee area with a sponge. Or, stuff an old hot water bottle with stockings to kneel on.

## Pestproofing

Some folks plant marigolds in their vegetable gardens to repel insects.

*    *    *

P      *Rabbits seem to love my garden and I can't keep them out.*

S      I've heard that planting garlic amidst your vegetables will make them feel "unwelcome" and they'll leave!

## Planters

No room for a garden? A wheelbarrow makes a wonderful moveable bed, and hanging baskets can grow certain types of vegetables.

## Row Markers

P      *My row markers get blown over or torn up.*

S      Use plastic spoons (write with a waterproof marker)—they're sturdy and last. Better still, make a diagram of your garden and keep it in a notebook. Last month's calendar can be used and the squares are already marked off.

## Stakes

P      *My gladiolas grow tall and then fall over.*

S      Straighten a coat hanger and make a loop at one end. Stick the straight end into the ground and let the flower come up through the loop; it will support the flower. If your flower is already kinda tall, don't close the loop until you stick the coat hanger in the ground next to the flower.

# GRASS

| | |
|---|---|
| **P** | *I was trying to sow grass seed in my yard and could not tell if I had covered it evenly.* |
| **S** | If you mix your grass seed with a little kitchen flour, you can see where you have sown the seed. |

\* \* \*

| | |
|---|---|
| **P** | *Mowing my sloped lawn is getting the best of me.* |
| **S** | Get you some old golf shoes. The spikes will give you traction and they certainly won't hurt the grass. Always mow crosswise and not up and down. |

\* \* \*

Got a lot of grass to trim along a sidewalk? Sit on a skateboard and roll yourself along.

## Grass in Cracks

| | |
|---|---|
| **P** | *What will kill grass in sidewalk cracks?* |
| **S** | Plain old table salt will do it. Just pour a generous amount anywhere you don't want grass. (It will kill most other plants, too.) |

\* \* \*

An old linoleum knife is good for getting out weeds and grasses in borders, cracks and hard-to-get-at places. The hooked blade works great.

## Seeds
*(planting, starting, watering)*

Put your seeds in some soil and water in the cups of a plastic foam egg carton. Place plastic over it and you have a neat little "hot house" to help them sprout.

P          *Any way to get seeds to sprout fast?*

S          Place seeds on a plastic-coated paper plate between two wet paper towels and cover with plastic wrap. Keep them damp and warm.

\*     \*     \*

For small seedlings use 3-ounce paper bathroom cups with drain holes punched in the sides and bottom. You can plant cup and all outside in the garden without having to disturb the roots.

\*     \*     \*

P          *It may sound dumb but I can't remember when to plant my seeds.*

S          With all folks have to remember these days, don't feel bad! Tape your seed packs to your calendar on the appropriate planting dates.

\*     \*     \*

Retain the seed packets and staple or glue them to an index file card or place in a notebook. Comes in handy next planting time—you can note whether you liked that variety, how well it did, etc.

\*     \*     \*

P          *I have a horrible time getting tiny seeds sown properly.*

S          Punch holes in the soil with an old ballpoint pen or chopstick. Then, use a salt or pepper shaker (a Parmesan cheese can works well, too) to shake small seeds into the holes.

\*     \*     \*

Seeds planted in mid-summer should be planted deeper so they are protected from the hot sun while they germinate.

\*     \*     \*

P          *Birds won't leave my seeds alone.*

S          Spread nylon net over the soil. Some folks say placing artificial snakes along the garden rows frightens away birds.

**P**     *I practically kill seedlings trying to water them.*

**S**     Use a sprinkler bottle or an eyedropper. You are
using too high a water pressure on the little things.

## HOSES AND WATERING

**P**     *I lose my temper every time I hook up the hose
because the faucet is right over my flower bed and
the hose smashes my plants.*

**S**     Twist a coat hanger into an M-shape and stick it
in the flower bed. Then, let the hose lie in the
M-groove . . . instead of resting on the plants.

*     *     *

**P**     *My hose turns into a fighting snake when I try to
roll it up.*

**S**     Get an old tire and wind the hose around and
around inside the tire. It'll stay put.

*     *     *

**P**     *How can I repair a leak in a water hose?*

**S**     Pour some melted paraffin on the leak and let it
harden. Then, wrap tape around the leak.

P      *I don't have time to water my garden by hand.*

S      Get an old water hose and poke holes all along it. Just lay the hose alongside the row and you'll have a nice "soaker."

## INDOOR PLANTS

Haven't we all gone plant crazy!

It used to be that the only place you saw real live growing plants was at your grandmother's or the flower shop. Now they are everywhere, from your favorite restaurant to the dentist's office. Why, I even saw a few in my neighborhood gas station!

Plants are growing, living things, and I am of the belief that plants can feel and tell good vibes from bad ones. (You may think I am crazy, but there are a lot of people who think like I do.)

Do you think that plants are like animals, that they can tell a good person from bad? I mean, why is it some people have green luscious plants no matter what they do or don't do to them. Then, there are the poor souls who read every book, who pinch, trim, feed, water, repot and pray. Nothing grows, not even weeds. Does that mean that they have bad vibes?

I must have changed, or at least changed my attitude towards plants, because I used to kill everything, and I mean everything. I even killed a cactus once. Do you know how hard that is . . . those buggers live in the desert all alone for years and survive, and I would bring them into my house and bingo . . . el-dead-o!

Now, boy, oh, boy! Do I have a green thumb, maybe not deep green, but green enough. My best luck is with avocados. You say those are very hard to grow? Not so, at least not for me.

As I said just a minute ago, I think what has changed is my attitude. That must be the key. Plants are like horses. If they know you are afraid of them, or afraid of taking care of them, they will prove you right.

I once threatened a plant that was kinda looking frumpy that if it didn't perk up I was going to put it down the garbage disposal.

Do you know that little devil came back to life and sprouted a bunch in the next few weeks. Maybe it was my imagination, but I swear they know.

The key to having healthy plants is to decide exactly how much time and effort you can put into taking care of them. If you know that all you are going to do is water them once a week and maybe feed them once a year, then for heaven's sake, get good, hardy plants which will survive, even if neglected. I like corn plants—they will take all kinds of abuse and still reward you by growing. They are nice to have around, aren't they!

*     *     *

An old swing set will hold lots of hanging baskets.

*     *     *

An old aquarium is a good place to plant an herb garden.

### Drainage

P    *The drain holes are so large that when I water my plants I am losing soil each time.*

S    Tear off a small piece of steel wool pad or use some nylon net and stuff it up in those holes; the water will drain but no soil will escape.

*     *     *

P    *I need something to use for a lightweight drainage layer in the bottom of hanging planters.*

S    Use the plastic foam leftover from meat trays (cut up in small pieces) and packing boxes.

### Fertilizers

P    *How can I use egg shells to fertilize my plants?*

S    Put your egg shells in a pan or some container with a lid, add water to cover and let sit a day or so. Water your plants with this and they will be strong and pretty.

P       *Any home-style fertilizers?*

S       I have always put my leftover tea and coffee (no
        cream or sugar, please) diluted with tap water on
        my plants every now and then and they look super.
        No, my plants don't stay awake at night from too
        much caffeine!


## Freeze-proofing

P       *During the winter my plants that sit in the window
        for sun sometimes "catch cold" at night.*

S       Place a piece of large cardboard between the glass
        and your plants at night to protect them from the
        cold coming through the window. Remove during
        the day.


## Leaf cleaning

Leaves of plants should be dusted every now and then. A great way
to clean plants with big leaves is to pull those mismatched socks over
your hands and wipe away—you get both sides with one swipe.

\*       \*       \*

P       *How can I dry my plastic flowers after hand wash-
        ing them?*

S       Put them in a pillow slip and hang them on your
        clothesline or from the shower head nozzle. (If
        hung in the sun, the pillow slip will keep them
        from fading.)


## Pestproofing

P       *One of my plants got infected and the others
        around it caught the bugs.*

S       When any plant gets attacked by bugs, always
        move it away from the other plants. Putting a clear
        plastic cleaner bag over the plant will help keep the
        little critters from spreading.

You don't have to go out and buy all kinds of insecticides for many of the bugs and insects on your house plants. You can simply use a mild solution of liquid detergent and water and wipe the leaves and affected area. Then wipe with clear water.

## Potting

**P**     *Do I have to start my avocado in a glass of water?*

**S**     No, you can pop the seed right into the soil and keep it well watered. I sometimes start mine out by putting it in a pot with another plant and wait until it gets its first good growth before transferring it to its own pot with soil.

*       *       *

**P**     *I do all of my potting on the balcony and don't have room for large bags of soil, rocks, etc. Any space-saving ideas?*

**S**     You can use old sponges, broken pieces of pottery or even nylon net to cover the holes in pots instead of rocks. When I plant, I put everything in a flat cardboard box (the kind that a case of soft drinks comes in) and work from there. Soil in one corner, gravel or rocks in the others, and hardly any mess to clean up.

*       *       *

**P**     *Do I have to repot my plants completely?*

**S**     No, scrape away the top inch or two and work around the roots with a small spoon. Apply new potting soil the same depth as that removed. This is, however, a short-term solution.

*       *       *

**P**     *I love to start new plants from old ones but flower pots cost so much.*

**S**     Have I got a goodie for you. The 2-liter plastic bottles that soft drinks come in are a boon to the home gardener. You can make almost any depth container that you want by cutting off the top of the bottle with a serrated knife. Then using a heated metal ice pick (careful here), punch holes in the bottom for drainage.

I absolutely love these for my avocados. You can plant them near the top of the bottle and watch the roots grow.

*       *       *

P      *I hate transplanting my tiny plants—it always disturbs the roots when I have to pull the plant out of the starter pot.*

S      Start your plants in paper cups and you can just cut the cup away from the root system. Using juice cans with both ends cut out (and set on a tray) makes it easy to gently push all the dirt and roots through without hurting the roots or plant.

## Shaping and Staking

P      *My ivy plant hangs down into the kitchen sink— yet I don't want to cut it off.*

S      Use a U-shaped hairpin to anchor the trailing vines back into the dirt.

*       *       *

Hang onto any kind of broken plastic-type recorder tape. They can be used to tie and stake all kinds of plants. The tape stretches and doesn't damage tender stems.

## Watering and Misting

P      *When I water my hanging plants, the water drips all over the place.*

S      Instead of pouring on lots of water, place a handful of ice cubes on top of the soil. They will slowly melt and nary a drop to drip.

If you need to pour on water and are afraid of drips on the carpet, put your old plastic shower

curtain or a few plastic cleaner bags on the floor
to catch the drips.

*    *    *

Want to give all your house plants a nice rainy day—bring them all
into the shower or tub, turn the shower on low and it's raining inside!
After turning off the water, close the door and let them soak up the
moisture while they drain.

*    *    *

**P**    *How often should potted plants be watered?*
**S**    A good way to tell is to thump the pot or container. If it sounds hollow, chances are the soil is
dry and needs water. If it thuds, then there is some
moisture in the soil.

*    *    *

**P**    *I want to take a trip, but there is no one to water
my plants while I am gone.*
**S**    Never fear. You can water your plants well, and
then tie clear plastic cleaner bags around the
plants and make a mini-terrarium. You won't even
have to move your hanging plants. Be sure they
are not in direct sunlight, and when you come
home, gently open the bag and let the plant adjust
before ripping it off and exposing it to a sudden
change in air.
   If you have a lot of plants, you can do about the
same thing in the bathtub or kitchen sink. Put
something like an old towel down so you won't
scratch the tub, place all your plants in there and
water heavily, cover with plastic, and off you go.
If you want, you can run about an inch of water
in the tub for extra moisture (be sure the stopper
is in). My plants survived two weeks like this.

*    *    *

An easy way to slowly water outdoor and indoor plants is to use a
2-liter plastic bottle and poke a small hole in the side near the

bottom. Fill it with water and set this right down in your plant, or just on top of the soil where it won't mash the plant. Drip, drip, drip . . . great for when you go away from home for awhile.

\*    \*    \*

P        *What if I have small plants I want to water slowly?*

S        Grab a paper cup and punch a small hole in the side near the bottom. Push it down about one-half inch into the soil and fill it with water.

\*    \*    \*

P        *I need a watering can with a spout, but they cost too much.*

S        Save a plastic bottle that dishwashing liquid came in, or a large shampoo bottle with a little spout that opens and closes. Be sure and rinse it well. You can direct the stream of water and even control the flow. Didn't cost you a penny!

\*    \*    \*

P        *I know I should mist my plants, but I don't want to spend the money for a mister.*

S        Use your plastic bottle that window cleaner comes in, after washing and rinsing it well. Some of them even have an adjustable spray nozzle.

## TOOLS

During the months the garden tools are in frequent use, you will find it handy to keep a bucket filled with sand mixed with any type of oil so that the tools can be dipped in for a quick cleaning and oiling. Be sure to wipe off any oil before using them.

### Cleaning

P        *I have a time getting the "goo" off my pruners.*

S        Spray your pruning shears with a vegetable oil

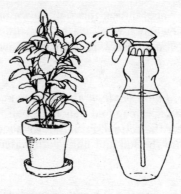

spray *before* use and the goo will slide right off for easy cleanup.

\*    \*    \*

P     *I lose small tools in the grass or else I step on rakes and stuff.*

S     For safety's sake, paint the handles of those tools a real bright color or wrap bright colored plastic tape around the handles. Added bonus: you will always know your tools on sight.

## Money-savers

Don't know what to do with a worn-out lawn mower? Convert it to a gardening carryall, or use it to haul garbage cans on.

\*    \*    \*

P     *I don't have much of a garden and hate to spend a lot of money on tools.*

S     A crow bar or some jacks from the car will work as a digger. I use a pencil to break up the soil in my potted plants when they need to be aerated. A beverage can opener that has a point makes a dandy weeder.

*7*

# *Auto Care*

The life and well-being of your auto is strictly up to you. Plants, pets and children seem to have a way of taking care of themselves when they have to, but your car will just sit there and die if you let it. This chapter deals with little problems that we all have, from smelly cars to losing the key and getting locked out. There are some very good preventive tips that I hope you'll keep in mind.

We are all concerned about how to save money and nowadays anything to do with a car is going to cost you money. Most of us are keeping cars longer, which means that you must maintain one as best you can for it to serve you well.

If you are a single woman and don't know anything about car care, take the time to learn as much as you can. No matter how simple, every little bit helps. Take an auto class for women; they really teach you a lot. Even if you don't do it yourself, you will know what they are talking about when you go to have your car worked on.

A very important thing to remember when it comes to your car ... if there is something wrong or you suspect that there is something wrong, don't hesitate to take it to be checked out. The longer you wait, the worse it will probably get. It's not going to go away and will most likely end up costing you more.

Always keep good records. Keep a maintenance book either in the car or someplace in the house that you can get to easily. Record everything from dates of oil changes, tire rotations, to tune-ups. Keep your receipts, too!

I suggest that you leave the major problems like repairing your transmission to the professional. May all your problems be small.

## DOORS, KEYS AND LOCKS

### *Doors, sticking and squeaking*

**Problem**   *The doors on my car do not close easily.*
**Solution**   Roll your car window down a little, and then close the door. It's the tight-fitting doors and windows designed to keep water out that also traps air inside the car.

*        *        *

**P**   *Squeaky doors bug me. I squirted some oil on the hinges and had to keep wiping off the drips. They still squeak.*
**S**   Maybe the oil you used was too thick and didn't get far enough into the hinges where the squeak was. Trying using a light oil in an aerosol can. It should penetrate the hinges and be less messy.

### *Keys and Key Rings*

**P**   *I'm afraid I'll lock my keys in my car—what should I do if this happens?*

S      The best advice is to carry an extra key in your purse or wallet. There are little metal boxes with magnets that will attach someplace where you can hide a key.

\*    \*    \*

P      *I hate leaving my entire key ring when they park my car for me at the garage.*

S      Use two key rings and put just the ignition key on one and give them that. I carry a safety pin on my key ring and take off only the ignition key and slip it on the safety pin.

\*    \*    \*

P      *I carry a lot of keys and I need to change them often, but all the key rings are hard for me to open.*

S      Use a metal-type shower curtain hook that opens like a safety pin. You can easily slip as many keys as you want off or on. An added bonus: you can hook it to your belt loop.

\*    \*    \*

If you stop at a friend's house and don't want to forget something, leave your car keys with the item. You won't get very far without your keys!

\*    \*    \*

If you have a lot of different keys in your family you should always clearly mark or code them. Don't put your name and address on your set of house keys, put your neighbor's or your business phone. If they are lost, you don't want the finder to know which house they open up, do you?

\*    \*    \*

P      *My car lock sticks sometimes.*

S      Don't ever oil the lock—it really will mess it up. Instead, rub your key with a soft lead pencil really well. When you insert the key in the lock you will "treat" the sticky lock with graphite from the pencil lead. You can buy a small tube of graphite at the auto parts store.

*        *        *

P    *My door lock freezes in winter.*

S    There's not much you can do about the freezing weather, but you can heat your key with a match or cigarette lighter before putting the key in the lock. The hot key will melt the ice. Caution: the key will be very hot—handle with care.

## GARAGE
**(Also see Garage as storage space, p. 214)**

P    *There is enough junk (valuable, I am sure) on the floor of my garage to outfit an entire family—I can't even get my car in.*

S    Hang as much as you can on the garage walls and even the ceiling. Things that you don't use often should be the highest up. Get that stuff off the floor and your garage will look a whole lot bigger. Be sure the things are hung securely so they won't fall on your car.

### In and Out

P    *Driving into and out of my garage is terrible— the space is so narrow (I have scraped the car twice).*

S    Attach some pieces of rubber or foam rubber to the sides of the garage where you are most likely to "get" a fender or side. It sure saves the paint.

*        *        *

P   *I either bump the front of the car or else I can't close the door when I put the car in the garage.*

S   Park the car just perfect and then suspend a ping-pong ball on a string down from the ceiling where it touches right in front of your windshield. You now have a perfect "liner-upper."

\* \* \*

P   *The new drivers in my family can't judge distance very well and keep "nudging" the wall with the front bumper.*

S   Hang an old tire right where the bumper would hit, and no problems—just like parking a boat.

## Floor Protection
*(Also see Mats for the car, p. 250)*

Save old floor mats to put on your garage floor to catch oil drips; even leftover strips of carpet help. Or, place an old cookie sheet or large flat pan filled with sand or wood shavings on the garage floor. It will catch the oil drips from your car and protect your floor. It looks neat and the sand or shavings can easily be replaced when they get saturated with oil.

\* \* \*

P   *I have terrible black oil spots on the floor of my garage, and I have tried everything to clean them up.*

S   If you can't clean it, cover it. Clean up as much as you can and then paint a large black strip and tell everyone it's your personal parking place!

\* \* \*

If you have to walk across the lawn to get to the garage, put an old throw rug on the garage floor in front of each car door. Helps keep the tracking down from sandy or wet shoes.

## INTERIORS

Write the date your inspection sticker is due and your license renewal date on a strip of adhesive tape and stick it by your speedometer. No fines for you! They are not tax deductible!

\*    \*    \*

A small thing, but it will sure save wear and tear and steps for a gas attendant: write your license number on a strip of adhesive tape and put it on your gas credit card, or use punch tape.

### Mats
*(Also see Floor Protection for the garage, p. 249)*

P        *In rainy weather water gets tracked in on the floor mats and just sits there, with no place to go.*

S        Carry a large kitchen sponge under the seat. Throw it down to sop up the water.

\*    \*    \*

P        *Floor mats—I absolutely hate washing them.*

S        If you wash the car at the car wash the high power spray will clean them in a jiffy. When washing your car at home, just use an old toilet bowl brush, or your work broom to sweep away the dirt.

### Odors

P        *Quite bluntly, my car has a bad odor.*

S        After cleaning it thoroughly, put baking soda in the ashtray. Also, tucking a bar of fragrant soap in the car will freshen it.

### Organizers

Don't smoke? Convert the car ash tray to a candy or gum dish or a loose change tray. I taped a fabric softener sheet in mine so the change would not rattle around.

P     *My car needs a "hump" to fit a car caddie on.*

S     Some just don't have them—buy a small TV lap tray; glue two plastic foam beverage cups to the tray. The tray sits on the floor of the car and the cups stick up. Set your canned drinks in the plastic foam cups. Glue on another cup to hold pen, paper and change.

\*    \*    \*

P     *I have a car pocket which hooks over the back of the front seat—the side seams have split open.*

S     To repair and reinforce it, put about four thicknesses of nylon net strips between the split pieces and sew them together.

\*    \*    \*

P     *I get rattled trying to keep track of tickets, directions, pen, paper, etc.*

S     Stretch two large rubber bands around the driver's visor, slip the items you need under them.

\*    \*    \*

P     *I hate fumbling through a glove compartment— and everything falls out.*

S     Group things in plastic bags and close the bags with twisties. Maps, pens, glasses, etc. You can then see what you need without emptying the whole compartment.

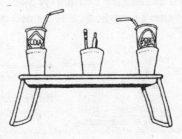

*Upholstery*

**P**     *My grandchildren's shoes make polish marks on my car's upholstery.*

**S**     Keep a clean pair of socks around to slip on *over* their shoes in the car. No fuss about getting little ones' shoes back on.

## MAINTENANCE
**(Also see Camper and Trailer Safety, p. 279)**

*Air Conditioner*

**P**     *The air conditioning won't work.*

**S**     Check the fuses. The fuses are usually under the car dash on the left side. The markings "A.C." mean air conditioner, of course. It's a good idea to keep some spare fuses in your glove compartment. Some sizes of fuses are used for two or more accessories. If the fuses don't solve the problem, see your serviceman.

*Antenna*

To keep your antenna moving up and down more easily, rub it with a piece of wax paper every now and then.

*Batteries*

Need to clean a car battery in a hurry? Pour a bottle of cola on it and brush the battery posts and cable connectors. Then flush it off with clean water.

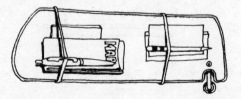

**P**      *How can I tell if I have battery trouble?*

**S**      If the starter works normally there is usually no battery problem. If the starter is sluggish, turn on lights and as you watch one light (dash, dome, etc.) try the starter for a second or two; if the light goes very dim the battery is probably weak. Further check requires equipment.

### Belts, engine

The belts that are turned by the crankshaft pulley of your engine operate your generator (or alternator), power steering, air conditioner, radiator fan, etc., are necessary for your car to operate properly. Some older cars have one belt; some have two and three. Have the belts checked by a mechanic every now and then, especially when you have your car greased and the oil changed. Most service stations routinely check them at that time. Have them tightened or replaced if needed. It's no fun to be on the road or in traffic and have a belt break.

### Convertible Top

**P**      *I have a sportscar with a leaky canvas top.*

**S**      Try mending it with dental floss or nylon fishing line. It's probably going to take two people to "push and pull" the needle through the top. You might try sturdy iron-on patches used on blue jeans if you can get the right color.

### Dents

**P**      *I got a dent in my car the other day at the supermarket. Can I fix it myself?*

**S**      Try securing a rubber suction-type "plumber's helper" over the dent and pull. Sometimes the dent will pop out. This will not work on all dents, but it's sure worth a try.

*Fluid and Oil Changing*

P    *I can't ever find the funnel when I fill up the "fluids" on my car.*

S    A plastic detergent bottle works well. Cut off the bottom, stick the neck in the filler hole and pour away!

\*    \*    \*

P    *I change my own oil—what can I use to dispose of old oil?*

S    Plastic beverage containers or plastic milk jars are good to catch the old oil in. Some service stations are accepting old oil for reprocessing; find one nearby and donate your used oil for recycling.

\*    \*    \*

P    *I can't remember when I need to change the oil, rotate the tires, replace the air filter, etc.*

S    Install a blackboard on a wall of your garage. When you drive your car, you can glance at the board to jog your memory.

\*    \*    \*

There may be times when you don't use a whole quart of oil. Save the leftover. The plastic lid from a one-pound can of coffee fits perfectly over the opened oil can.

## Guarantees

Keep your repair bills handy. Your guarantee may still be good —no use paying for the same job twice.

## Radiator

P    *I want to make sure my radiator is in good condition—how can I check it?*

S    Look for water under the car for a large leak. Check the water level frequently for small leakage and look for wet spots around the radiator, hoses and water pump.

## Tires

Tires should be inspected every now and then, and each time you have the oil changed. The car is put up on a lift to change the oil and the tires can easily be checked all around. Look for nails, glass, cuts, blisters, cracks in the sidewalls and how the tires are wearing. Uneven wear usually means that you need the wheels aligned and balanced or rotated. These jobs cost much less than new tires!

\* \* \*

Soft Top (See Convertible Top, p. 253)

## Water Hose

**P**      *Can I repair a water hose temporarily?*

**S**      Drain the water out first and let it cool. Wipe the outside of the hose dry, and wrap two or three layers of duct tape tightly around the leak. Refill the water and drive slowly to the nearest repair place.

## Windshield Wipers
*(See Windows and Windshields, p. 264)*

# ON THE ROAD

## Breakdown at Night
*(Also see Trunk Supplies, p. 259)*

**P**      *For safety's sake is there something I can do to make my car seen at night should I become stranded?*

S            Put a large X of reflector tape across the inside of
             your trunk lid and inside the hood. Lift the trunk
             and hood, and your car can be more readily seen
             from a distance.

*    *    *

No flares? Flatten clean dry milk cartons and store them in the car
trunk. When needed, pull them open and add a little dirt or gravel
to the carton to keep it from tipping over. Ignite the milk cartons and
they will burn for a few minutes.

### Following Another Car

P            *I always lose someone in a strange town when I
             have to follow them in my car.*
S            Attach a colored cloth or scarf on the lead car,
             making it easy to spot. If they have a radio antenna
             that sticks up, tie it to the top of that.

### Gas Cap

Lost a gas cap at a self-serve? Why not use clear tape and stick
an address label sticker to the gas cap—write your phone number on
it, too. You'll get a call from the station.

### Hatchback

Got a hatchback? When you go to the drive-in, park the car with
the rear facing the screen, fold down the back seat and you've got
a neat place to lean back and enjoy the movie. A cooler of drinks,
some snacks, and the fresh air—good summer fun!

### Lights

P            *Help! I always forget to turn the car lights off.*
S            Put a clothespin on your ignition key as a re-
             minder, or if you have a pull-out light switch hang
             a tissue on the switch.

## Out of Gas

P    *I got stuck on the road with no funnel to use for pouring gas in the car.*

S    In a real pinch you can use rolled-up newspaper, foil, or even the road map out of your car. These make a very good makeshift funnel. Be sure to dispose of any gas-soaked material safely.

## Parking

P    *I really have trouble remembering where I've parked at these huge shopping malls.*

S    Look at the huge letters of the store nearest you. Make a mental note of which letter your row is closest to.

## Seat Belts

P    *Disappearing seat belt buckles drive me up the wall.*

S    Cut a slit in plastic coffee can lids just big enough to slip the buckle part through—the lids will keep them from sliding between the seats. Smaller plastic lids may do the trick and not get in your way.

\*    \*    \*

P    *My shoulder harness seat belt is so tight it is really uncomfortable and pins me back in the seat—so I don't use it.*

S    Put a spring-type clothespin on the belt in *front* of where it goes through the guide on top of the seat back or the top of the car. Make it comfort-

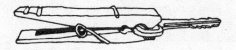

able, but not real loose—just so you won't be tied down.

When you come to a quick stop, the belt will hold you. The pin will not interfere with the belt reel from catching and stopping you from going forward abruptly. It just stops the belt from going back into the reel and being tight across your shoulder.

Seat and shoulder belts should be worn at ALL times to prevent deaths and injuries.

## Shoes for Driving

P    *I always mark up my new shoes when I am driving.*

S    Carry an extra pair to change into when you get into the car. That black from the pedal is hard to get off.

## Starting

P    *What should I do when my car won't start?*

S    Make sure the key is on and inserted all the way in. Some cars won't start unless they are in park or neutral gear. If the car won't crank at all, check out the battery by hitting the horn or turning on the lights. If the horn won't honk or the lights won't come on, it's probably the battery.

If you suspect battery problems, check the battery cables where they connect to the battery to make sure they're tight.

If the battery is strong enough for the starter to "turn over" the engine and it won't start, check to see if you have gas.

Get qualified help if none of the above solves the problem.

## Stuck Wheels

P        *What can I do if I get my car stuck in mud?*
S        Find something you can use to get traction—dry
         sand, boards, newspapers—anything handy that
         causes traction. Don't spin your rear wheels—
         you'll just dig in deeper.

## Theft

Thieves can make a stolen car almost untraceable. Cut one of your old plastic credit cards so it can't be used and drop it down a side window. Water won't hurt the plastic. Very few thieves will take time to dismantle a car door. If it's found, your card will be positive identification that the car is yours.

## Trunk Supplies

Got an old flannel-backed tablecloth? Use it to wrap tools you want to keep in the trunk of your car. It keeps them from sliding around on sharp turns.

\*     \*     \*

Always keep an old blanket in the trunk of your car. You can use it if you get stranded in the cold, for sun protection from the heat, or to keep your clothes clean if you have to crawl under your car.

\*     \*     \*

A spur-of-the-moment picnic is great fun. If you have a supply of paper plates, cups, paper towels, a can and bottle opener stored in an empty ice chest in your car, all you have to do is stop and buy sandwich fixings, drinks and ice—not too great a cash outlay.

\*     \*     \*

You should always keep a few emergency-type supplies in your car trunk. I don't mean a whole auto supply store-just some simple things that may save you a lot of trouble:

1. A small roll of yellow reflector tape. If a headlight goes out, put some on the bulb and at least it will pick up light from oncoming cars and they will know you are not on a motorcycle.

2. Flares or milk cartons (See *Breakdown at Night,* p. 255.)

3. A few thick rubber bands . . . great for holding a flashlight to your wrist if you have to change a tire alone at night.

4. Baking soda for small electrical fires. Never put water on an electrical fire.

5. Always have spare fuses handy . . . sometimes you can't get to a station to replace one that burned out or they may not have the right size.

6. Be sure your car has the proper jack and tools needed to change a tire; there are certain things you just can't substitute.

Oh, yes—become familiar with the instructions on how to change a tire or at least know where they are so you can show them to some kind soul who is willing to change it for you. Three cheers for kind souls!!!

## Waiting Line

P    *I get so frustrated and edgy waiting in lines at the bank, the gas station, etc.*

S    Make yourself a kit or box to keep in the front seat for times like these. You can make out a grocery list, write a letter, do your nails, read a book, munch on something, clip coupons—anything to pass the time and let you relax a bit. Caution: be sure your car is in neutral and your brake is engaged so that you do not roll into the car ahead of you.

## Weather, hot

P    *The steering wheel becomes so hot in the summer —ouch!*

S            Keep an old pair of gloves in the glove compartment to drive with until it cools down. Or, lay something over it before getting out of the car.

\*　　\*　　\*

P            *Glare and reflection are a problem to me in the summer when I drive.*

S            Place a piece of dark felt on the dashboard to help cut the sun's rays.

\*　　\*　　\*

P            *I don't want to wear long sleeves in the summer, but I don't like "driver's arm" sunburn on long trips.*

S            Make a loose-fitting sleeve out of remnants and carry the sleeve in your glove compartment. Before starting out, slip the sleeve over your arm and pin it to the shoulder of your garment.

\*　　\*　　\*

That straw cushion you use in the summer will also insulate you against a cold plastic seat in the winter!

*Weather, cold*
*(Also see Doors, Sticking and Squeaking, p. 246—247 and*
*Windows and Windshields, p. 264)*

When starting up in cold weather, pump that old accelerator a couple of times first. It gets the intake system charged with fuel.

## WASHING YOUR CAR

*Bumpers*

P            *How do I get rust off my car bumper?*

S            Wad up a piece of aluminum foil and rub the spot briskly. This will not fill up the pits, but it will make for a nicer appearance.

**P**          *Old bumper stickers—how can I get them off?*

**S**          Spray the sticker with prewash spray, let it sit for
               a few minutes, and then, using a little elbow
               grease, rub it with stiff brush or a piece of nylon
               net.

### Decals
(see p. 264)

### Cleaning Supplies

**P**          *Mechanic's hand cleaner is expensive to buy and
               my family goes through it like it's free.*

**S**          There are a few things you have right in your
               kitchen that will do the job. Did you know that
               sugar or salt work well as an abrasive cleaner when
               mixed with a little liquid detergent, vegetable oil
               or cooking lard?

               Your family may look at you funny at first, but
               just mix some up and let them give it a try. Put
               some lard, and sugar or salt in an old coffee can
               and leave it by the outside sink or faucet.

*          *          *

An old diaper pail is good to store all your cleaning supplies and rags
in when going to the car wash. (Also see Scrubbers, p. 28)

*          *          *

Socks that have lost their mate make super wash rags, or use them
to apply wax and buff the car.

*          *          *

If you have kids and soda pop in the car, you're gonna need a couple
of disposable diapers under the seat to wipe up spills—they absorb
like super!

*          *          *

P      *I'm short and I can't reach the top of my pickup
to wash it.*

S      Grab that old kitchen string mop—dip it in some
soapy water and wipe away!

*   *   *

P      *Yuck! My hands get so dirty when I do the simplest
chore on my car. I'm a lady and really enjoy doing
these things but oh, the condition of my hands.*

S      Rub a thin layer of petroleum jelly on your hands
before starting, and the grease and grime won't get
embedded in your skin.

## Grills

P      *Ick! Bugs on my car's grill are so hard to get off.*

S      Using baking soda and a damp sponge, or baking
soda paste and a piece of nylon, scrub them away.

*   *   *

P      *I hate cleaning my car's grill.*

S      Use an old vegetable brush or even a toilet bowl
brush to scrub the gunk off.

## Headlights

Speaking of headlights . . . if they are dirty and covered with bugs,
the maximum amount of light is not going to shine through. So don't
forget to clean the lights when the rest of the car gets a bath.

## Undercarriage

P      *My car is caked on the bottom with goop—how can
I possibly get under there and get it off?*

S      Put your lawn sprinkler under the car and turn the
water on full blast. No sense breaking your back!
This will get lots of it off, but the buildup of grease

and oil will have to be cleaned off by a professional.

*Wheels*

P     *Spoke wheels are a pain to clean.*
S     Not if you use foamy-type bathtub cleaner and a toilet bowl brush.

*Windows*
*(See Windows and Windshields, below.)*

*Woodgrain*

P     *The woodgrain on our station wagon has lost its sheen and looks kind of tacky.*
S     Rub in some good neutral shoe wax and buff.

## WINDOWS AND WINDSHIELDS

Going on a long trip? Keep the windshield clean by using premoistened towelettes. The greasy film comes off easily.

\*     \*     \*

When you replace your windshield wiper blades, save an old one—put it under the seat for a quick swipe inside of the windows when they fog up. Did you know it's not how much you use your wiper blades that determines if they should be changed, but how long they have been on your car? It's exposure to the air, sun and all the bad things that are floating around that cause them to deteriorate. So check them often because when you want them to work well on a dark rainy night, that's not the time to find out you need new ones.

*Decals*

P     *I have a decal on my window that just won't come off.*

S         Spray it with prewash spray and tape a wet sponge over it . . . let it sit awhile and usually this will help dissolve the paper and glue. Don't ever scrape at it with a sharp knife, etc. Some windows and windshields are covered with a plastic film and you might scratch it and the glass.

## Fogging Up

If your windshield and windows fog up or collect a lot of moisture while you are driving, don't use your hand—all you do is smear that stuff around and the oil from your hand will cause a real mess. Stuff an old oven mitt under the seat, slip it on and wipe away . . . it absorbs a lot of moisture.

*   *   *

P         *My windows fog up.*

S         Turn on the air conditioning system. The other choice is to open a window.

## Icing Over

P         *In icy weather I have to go to a parked car with iced-over windshields and windows.*

S         If you think there will be ice on your car when you return to your parked car, here's a way to try to prevent it. Spread a piece of plastic over the windshield and secure it with small magnets on the metal windshield molding. Closing the doors on the sides of the plastic will hold it that way.

         Also, you need to see out the front side windows so hang a plastic trash bag out each window and roll them up to hold the bags in place. If the wind is blowing, a few paper clips or bobby pins stuck in between the window and the rubber molding on the door will hold the bag down.

It's a lot easier than scraping thick ice off when you are in a hurry to get to work or go home.

\*     \*     \*

P     *What can I do when the windshield and windows ice over?*

S     If you don't have a plastic or hard rubber scraper, a plastic credit card makes an emergency ice scraper. Do *not* use metal to scrape a windshield 'cause it will scratch it. Start your car up and turn on your defroster while you are scraping.

## Wax

P     *A film of hot wax from the car wash is on the windshield of my car.*

S     Wet a cloth with vinegar and wipe the windshield and windows clean.

# 8

## Camping and RV's

The call to the wild, getting back to nature, or getting away from it all. The different kinds of "camping" are about as varied as the different flavors of ice cream.

I have a little Hill Country lakeside cabin that I call my retreat and to me that's roughing it. I do have an almost complete kitchen (that means no microwave) and indoor plumbing and even a bathtub to soak in. Some people will say that's just going to another house, and maybe it is to you, but to me it's "getting away from it all."

Whatever makes you happy is what's important. If you really like to rough it and carry everything into the wilderness on your back, GREAT! Maybe you like to go by trailer, or pop-up camper, and set up with a few conveniences. You might be like me—just going to another location with fresh air, a fireplace and the smell of the woods is enough.

Many of the problems are all the same whichever way you do it. They usually center around food, cooking and keeping track of things. When you go away, remember that this is supposed to be an enjoyable time for you and the family. The secret to having a good time is to make it as easy as possible. That means: If you can't eat it, wear it or sleep in it, don't drag it with you. The more you take, the more you have to keep up with and pack up.

If you go for a day or a week, please remember what you are there for. To enjoy Mother Nature, relax, and have a good time. If you spend all your time cooking or cleaning up, it's a drag. Take a few minutes to plan and figure out how you can make everything as easy as possible and thereby avoid all the "boring" stuff.

Last but not least, if you can bring a little nature home with you, like a pine cone or sea shell or a pretty leaf, you can look at them and enjoy your good memories for a long time.

## ADVANCE PREPARATION
**(Also see Advance Planning for moving, p. 293 and Loading the Car, p. 307)**

When you know you're going camping quite a few weeks in advance, why not write or call the Chamber of Commerce in the area for anything of special interest to see.

You might be surprised what's available just down the road, or just a few miles away.

\*    \*    \*

**Problem**      *I always forget something we really need.*

**Solution**      Some day when you're not rushed, sit down and "think through" an entire camping trip. Write down everything you need to cook with, menus for a week or so and all the food and seasonings to cook them with, what clothes each member of your family needs, all the toiletries needed, etc. Include flashlights, extension cords, light bulbs, perhaps a radio or fan, a rope with clothespins, coat hangers, matches in a waterproof container, and so on. Make lists and put them in a safe place.

When camping time comes, you can pack knowing
you haven't forgotten anything.

*　　*　　*

Don't throw the plastic liquid detergent bottle away when you are
finished. Take it on your next outing. Fill it with water when you get
there and you have a handy dispenser for soapy water for quick
cleanups.

*　　*　　*

Start a "camping box." Fill a box with one-of-a-kind dishes, pots,
pans or broken sets of dishes that you have gotten at garage sales.
After a while, you'll have a complete camping set that you can keep
stored separately, ready to go on a moment's notice.

*　　*　　*

Save all the old tennis shoes to use for "river shoes." Even old, torn,
shot tennies your kids have outgrown could be passed on down to
other "camping" families' kids.

*　　*　　*

P　　*Toothpaste, soap, deodorant, shampoo costs so
much in the individual sizes needed for camping.*

S　　Save that little dab still left in each tube or container before it's completely gone and stash it
away. The old budget won't be hit so hard come
vacation time. You'll have enough grooming aids
to give to everyone.

*　　*　　*

P　　*If I can survive the first meal on a camping trip,
I've got it made.*

S　　Don't let it get you down. When you're tired from
the trip and the kids are starving, don't try to hunt
for ingredients and cook. Take that first meal already prepared from home (fried chicken or sandwiches or such). Eat and then set up camp. Sure
saves wear and tear on the nerves.

*　　*　　*

P       *Buying food to take on a camping trip wrecks my*
        *budget because of all the extras involved.*

S       Those "extras" are expensive but really add to
        everyone's enjoyment, don't they! To keep the old
        budget more in line, buy a dab of this or a can of
        that each payday, or whenever, two or three
        months before your vacation. Put them someplace
        where you won't be tempted to use 'em.

        One more word of advice . . . take along enough
        food for the entire stay if no major food store is
        nearby. Having to purchase food in tourist areas
        will wreck the budget even more.

*    *    *

If you know there's an electrical hookup at the campsite, take along
your electric skillet. Fantastic!

## AT THE SITE

### Camping Etiquette

FOOD FOR THOUGHT: We go camping to get away from the
day-to-day routine of life—right? I realize we all have our likes and
dislikes, but if you're camped right next to several other adventurous

families, be considerate of their feelings. After all, they came to get away from it all, too.

If you have radios or TV's, keep them low. Everyone may not have your taste in music. You "country kickers" may be camped next to the "Boston Pops"!

Lights? Turn them out at a reasonable time, so those "early birds" can get enough sleep.

\* \* \*

P      *I love to go camping but I'm bashful meeting other campers.*

S      Bumper stickers telling what campgrounds you've been to would be a good conversation starter. Also, the old standby "May I borrow a cup of . . . ?" or "How can we get there from here?" are icebreakers.

## Cleaning Cookware

P      *Camping is fun, but cleaning the camp stove afterwards almost spoils it all.*

S      Camping was meant to be fun, not drudgery. So line every possible square inch of that stove with aluminum foil before using.

     When it's time to pack up, cleanup will be a breeze.

\* \* \*

P      *I have to use my good cookware and it gets blackened on the bottoms.*

S      Line the pans with foil on the *outside* and just toss the foil into the trash when finished. Or, coat the bottom and sides of each pan with dishwashing detergent; the soot will wipe off the pans with a wet cloth.

*Dressing and Bathing Area*
*(Also see Keeping Dry, p. 273)*

P       *We need extra dressing-area space as our tent is
        rather small and our family is rather large.*

S       Pack a large umbrella and an old (but good)
        shower curtain. Hang the umbrella by the handle
        (upside down) on a tree limb and hook the shower
        curtain onto the tip of each metal rib of the um-
        brella. It's practically custom-made for this pur-
        pose.

            You'll have a dressing area which is completely
        private and so easy to take down again when you
        get ready to move on.

            A word of caution: Take the whole thing down
        if it looks like rain. This is a fair-weather tip only.

✿   ✳   ✳

Hate to wait in line for family members to finish with their morning
shower in the *one* shower stall? Have each one wear only a beach
robe to the shower house and dress upon returning to camp.

Saves time and keeps from getting clothes wet on the shower floor.

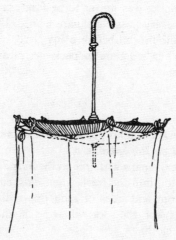

P       *How does a person keep his sanity trying to wash his hands or take a shower when there's no place to lay the soap except in the dirt or shower floor?*

S       Try this! Save those last little pieces and slivers of soap from home (or use a new bar). Put the soap in a nylon stocking and tie shut. Tie the stocking around the faucet or the shower head. Or, tie it to a tree branch near the water bucket or faucet.

## Keeping Dry
*(Also see Sleeping Bags. p. 278)*

P       *Our clothes always get damp when we are camping.*
S       If you'll store them in plastic zippered pillow protectors. they will keep clean and dry.

*       *       *

P       *I never manage to keep my clothes dry when I go to the campground shower—there's never any place to stash them while showering.*

S       I could have kicked myself when I came across the solution to this one. I was the person who tried to

hang a towel, washcloth and a complete change of clothes on one tiny nail—unsuccessfully each time I tried it. All you have to do is carry along a plastic shopping bag with all your things in it and hang the bag on that one tiny nail!

*     *     *

**P**      *All our clothes wind up on the floor of the tent— usually damp and dirty.*

**S**      Fasten a screw-type hook in the main pole of the tent. Hang a garment bag or a plastic shoe bag with shelves on the hook. The clothes won't fall to the ground and the see-through plastic will elimi- nate the "tossing around" to get to them.

*     *     *

**P**      *At our last picnic we had a sudden shower and all our supplies got wet.*

**S**      If you'll buy a small plastic trash can with a tight- fitting lid, you can store all your paper goods in it with no need to worry about sudden showers.

*     *     *

**P**      *The bottom of my tent gets wet.*

**S**      Plastic drop cloths that painters use are pretty cheap. Throw one on the ground before setting up your tent.

### Labeling Tent

**P**      *It is really hard for the little ones (and adults) to find our tent in the camping area, they all look alike after awhile.*

**S**      Attach a small flag or colored handkerchief or something distinguishable to the highest point of the tent or to a car antenna or trailer top. Most anyone will be able to spot their home base if it's marked with a brightly colored flag.

*Signals*
*(See signals for children, p. 274)*

*Storage*

**P**    *Since we won't damage trees by driving nails into them, not having a place to hang numerous items is very inconvenient.*

**S**    Punch several holes in a man's leather belt. Buckle it around the tree trunk, then insert pegboard hooks in the holes. You'll have space to hold several pieces of camping equipment, or whatever.

*       *       *

**P**    *There's no cabinet space in my trailer's little bath —toothpaste and such rattles around—it drives me crazy!*

**S**    Mount spice racks inside the bathroom door or on the bath wall to stick personal items in.

*       *       *

**P**    *My mom bought me a plastic tote bag to carry my swimsuit and towel to the pool. I lost it (and the one before it, too)*

**S**    Sounds to me like you've got a mom who's not too happy about that! Save those plastic rings that hold six-pack cans of drinks together. Remove the entire plastic as one piece. When you've got a bunch of them, get some string and just start tying them together in the shape of a tote bag. Two of the plastic holders will make the bottom. Cut a handle from another. If you lose this one, at least it was free!

*       *       *

**P**    *My spray deodorant, etc., as well as my underclothes are so cold early mornings. Brrrrr!*

S        Before you crawl into your sleeping bag at night, place the deodorant and underclothes at the foot or bottom of your sleeping bag. Next morning both are nice and warm—well worth any inconvenience from sleeping with a can of deodorant!

\*    \*    \*

P        *The kids can't find the shampoo, etc., since it is never put back twice in the same place after someone uses it.*

S        Take along a plastic shoebag to keep all these personal items in place. And label each pocket as to contents. A shoebag is also a dandy place to keep first-aid necessities handy, too. You can hang it from any convenient spot.

\*    \*    \*

A neat carrier for knives, forks and spoons on camping trips or picnics is a lunch kit—either metal or plastic. The flat, square type works best.

Just set it out on the table come mealtime and let everyone help themselves.

\*    \*    \*

Large coffee cans or fruit juice cans are great to store utensils in.

\*    \*    \*

Place your opened milk cartons and cans of juice in plastic bags and twist-tie shut, just in case of spills in your ice chest.

\*    \*    \*

P        *I can't seem to keep track of my roll of paper towels. It keeps coming unwound or rolling off the picnic table.*

S        Just put a rope or twine through the cardboard tube in the center of the roll of towels and tie it fast to a tree. Real handy and no lost towels. (No laundry to do later, either.)

## Sunburn Protection

P    *I love outdoor camping activities, but the sun doesn't like me. My skin sunburns severely, even though I use a sunscreen lotion.*

S    The amount of sunscreen protectives in a lotion vary, so learn to read labels. If your skin is extremely sensitive to the sun, choose one with a high "SPF" (sun protection factor).

For example, one with an SPF of 8 means you can stay in the sun eight times longer than you could with no protection.

It would also provide maximum protection against the sun while permitting limited tanning. Lesser numbers would provide less protection and allow for more gradual tanning, so know your skin type.

Also, choose a sunscreen with a "water resistant" label. These claims can only be put on products that meet government testing, requiring that the sunscreen maintain the initial SPF during a forty-minute period of water immersion.

This means it won't wash off in the water and you won't have to reapply your sunscreen every time you go for a dip—at least for forty minutes!

# BEDDING

## Mosquito Protection

P    *We sleep in our station wagon but we have to keep the windows rolled up because of mosquitoes and that makes it miserably hot.*

S    Get some long, small-holed nylon net pieces wider than the car door and hang them over the inside of your doors. Then close the doors and roll the

windows down. If the net blows, place magnets on
the window frames to hold the net in place.

\*    \*    \*

P    *How can I keep mosquitoes and insects away from
my baby at night?*

S    Put nylon net over the baby's crib or playpen.

## Sleeping Bags
### (Also see Baby Bed for camping, p. 289)

To keep sleeping bags from slipping off the mattress at night or to
make the ground "softer" carry inch-thick pieces of foam along that
match the length and width of the sleeping bags.

These take up very little space when rolled tightly.

\*    \*    \*

P    *The damp ground gets my sleeping bag clammy.*
S    Before putting your sleeping bag down, put an old
plastic shower curtain on the ground, then spread
a lot of newspapers for extra insulation.

\*    \*    \*

P    *My sleeping bag never smells really fresh when I
pull it out to use.*

S    You can air it out in the sunshine. Better yet,
sprinkling some baking soda inside, or putting in
a few fabric softener sheets before storing it will
help keep it sweet smelling.

## Sleeping in Car

P    *We sleep in our station wagon but have no curtains
for privacy.*

S    Pack a can of the window cleaner that leaves an
opaque film after applying. Rub this on the windows at night; just wipe it off in the morning.

Not only will you have privacy during the night but you will also have the cleanest windows in the camp!

## CAMPER AND TRAILER SAFETY
### (Also see Maintenance for the auto, p. 252)

Word of Caution: If you are pulling a trailer with a car, never, never let anyone ride inside the trailer ... you never know when something might happen and sudden stops can be dangerous.

*   *   *

If you're traveling in a pickup camper and there's children riding in the back, it's a good safety idea to replace thin camper glass with safety plastic.

## CLOTHING

### Clean Clothes

**P**      *My kids always look like "river rats" on the trip home.*

**S**      Pack a clean set of clothes (minimum a shirt) and tennis shoes (at least a clean pair of shoelaces if you don't have other tennies). Don't let the kids know you've got them until time to go home. They'll look spic and span if you make any restaurant stops or visits to friends on the way home.

*   *   *

This is a wonderful hint! When I was small and we were traveling and camping, my shirt got so dirty that my mother turned it around so the dirty part was in back—you know how important first impressions are! So at least when someone saw me from the front I looked OK.

The real kicker was—when the front (really the back) got awful, she turned my shirt inside out and I looked all clean (on the outside) for a day or so more. This may be funny, and it was, but it sure kept me looking half decent for a while.

*Laundry*
*(Also see Chapter 3, The Laundry, p. 130)*

P        *I like camping but I don't like the smell of the clothes to be laundered after the trip.*

S        Put two or three fabric softener sheets in with the soiled clothes. They will smell much fresher.

      \*     \*     \*

P        *Doing laundry while camping out is for the birds.*

S        Save your old clothes, the ones that you won't wear any longer or ones that are not in the best of condition. Wear them while camping; when soiled, add them to the fire or just throw away. I agree—who wants to wash clothes? You are supposed to be getting away from it all!

      \*     \*     \*

Use a clean garbage can or diaper pail with a tight-fitting lid. Place your dirty clothes in it along with soap and water and put the can in the trunk of your car. When you get to your next campsite, all you'll have to do is rinse them out and hang them up to dry. Viola! The jostling of the car acts like a washing machine.

## COOKING OUT
**(Also see Food Preparation, p. 69)**

*Camping Menu*

When making up your camping menu, put a number by each meal and the corresponding number on top of the cans for that particular meal.

Tape the menu somewhere in the cooking area at the campsite;

then sometime when the kids want to prepare the meal or you just want to be lazy for a change, just tell them to match the numbers and fix the meal.

You'll get to enjoy your vacation, too, by doing this little bit of extra planning ahead of time.

### *Charcoal*

To quickly start a charcoal fire in the barbecue grill, get a large (46-ounce) juice can and cut out both ends. Punch three or four rows of large holes around one end of the can.

Place the can upright in the bottom of the grill with the holes of the can at the bottom. Stuff a sheet of crumpled newspaper in the can, then fill with the desired amount of charcoal, leaving two or three inches of space at the top. Light the paper through the holes in the can with a match.

The holes in the can let the fire draw and the charcoal will begin to burn very quickly. After it takes on the familiar gray look, remove the can with tongs or a thick mitt. Replace the grate and you're ready to bring on the goodies to grill.

\*   \*   \*

P       *We love to grill but charcoal bags are so bulky and spills can mess up the car (not to mention your hands when you're picking it up).*

S                    Store charcoal in egg cartons or put it in plastic bags and close with a twistie.

## Condiments
*(See Food Storage, p. 284)*

Keep all those packets of salt, pepper and catsup you get from fast-food places to use on your picnics. They are free, sealed and disposable.

\*    \*    \*

Use the cups in a muffin tin to hold pickles, onions, relish, mustard, etc., on the picnic table. After a meal, just cover the whole tin with plastic wrap or foil and it's ready to use next time.

\*    \*    \*

P                    *I dislike dragging condiments from the camp "pantry" to the camp table.*

S                    Put jelly, coffee cream, mustard, etc. in an empty plastic soda pop carton. Makes a nifty tote, or just leave the carton on the table.

## Covers, Food

P                    *I cover the food left on the table to keep flies off but the kids come along to look and uncover everything.*

S                    If you'll just toss a large doubled piece of small holed nylon net over the food and weight the net down, they can find what they want and reach under the net. Or, use clear plastic wrap that kids can see through without uncovering the dish.

## Eggs

P                    *I'm a city boy who doesn't like cold eggs and bacon on a camp-out.*

S        No one does! Put your bacon and eggs in a plastic foam cup and they'll stay warm for quite awhile.

\*    \*    \*

P        *Help! How can I travel without breaking eggs and spoiling them?*

S        Why not break the eggs into a bowl before you leave and then pour the eggs into a hollow plastic rolling pin and keep it cold? Pour the eggs out as you need them.

### Hot Dog/Marshmallow Roast

P        *The kids always complain their hands get too hot when they roast weiners or marshmallows.*

S        Get some aluminum pie tins or heavy-duty paper plates and run the roasting stick through the middle and down near where they hold it. This will reflect the heat and keep those little hands cool. They will have roasted weiners, not fingers.

\*    \*    \*

Take along sticks or wire coat hangers for roasting marshmallows or weiners. Invariably, if you get to the campsite at night the kids want to do the roasting first thing, and sticks are sometimes nowhere to be found, or hard to find in the dark.

*Ice*

If ice cubes melt too quickly in your gallon jug of lemonade or whatever, freeze ice in margarine tubs or whipped topping containers, etc.

The larger size of cubes will last longer and won't dilute your drink so readily.

❊   ❊   ❊

**P**    *A friend told me to pack my food in dry ice—will dry ice harm my food?*

**S**    Heavens no! Dry ice is carbon dioxide in a solid form. However, it will freeze anything it comes in contact with. It's terrific for keeping food frozen or extremely cold. Don't put vegetables and such in contact with it. Don't handle dry ice barehanded. A few chunks tossed in with your "wet ice" will keep it from melting so quickly. You can find out where dry ice is sold in your ad pages in the phone book.

❊   ❊   ❊

**P**    *How can I keep my salad fresh until we get to the campsite?*

**S**    Put your salad in the top part of a double boiler and fill the bottom with ice. If you have a set of bowls that fit one inside each other, you can use the largest one to hold ice and then place the smaller one inside it with the salad in it.

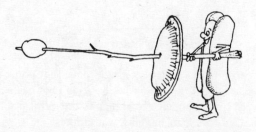

*Water*

| | |
|---|---|
| **P** | *It seems I spend all my time boiling water for this and that when camping.* |
| **S** | If you have electricity, take the biggest electric coffee pot or urn you can find and keep it "churning" all the time. You'll have plenty of hot water when you need it. |

\* \* \*

| | |
|---|---|
| **P** | *I like to back pack but I can't figure out how to get really cold water in a canteen.* |
| **S** | Fill the canteen one-third full of water the night before and place it in your freezer (leave the cap off the canteen). Next morning, fill it the rest of the way up with water and put the cap on. Juice can also be done this way. |

\* \* \*

Freeze water in clean milk cartons for ice. When the ice thaws you'll have nice cool drinking water. While it's thawing it will keep other perishables cool.

## EQUIPMENT

### Canvas

Don't spoil a camping trip by having a leaky canvas roof. Check out your pop-up camper *before* you leave. It's a good idea to store those campers under a shed to prolong the roof's life.

### Clothespins

Always carry a large supply of clothespins; they come in so handy for everything—from clipping your napkins together so they don't blow away, to clipping open a road map to the right spot. And natch, the old standby to use in hanging wet clothes!

## Cups

Never have enough cups for a large thermos bottle? Hang a few extra cups on the thermos with a shower curtain ring.

*       *       *

P           *The cost of paper cups for a camping trip for our bunch looks like the national debt.*

S           And invariably you run out, right? Why not get a different color or design plastic glass for each member of the family (plus a few extra) and have each one use the same glass all day long.

## Flashlights

Keep your flashlight in a plastic bag twisted shut. A sudden shower won't do it a bit of good nor will dropping it in the river or lake.

## Glassware, transporting

P           *I am always worried about the glass jars and things breaking.*

S           When you pack your camping or trailer things, use all those old socks that hang around. Cut off the foot part and slip the rest around each glass thing. This cushions the jars and will keep them from banging together.

## Utensils

P           *I can't afford two sets of utensils, and when we go roughing it I end up "missing" a few things here and there.*

S           Take the time to clearly mark all your items, down to knives, stirring spoons, pots and pans. You can either tape an address sticker with your phone number using clear, see-through tops. Or, mark them with your name or initial using bright red nail polish. When something ends up in another campsite, it's a dead giveaway that it belongs to the "Joneses."

I have a Chinese-style knife that was made for my mother in China in 1948 that is perfect for slicing vegetables, etc. I put my name and phone number on it per above instructions, and took it to a chili cookoff. Naturally, it disappeared from our spot and I was sick—do you know I got a phone call a few days later and it was returned—it's worth the effort.

\* \* \*

P    *I hate washing forks and knives when camping— I am supposed to be on vacation.*

S    Save all the little plastic utensils you get from drive-ins, etc., and take them along. After one use, you can toss them in the garbage if you don't feel like washing—that's what paper plates and plastic forks are for, dear!

\* \* \*

P    *I dislike having to wash my dishes and silverware before every meal, yet I want to insure that they are clean.*

S    Just place the dishes and eating utensils in a plastic bag and close it with a twistie. You can remove those needed for each meal, reclose the bag and nary a pesky fly or crawly bug will have a chance to cause you all that extra work.

\* \* \*

If you don't have a water faucet at the campsite, use a plastic gallon milk jug or bleach bottle (wash it thoroughly) and poke a small hole in the bottom. Plug the hole with a golf tee or small cork. Be sure to tie these to the jug or you may lose the stopper and your water.

Fill the jug with water and tie it around a low-hanging tree limb. Put a bar of soap in a nylon stocking and tie it to the tree.

Now, to wash your hands, just remove the stopper and grab the bar of soap. Really works great!

## FUN ACTIVITIES
### (See Playtime for children, p. 305)

Take along bottles of bubbles—the dime store variety. While spending time around the campfire, blow bubbles into the smoke. It's fun to watch them rise with the hot air and float around.

At night, let the kids follow them with the flashlight and watch the pretty colors they make. (Should go without saying, but NEVER let the kids get close to a campfire, of course.)

\*     \*     \*

Smaller children can get bored camping after a day or two, so take along a small riding toy or tricycle.

They'll have a grand time riding around the campsite and will be entertained if they are too small to swim unsupervised.

\*     \*     \*

Waterlogged and wanting do so something a little less strenuous, yet keep those kiddos (and some adults) entertained?

Try a game of pitching washers. All it takes is six or eight large washers about 2½ inches in diameter (available at hardware stores) and two holes dug in the dirt. The holes should be slightly larger than the washers and a couple of inches deep.

The game is played the same as horseshoes, so put the holes about twelve to twenty feet apart (depending on the age and size of the players). Every washer that lands in the hole is a point. Two players compete against each other, using three or four washers each.

Lots of fun and the washers take up next to "nil" storage space, are easily available, and ever so easy to carry with you.

\*     \*     \*

When the family is sunburned and tired of swimming and hiking, take a little side trip and see what the country has to offer.

## PACKING
**(Also see Packing for moving, p. 303 and Loading the Car,- p. 307)**

Plastic bags are space savers. If you eliminate large bulky boxes and cartons, you'll have a lot more room. Remember, many boxes of food are not completely full. Put meal-size servings of instant mashed potatoes (you can even put in powdered milk and salt and add the water and butter later), noodles, macaroni, biscuit mix and so on in plastic bags and close them securely. They tuck under things and in corners nicely.

*       *       *

Carry soap in a margarine tub to keep it dry.

*       *       *

Duffle bags or pillow cases "stuff" in the car trunk and under cots much better than suitcases.

## SUBSTITUTIONS

### Baby Bed

Take along your baby's playpen. It can serve as a bed or a supervised play area, and you can put a sheet over the top for shade. It is a safe way to take your baby along with you to the swimming hole to watch while you swim.

### Colander

A plastic woven box that strawberries come in makes a camping colander that doesn't take up much space and can be discarded before returning home.

### Grill

P        *There is no room in our subcompact car to carry along a grill for barbecuing.*

S        Stuff four 3-pound coffee cans and your oven rack

into the car. When you want to barbecue, fill the cans with water or sand, place the oven rack over them, and you're ready to go! You could even carry charcoal briquets in the cans and use them for cooking. More space saved.

## Napkin Holder

An empty coffee can makes a good napkin holder.

## Table

Need a "table"? Place a board between two tree forks—makes a good dishwashing center or storage table. Tie the board securely so it doesn't "tump" over.

## Tablecloth

P    *Our tablecloth always blows and flaps in the wind.*

S    Use an old fitted bedsheet and just slip it over the corners of the table. If you already have a pretty tablecloth that you want to use, get some double-sided sticky tape and tape that bugger down.

## Tent Maintenance

P    *Our last tent tore at the top center pole. I don't want this to happen to our new one as replacement is too expensive.*

S    Invert a tin or plastic funnel over the center pole before inserting it in the hole to raise the tent; it will reinforce the ring at the top of the tent and help to prevent its ripping out.

## Towels

P    *Towels and washcloths take a beating when camping. Worse yet, many times they get lost.*

**S**     Save all your old, frayed towels, etc.,—those you
have to replace from time to time. Just put them
aside and on the next camping trip drag them out
and take them along instead of your good ones.
You won't cringe if you see one down in the dirt
or feel too badly if one disappears.

# On the Move

When it comes to problems about traveling and packing and moving to a new location, I know how it feels, and I can sure help you solve them. The first place to start is getting ready to leave. If you are just going on a short trip it doesn't take too much planning to get organized. If you are making a major move, then settle in and read this chapter and get ready to get it done. The questions in this part are the ones that I receive time and time again, the ones everyone has troubles with.

I like moving. It is the only way to really clean out closets and sort through all that stuff in the "catchall" drawer and honestly—now I mean honestly—get the garage or attic "gone through."

I have always told you, "Clean when you are in the mood," but this is an exception. You are being forced to get it done. Do plan ahead and do a little bit at a time. Do one closet, one drawer or one shelf at a time. When the "big day" comes, most of it should be ready to pack. The other section in this chapter deals with traveling, both business and pleasure. Getting between here and there really can be a nice experience. I've had to learn how to make it both efficient and enjoyable since I travel a lot for business, doing spots on TV shows, going on book tours, and giving speeches. I have learned, sometimes the hard way, the ins and outs, the shortcuts and the ways to make it easy.

There are times that I am traveling so much that I am on a plane and in a different city every day. I never check luggage; I always carry it with me and so far have never missed a plane.

I promise you, your transit time doesn't have to be difficult . . . all you have to do is take it a step at a time. Don't be afraid to ask questions: "Is this plane going to San Antonio?" and "Is this the right way to the airport?" You will save a bundle of time and mistakes.

If you are traveling by car, current maps are important. Have someone, somewhere, that you can call in case you get lost.

Planning is very important; if you plan well, there will be no major problems. Above all, remember there is only so much you can control. If a plane or train or bus is late, or your luggage is lost, you had nothing to do with it. Do the best you can, but don't let it ruin your vacation or spoil the fun for others.

## ADVANCE PLANNING
### (Also see Advance Preparation for camping, p. 268)

| | |
|---|---|
| **Problem** | *We are moving cross-country and will be driving two cars. We need a way to communicate with my husband who will be in the lead car. We don't have CB radios.* |
| **Solution** | Buy little colored plastic flags, letting different colors represent messages (i.e., BLUE, stop for gas, YELLOW, let's eat). Let the kids be the flag wavers. |

*Moving Day Meals*

**P**     *Anything I can do to help my neighbors when they are moving?*

**S**     One of the nicest things you can do is fix a farewell meal for them on moving day. Nothing is worse than spending all day packing and then having to clean up to go out and eat. Put everything on disposable plates and they can enjoy their last meal in their home without having to wash a dish— what a thoughtful person you are!

*Newspapers*

**P**     *I always feel like a lost sheep in a new town.*

**S**     Subscribe to the newspaper in that town for a few weeks *before* you move. Things won't seem so strange to you when you arrive and you'll be familiar with the stores from their ads.

*Phone Directories*

Take a phone directory along with you when you leave a city. Frequently, you'll need the addresses of doctors, banks, schools, etc., in your old hometown.

*Prescriptions*

If you use prescription drugs, have them refilled before you leave (your doctor will probably need to send records to your new hometown doctor). Carry along your medications, extra eyeglasses, and important papers with you on the trip. You'll feel better knowing they're in your possession.

**LUGGAGE**

*Choosing luggage*

**P**     *I dread traveling by plane because it is so difficult for me to manage a heavy suitcase.*

S      Two smaller suitcases are easier to manage than
       one large one. If your luggage should decide to
       take another plane than the one you're on, at least
       you stand a chance of getting one suitcase on your
       flight!

## Extra Luggage

P      *We never have enough room for everything in our*
       *luggage on the return trip.*
S      Plan ahead and pack an extra bag in your suitcase.
       The cloth type that folds up is ideal; it won't take
       up much room and when you discover you have
       overstuffed your suitcase, you'll have instant extra
       luggage at no extra cost.

## Labeling

P      *I always have a terrible time distinguishing my*
       *luggage from all the others that look like mine.*
S      Mark yours with something different—a red yarn,
       pompom or a big green bow.

                    *    *    *

P      *My luggage tag came off and it took forever to find*
       *and identify my luggage.*
S      Always tape identification on the inside, just in
       case.

## Lost Luggage

P      *My bag got lost for days on my last airplane flight.*
S      Watch when you check in and be sure they put the
       correct destination on your luggage.

                    *    *    *

P      *It never fails that my luggage gets lost or arrives a*
       *day late.*

S          Prevention is the key. Never put anything in your
           suitcase that you must have—medicine, money,
           traveler's checks, house keys, etc. Take a very light
           carry-on bag that will fit under the seat. Fill it with
           makeup, shaving gear, toothbrush and paste, any
           medicine that you must take, and an extra shirt
           and change of underwear—just in case. Enough to
           see you through until the "misrouted" suitcase
           arrives.

## Luggage, substitutions

P          *We're making extended visits to our children but
           we don't like living out of a suitcase, and they have
           no extra drawer space.*
S          You could purchase a lightweight fiberboard chest
           of drawers and pack your things in that instead of
           a suitcase. Lay the chest in the back seat or trunk.
           Clothes can be carried in the car on hangers. Use
           the chest at your children's homes.

## MOTELS AND HOTELS

P          *Our motel room is a mess only a few minutes after
           we get there and looks like a whirlwind hit it.*
S          If you are only staying for a night or two, there is
           no need to unpack everything. Pull out only what
           you need and then try and put it back when you
           are finished with that article. When it's time to go,
           packing is a snap!

## Carrying ID

When you're traveling, always have your "staying address" on
your person. Your driver's license showing your address back home
is not going to help the police locate a relative staying back at the
hotel if something should happen to you.

Be sure your child has some kind of identification on his or her person when traveling.

### Correspondence

**P**      *I like to send postcards to my friends but it's hard to get around to addressing them while on my trips.*

**S**      Type or write friends' addresses on those adhesive address label sheets before you leave on your trip. When you want to send a card, peel a label off and stick it on the card and mail away. You could have your friends give you a few of their address labels. This would be easier on you!

### Fire Exits

Always check where the fire exit is in your hotel or motel . . . . make a mental note how many doors down and which way. If the halls are filled with smoke it's hard to read the exit sign.

### Ironing
### (See Ironing, p. 139)

**P**      *How can I do touch-up ironing in a hotel room with no board?*

S      Take along a travel iron and a pillow case. Buy a newspaper at the hotel, put it in the pillow case, and you have a small "ironing board" to do touch-ups on.

\*    \*    \*

P      *Any way to unwrinkle clothes?*
S      Hang them in the shower away from the stream of water (close the bathroom door) and steam them a few minutes with real hot water.

## Laundry

P      *I hate putting my soiled clothes in with my clean ones when traveling.*
S      Pillow cases or zippered laundry bags are great. The cases tuck nicely in corners and don't take up much space.

\*    \*    \*

P      *Dragging along a bottle of detergent to do a small amount of hand laundry takes so much room.*
S      Use a little squirt of your hair shampoo.

\*    \*    \*

P      *I wash clothes in the motel sink—but they never seem to dry.*
S      Before hanging them up, roll them in a towel and squeeze as much moisture out as possible; then use your hair dryer to blow them dry if you are in a hurry.

\*    \*    \*

When traveling, to solve the problem of never having enough hooks to hang things on in the motel bathroom, take along a few of those plastic clothespins with the hook at the top.

These can be hung over towel bars, shower rods and cabinet knobs.

## Lost and Found

Take a matchbook from each motel or hotel that you visit. If you should leave something behind, you will have the name and address of the motel handy.

## Night-lights

Dark motels or strange bedrooms can upset small children. When you travel, carry a night-light along. Even *you* can make your way to the bathrooms more readily.

\* \* \*

Carry along a lightbulb with sufficient wattage in case you want to read and the light in the motel room is not bright enough.

## Soap

P      *Tiny bars of soap in hotels and motels are such a nuisance to use when showering.*

S      Take along a regular-size bar of soap to use in the motel and drop the motel bars into your handbag to use at service station stops.

\* \* \*

Tuck away the small bars of soap and a cloth in a plastic bag for roadside restroom stops.

## Towels

P      *My husband and I get our towels mixed up in hotels.*

S      Follow one easy-to-remember rule in traveling . . . let your husband's things always be on the right and yours on the left. This goes for towels, drinking glasses, clothes in the closet, clothes in the drawers, and even as nearly as possible, when packing the suitcases. This will be his big chance to *always be right!*

## PACKING
### (Also see Packing, p. 303)

*Bed Linens*

**P**     *When moving it's really a pain to locate bed linens in a hurry to get the bed made for the little ones.*

**S**     Leave an old fitted sheet on the mattress . . . slip the top sheet and pillowslips and maybe a light blanket inside it. It's all there ready for you when you want to put them to bed.

*Cleaning Supplies*

Put all your cleaning supplies in a wastebasket along with the mop and broom, and make sure it's the *last* thing on the moving van (remember, last things in, first things out).

*Clothes*

**P**     *I have to pack some clothes for moving and I don't want them to get a musty smell.*

**S**     Place bars of soap in with your clothes (of course, be sure that the clothes are clean before packing them).

*Dishes and Glassware*

**P**     *Washing dishes and glasses that have been wrapped in newspapers is a lot of trouble and sure takes a lot of time.*

**S**     Watch for a sale on paper towels and stock up. When you are packing to move, wrap all your "kitchen" things in the paper towels and you won't have to wash a thing when you start unpacking . . . bonus, you will have a lot of paper towels for all those dirty hands at your new home!

\*   \*   \*

Bath and kitchen towels are good to pack dishes and crystal in when preparing to move.

## Drawers

P    *It takes me forever to arrange kitchen drawers when I move in.*

S    Dump the contents of each drawer into a plastic bag (you've probably got them arranged like you want them) *before* you move. Then, at your new house just place the bags in a drawer and unpack at leisure. You'll pretty much know exactly where stuff is and just about where it was at the old house.

## Essentials

P    *Last move we made, we arrived dead tired and had to unpack boxes before we could do anything.*

S    Take a box along with you in the car that has essentials like toilet paper, towels, soap, washcloths, can opener, tableware, coffee pot, etc. When you get there you can open a can of something and feed a hungry child. You will probably be too tired to eat out!

## Hardware

P    *Every time we move, buying nuts and bolts and picture hangers costs a fortune.*

S    As soon as you take a picture down or remove a
curtain rod, put the hangers, etc., in a little plastic
bag and tape the bag directly to the picture or rod.
They will be right there when it's time to rehang.
Don't forget where you packed the hammer!

## Labeling

P    *Even though I color-coded my packing boxes, I
can't find what I want easily without having to go
through twenty kitchen boxes.*

S    When you are packing, number each box K-1 or
B-2 and so on, and keep a list of approximately
what goes in it. When you want the blankets for
your son's room, you know which room and which
color-coded box it's in. Look at your list and you
can find the number.

\* \* \*

P    *Any way to make the move any easier—I wound up
with forty boxes marked "miscellaneous."*

S    Yes, there sure is, for you and the mover. When you start moving, assign each room a color. Yellow for the kitchen, blue for the first bedroom, green for the living room, etc. When you pack a box or carton, put a strip of that color tape on the box to indicate which room it goes in. Colored felt-tip markers can also be used. You should put a strip of the colored tape or a colored piece of paper over the door jambs in the new house to direct the mover. When the mover unloads the cartons he'll know which room to place the boxes in.

*       *       *

P    *I don't want my refrigerator to smell after being closed up for so long during our move.*

S    Be sure it is clean, clean, clean, and put some charcoal in some panty hose and then tie them in the door; also put some in the freezer. Stuffing the whole thing with newspaper helps absorb odors also.
(Also see Refrigerator, p. 38)

## On Arrival

P    *We are moving and I have to go house-hunting in a strange city; how will I remember what's what and where's where?*

S    First thing, buy yourself a map of that city and a little notebook. For every house you look at, trace the route to the house on your map and circle the location. Make a few notes about the house in your notebook (address, color, size, price, distance from schools, churches, shopping, etc.). You'll be able to easily decide which houses you want to go back and look at again.

*       *       *

When moving into a new neighborhood, it is very important to teach your children their new phone number and address. You think you get confused—think how a small child feels! If they can't remember this information, it is a good idea to have them wear an ID bracelet (homemade is fine). Or, you can even have them wear a little name tag showing their name and address. This will turn out to be an icebreaker in meeting other kids in your area.

## TRIPTAKING

*Children*
*(Also see Identification, Child, p. 306)*

P   *We love to travel with our child, but the car does get pretty cluttered.*

S   Hang a shoe bag over the back seat to hold small toys, crayons, bottles, etc.

\* \* \*

In the summertime, the first things kids want to do when they get to the motel is swim, so tuck their swimwear in a little bag and have it handy. You won't have to unpack or unload all those suitcases right away.

\* \* \*

P   *How can I make a sleeping or play area in my car for my small child.*

S   Place the suitcases on the floor of the car of the back seat. Then lay a baby mattress across them to make the "floor" level with the seat. By spreading a quilt or two across them you have a good area for the baby to sleep or play in during stops. Remember, a baby, too, should be protected by a restraining device.

\* \* \*

A metal cake pan with a sliding lid is a good lap desk for traveling children. Crayons, color books, etc., will store inside the pan, and the lid makes a good writing surface.

\* \* \*

Older children might enjoy taking along a notebook and making a journal of the trip. The journal can be used for a souvenir or for a school report.

\* \* \*

P   *We need a way to help keep our two older children occupied.*

S   Give each of them a large map of the United States and a colored pencil. They can watch for license plates from the various states and as they spy one, mark it on the corresponding state on the map.
   Not only will they have fun spotting the different plates, but it will help them to learn the location of each state.

\* \* \*

Stop and buy sandwich makings and drinks, then find a nice roadside park. While you are eating your snack you can walk around and rest your back and legs. It's great to let the kids "let off steam."

\* \* \*

P  *We love to stop for picnics, but sometimes we can't find a table.*

S  Put a folding TV tray in your trunk . . . just set it up and you have a place to put all your lunch goodies on.

\*   \*   \*

P  *I give my kids a drink when traveling, but then minutes later they are asking for another.*

S  If you will give them a cup of crushed ice instead of water, it will occupy them longer and still quench their thirst (real or imagined!). Keep a small foam chest full of crushed ice and a few cups inside the car.

\*   \*   \*

Put ice cubes in a plastic bag closed tightly with a rubber band. Punch a hole in a corner to drink from. Less spills and mess than a cup of water and it keeps youngsters happy for awhile.

\*   \*   \*

P  *Our young children get so restless sitting in the restaurant waiting for our orders after they've sat in the car for so long on our trip*

S  Have one parent go in and order for everyone, letting the children have the freedom to move around outside (under supervision, of course). You won't have fussy children squirming or arguing about what to order.

\*   \*   \*

P  *I would like to provide my preschooler with some type of identification as I worry about her straying from the campsite.*

S  Make the child a wrist band out of twill tape. Use indelible, waterproof ink and write her full name and the number of your lot and campsite on it. Fit it on her wrist securely and stress to her that she must keep it on at all times.

P     *I'm always turning around to supervise the kids in the back seat while driving.*

S     That could be very dangerous. Clip a mirror on the dashboard or put one on the driver's sun visor.

*   *   *

P     *My kids could make a mud puddle in the Sahara Desert with just one teaspoon of water—they get so dirty when we travel.*

S     Resign yourself and just carry along a detergent bottle filled with a little soap and water and take a washcloth and towel. Easy to wash off little dirty faces and hands just before you arrive.

*   *   *

P     *My child always spills his drink in the car.*

S     Use one of those training cups with the lid and spout—even an older child enjoys drinking from them.

*   *   *

P     *My family loves to stop at the beach when traveling but I dislike sand tracked in the car by the kids.*

S     Dampen washcloths and put them in plastic bags fastened with a twistie. As the kiddos get in the car, have them wipe their feet off and put the sandy cloth back into the bag.

## Loading the Car

Take along an electric coffee pot or hot pot to heat water in. Use instant coffee, and you have "room service" right in your room. When your feet hit the floor, you can have that morning cup of coffee right there to enjoy while you dress for breakfast. Oh, so nice, and cheap!

*   *   *

Take pillows with several cases on them to make things more comfortable in the car. As one case becomes soiled, slip it off and the pillow will be ready to use with a fresh one already on. The dirty case can be used to hold dirty laundry.

\*　　\*　　\*

P　　*I don't have any garment bags but I need something to protect my suits in my car.*

S　　Button up the clothing inside an old raincoat or use several plastic cleaners' bags.

\*　　\*　　\*

P　　*I want to carry some dresses on a rod in the back seat of my car, but they hang down too far and drag.*

S　　Put cardboard tubes on the hangers and then lay your dresses across the hangers just as you do pants. They won't wrinkle or drag on the car floor.

## Map Reading

P　　*I can't drive and read the map at the same time. I need some navigating help.*

S　　If you are traveling alone, write out your travel route in advance. Pin the route to the seat of your car or tape it on the dash. No one can safely drive and read a map at the same time.

## Medicine

P　　*Traveling with large bottles of all my vitamins takes up room.*

S　　Count out the number of days you will be gone and take only what is needed in small suitable bottles or plastic bags.

## Money

Before leaving on a trip, accumulate some change and put it in a small purse. Have it handy for telephones, pay toilets, and drink machines along the way.

*Packing Suitcase*
*(Also see Loading the Car, p. 307, Packing, p. 300, and Personal Items, packing, p. 310)*

*Clothes*

P        *My clothes always arrive wrinkled.*

S        Roll your clothes or pack with plastic bags—put the heavier things in the bottom of the suitcase.

\*    \*    \*

A space saver when you are packing is to roll all belts, ties and even small things like slips, and put them inside your shoes. Don't let any space go to waste.

\*    \*    \*

Always prepare an itemized list of articles in your suitcases. In case they are lost, the carrier will ask for such a list and it will save you time and hassle. Keep the list in your purse or pocket.

\*    \*    \*

P        *I hate pulling everything out of my suitcase just to get one thing that always seems to be on the bottom.*

S        A really nifty way to pack it is to put everything in large, clear plastic bags. Shirts in one, pants in another, shoes, toilet articles, etc. Then all you have to do is slip just one bag out, and the rest stays neat.

\*    \*    \*

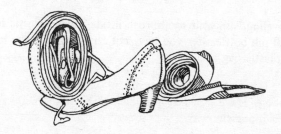

P  *I either take along too many clothes or not enough.*

S  You need to make out a "clothes menu" before you go. Plan each day's activities and what you will wear. Mix and match—all the same color scheme—and your accessories and outfits will "go further."

\*   \*   \*

P  *I'm always forgetting my slip or black shoes, etc.*

S  Write out a master list. Start thinking from shoes up—shoes, stockings, slip, dress, jewelry, etc.— and use this list to pack from.

\*   \*   \*

P  *Every time I go through the security check they practically have to dump out my handbag or purse.*

S  Plan for it, dear. Put all the things in your purse in several small plastic bags and they can just lift the bags out instead of digging around. Sometimes it's embarrassing, isn't it!

## Personal Items

A handful of safety pins and a few threaded needles stuck to the inside of your suitcase will come in handy when a button pops off or a hem comes undone.

\*   \*   \*

Travel often? Save time and space by buying sample-size toiletries and leaving them in your suitcase.

\*   \*   \*

For traveling, slip your toothbrush inside a clean plastic hair roller or small pill bottle after you have cut an opening in the top. Slip it into a plastic bag.

\*   \*   \*

P          *I hate packing a wet toothbrush.*
S          Blow it dry with your hair dryer.

✿   ✿   ✿

P          *I love the convenience of towelettes when I travel,*
           *but they cost too much.*
S          Moisten cotton pads with a mixture of rubbing
           alcohol and water (half water and half alcohol).
           Put them in a small jar with a tight-fitting lid.
           These are cooling, soothing, and you can throw
           away the jar prior to returning home.

✿   ✿   ✿

Those premoistened towelettes are not just for baby—use them to
remove makeup, wash your hands, or just revive tired feet!

✿   ✿   ✿

You can carry a wet paper towel in a plastic pill bottle—handy to
use for changing the baby, then just toss in the trash.

# PART THREE

# All Around the House

## INTRODUCTION

The third part of this book is about the people and pets in your life.

Putting together Chapter ten, "Babies and Children," was a simple matter of putting good information into logical order. Can you apply logic to children, though? That's one question I'm not going to even attempt to answer! But the information is all here for you—to help with those little wonders when they stump you! When you are frustrated and at wit's end, just remember that children (no matter what age) don't necessarily do things *to* parents, they do them just 'cuz they're kids.

There are no required courses on how to raise children; parents don't have to go to school or get a license somewhere. Parents just do their best, make the best judgment they can at the time, and hope. So if you have a problem with your kids, I hope the answers are here to help in your day-to-day battle to stay one step ahead of the children (sometimes one step behind, and that's called "picking up after").

Chapter eleven, "In Sickness and in Health," is for those among our family and friends who don't have it so easy. Sometimes, when someone we love is handicapped, even though it may be only temporary, it is difficult to deal with. What do you do when you have to have an ice pack in a hurry and you have none in the freezer ready and waiting? How do you help someone who has a broken leg and can't get up the stairs or carry out the garbage? This chapter of the book will help you solve these problems and many more.

To be handicapped doesn't mean to be totally dependent on others. There are a lot of hints in Chapter eleven to help those who are less able to do things for themselves.

The elderly—or Senior Citizens, if you will—are able to do a lot for themselves, and it helps them maintain a positive outlook to know that they can. We have some nifty hints for them as well.

If you own pets, you know that they are just like members of the family. I have a household full of them, so Chapter twelve, "Pets," has been a joy to put together. I used to say that I own a dog, but she really owns me—and that doesn't bother me in the least! Tequila is a little 3-pound chihuahua that has been my roommate and companion for over six years. She is twelve years old now and so she is quite an old lady but still in good health and perky as ever.

When I got married, I told my husband, David, that along with me came Tequila. That agreement was all right with him, because *he* had a macaw (large parrot) of whom *I* wasn't overly fond. So our family of animals now includes Rocky who has finally come to like me a bit . . . not a bite, just a bit.

To those, add little Fussy, a cockatiel who sings in the early morning and sometimes flies into the glass window when he is out of the cage. The only way I can keep him from doing this is to make sure the drapes are closed.

The last of our pet family, but most surely not least, is Fred the Ferret. You are probably asking yourself "Did she mean another parrot?" No, a ferret is a small animal, similar to a mink or weasel, and a real delight to watch. How, you ask, did Heloise end up with a ferret as a pet? Well, it's a long story but the ending is, I saw one in a pet store and the rest is history. Fred is a little unusual in that he is an albino, which has caused some problems. When we put him in his cage, we put newspaper down just like you do for hamsters, but the newsprint started turning his white coat of fur black. This was a problem for Heloise. Solution: I used shredded brown paper bags instead, and give old Fred a bath every few days.

How do you bathe a ferret? Just like you do a baby in the kitchen sink! The fun part is using the hair dryer to dry him.

So off we go—All Around the House.

—Hugs, Heloise

# 10

## Babies and Children

Children make the world go round and round, don't they? Sometimes you're tempted to ask yourself if they really are worth it—usually when they've just tracked mud in on your clean floor—but then a little one comes up with a posy and a hug for no special reason.

This chapter gives you the benefit of experience of mothers who have been through it all, from handling the 2:00 A.M. feeding to entertaining a bored preschooler on a rainy day.

Parenting calls on inner resources and strength and most of all, *love*. We all need to remember that no one is going to be a perfect mother or father, and that to do your best is all anyone, or any child, can ask. You may look back on the times when you didn't know to put ice on a bump or let a little one suck on a popsicle instead of holding an ice pack to his lip . . . but remember, love can more than make up for the mistakes you think you've made along the way. If children know you love them, some of the mechanics of mothering don't seem so important.

Give your children lots of hugs, and maybe they won't know that the toast was burnt and you scraped it off. I won't tell.

## BABIES

### Announcements

**Problem**    *Being nonsmokers, we would like a suggestion for something to pass out besides cigars when our new baby arrives.*

**Solution**    Why not have ball-points printed with "It's a girl" or "It's a boy."

### Baby Book

**P**    *Keeping my baby's book up-to-date is a real problem.*

**S**    If the book is handy, it will be easier. Keep it on a bedside table and enter things each night. Or, keep note pads around to jot things down, then transfer them to the book later. Use a kitchen calendar to make quick notes.

### Bathing

**P**    *My baby gets so bored when I bathe her in the sink.*

**S**    Cut out some pretty pictures and put them on the cabinet where she can see them. Or, hang a pretty mobile above so she can look up and see something besides blank wall space.

\*    \*    \*

**P**    *Drying my baby seems so difficult with his squirming around.*

S    Use a big beach towel and completely wrap baby
     up. He will be easy to hold and no problem with
     missed wet spots.

\* \* \*

Cold lotion doesn't feel too good on baby's skin. Put the plastic bottle
(with the cap on tightly) in the baby's tub (or other sink) during the
bath so it can warm. Warm the shampoo this way, also.

\* \* \*

P    *Baby powder is very expensive for me. Can I substi-*
     *tute?*
S    Mix the powder with a box of cornstarch or baking
     soda to make it go further. Both are wonderful and
     safe to use.

\* \* \*

If you bathe baby in the kitchen sink, place a hand towel or small
piece of foam rubber in the bottom and baby won't slip. Makes a soft
cushion, too.

\* \* \*

P    *My baby is so slippery when I bathe her—I am*
     *really afraid sometimes she will slip.*
S    If you will leave a T-shirt on when bathing the tiny
     one, you can hold on easily. No slippery skin.

\* \* \*

P    *My baby slips in his plastic bathtub.*
S    Lay a towel in the bottom of the tub; I think
     nonskid appliqués would be too rough and
     scratchy.

\* \* \*

P    *Every time I bathe my baby, she spits up.*
S    Some wee ones don't like to be jostled—are you
     bathing her right after a feeding? Why not bathe
     your baby before you feed her and see if that helps?

P       *My baby is too large for his infant tub and really too small for the family tub.*

S       Use a plastic laundry basket that is the woven type. You can put this in the tub and baby in it. The water flows in and out and he stays in one place. Never, never leave a child alone in water— no matter how shallow the water is.

## Beds and Cribs
*(Also see Baby Bed for Camping, p. 289)*

### Beds

A towel rack attached to the outside end of baby's crib is so handy to hold blankets, towels, and such. Just be sure that your baby can't pull them into the crib.

*     *     *

For a very tiny baby, you can keep all the things that you need close at hand, like powder, pins, wipes, etc., at the end of the crib. Just hook a bicycle basket at one end of the crib to hold all the essentials. Of course, when baby starts pulling himself up, move the basket to another spot.

*     *     *

Beach towels make good summer blankets for baby. Easy to wash and dry.

P       *Our baby's room is drafty. How can I keep the draft
        off the baby at night?*

S       Take the mattress out of the crib and slip a blanket
        under the springs. Pull up the sides of the blanket
        and secure the sides to the crib railings. Replace
        the mattress.

*        *        *

P       *Putting my baby back in a cold bed after an early
        morning feeding always wakes her up.*

S       Keep a plugged-in heating pad with a towel
        wrapped around it next to the baby's bed; as soon
        as she is lifted from the bed, put the heating pad
        in. When you return her bed is nice and warm.

*        *        *

P       *When the weather gets cool, the plastic liner that
        I use on the baby's crib makes the bed so cold.*

S       Place a large beach towel between the liner and the
        sheet.

*        *        *

P       *My baby kicks the covers off.*

S       Fasten men's suspenders to each side of the cover
        and secure loosely under the mattress. Or, using
        shower curtain rings, attach the blanket to the side
        rails. You can sew blanket "pillowcases" to slip
        the baby into.

*        *        *

Placing baby's crib at a diagonal from the corner of the room makes
it easy to change the sheets, etc. You can get to your baby from both
sides of the bed and there's no chance of little fingers touching the
wall.

*        *        *

P       *My little "darling" drives me up a wall shaking his
        bed and watching it walk across the room.*

S    It's amazing how those little ones can figure out things at such an early age. If you want to outsmart him, put sponges underneath each leg of the crib . . . that creepy, crawly crib won't crawl.

＊    ＊    ＊

P    *I hate to put my baby back in a damp bed—even though I have changed the sheets.*
S    Use your hand-held hair dryer to quickly dry out those damp spots and warm the bed.

＊    ＊    ＊

P    *The little ones in the neighborhood always seem to ring my doorbell during my baby's nap time.*
S    Post a picture of a sleeping baby on the door. Even the smallest tyke can tell that it's not the right time to ring the bell.

＊    ＊    ＊

P    *I have to wash so many sheets for such a tiny baby.*
S    Use only one sheet on the crib. Tuck the sheet in the top as usual, then fold it halfway back up the bed. It's kinda like "short-sheeting," but a tiny baby never gets down to the bottom anyway.

＊    ＊    ＊

Ever had to completely change a wet crib at three o'clock in the morning? Next time you make the bed, make it up "twice," with rubber pad, sheet, rubber pad, sheet, etc. When the bed gets wet, remove the top sheet and rubber pad. The dry bedding underneath is ready to use.

### Bottles

P    *How do I get that chalky deposit out of my baby's bottles?*
S    Boil the bottles in water with one or two cups of

vinegar added, for ten minutes or so. To prevent this chalky deposit, add a little vinegar to the water each time you sterilize the bottles.

\* \* \*

P   *The plastic bottles my baby uses have developed an odor.*

S   Boil the bottles for a few minutes in baking soda and water.

\* \* \*

P   *No matter how well I clean baby bottle nipples, they get so clogged.*

S   Use a toothpick to gently push through the hole.

\* \* \*

P   *Every time I wash bottles, caps and nipples in my dishwasher, they scatter.*

S   Put them in a nylon net bag with a drawstring closure.

\* \* \*

P   *My baby can't hold a bottle because it's slippery.*

S   Make a tube out of a small sock and slip the bottle inside.

\* \* \*

P   *Even though my baby can hold her playthings, her bottle seems to be impossible.*

S   Place one of the colored plastic rings around the bottle. It will attract her attention, and since she is used to holding it, she will want to hold the bottle.

\* \* \*

P   *The baby bottles in the fridge are always falling over and are really bothersome.*

S      Use a cardboard carton that soft drinks come in. The compartments will hold six bottles, and they won't fall over every time you reach in the fridge.

*   *   *

P      *When my friends and I visit, getting baby bottles mixed up is a disaster.*

S      Put a different colored rubber band or a small piece of tape on the bottles to color-code them.

*   *   *

P      *How can I keep plastic disposable bottles from leaking when traveling?*

S      Put a piece of plastic wrap over the bottle opening before putting on the nipple and cap.

     Remember, water temperature and bottle temperature should always be checked, using the crook of your elbow. Your hands are less sensitive to heat.

*   *   *

P      *I just dread dragging myself to the kitchen to warm the bottle for the 2:00 A.M. feeding.*

S      Before going to bed, heat the bottle to the right temperature, while at the same time filling a wide vacuum bottle with hot water to warm it. When the baby bottle is ready, pour out the hot water, pop in the bottle, and close the lid. Keep this by baby's crib and you won't have to take an extra step.

*   *   *

Heat baby's bottle in a coffee can. It's deeper and more narrow, and the bottle will heat faster. Remember, the can will be hot so don't touch.

*   *   *

P      *I want to go out but I worry about how to keep baby's bottle warm.*

S      After you warm the bottle to the right temp, put it in a clean, round. potato chip can, put the lid on and wrap in a towel. When it's time to eat, the bottle is still warm.

\*    \*    \*

P      *I hate to have to spend the money for a bottle warmer.*

S      If you have a slow cooker, this works just great. Keep it turned on low. The water isn't hot enough to boil, but warm enough to get the milk to the right temperature in no time.

\*    \*    \*

P      *Weaning my baby from her bottle is almost impossible.*

S      When it is time to start getting her away from the bottle, take the lid off and let the little one start drinking from her old favorite bottle, then move onto a cup.

\*    \*    \*

P      *My little one just refuses to drink from a cup and won't touch anything that isn't in his bottle.*

S      This just might do the trick . . . fill the bottle with something that doesn't taste as good as whatever you put in his cup . . . for example, put very diluted juice in his bottle, and the good stuff in the cup. When there is a "taste test"—guess which one will be picked!

## Bathtime

P      *My toddler loves to play with plastic toys in the bathtub, but oh, the mess afterwards.*

S        Keep a nylon net bag handy to put those drippy toys in after the fun's over. Just hang it over the faucet handle to drip dry.

To delight the small fry, cut animals such as frogs, turtles and fish out of colorful construction paper. Coat them with paraffin, let dry, and they will float on the water.

Fun at bathtime!

## Colds

P        *My young baby doesn't sleep well when she has a cold.*

S        Try propping up the head of the bed with books or pillows under the mattress; if your baby is very young, use the infant seat to keep baby's head elevated. The baby will breathe easier in an elevated position and will be able to sleep more comfortably.

## Diapers

There are always days when everything gets off schedule or seems to go wrong! Be prepared by having a supply of disposable diapers (even though you don't ordinarily use them) and ready-to-use formula on hand, prescribed by your pediatrician, of course.

\* \* \*

To keep those diaper pins gliding easily through the diaper, just stick the pin in a bar of soap before using.

\* \* \*

P        *I hate to throw away a new disposable diaper which can't be used because the tab's pulled off.*

S        Don't! Keep an adhesive bandage or some adhesive tape handy and make a new tab.

\* \* \*

P        *Occasionally I have to dry diapers indoors, but I
         don't really have the room to dry as many as my
         baby needs.*

S        Hang two coat hangers on your shower curtain
         rod. Pin one corner of a diaper to one hanger, and
         the other corner to the other hanger. Fill up the
         hangers (they're parallel), and it's just like two
         short clotheslines, side by side.

         When those two "clotheslines" are full, start
         with another two hangers. You can really hang a
         bunch this way.

*    *    *

Ever been caught with sopping wet plastic pants for baby and no dry
ones to be had? Wash them out, then dry them in a hurry, using your
electric hair dryer.

*    *    *

You like soft things next to your skin and so does your baby. Add
a fabric softener to your last rinse or use a softener in the dryer for
your diapers. Besides being soft and feeling good, the diapers will be
easier to pin.

*    *    *

P        *Sometimes while visiting, I can't find a place to lay
         a soiled diaper when changing a baby.*

S        A fancy bedspread or carpet just isn't the spot,
         right! Well, get one of those plastic "flying saucer"

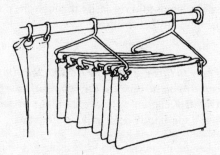

shaped toys with the curled edge and stick it in
your diaper bag.

It's a perfect place to plop the diaper down temporarily and the plastic toy is light and easily
washed.

\*     \*     \*

Take along some empty coffee cans with plastic lids to put soiled
diapers in when away from home.

\*     \*     \*

P        *I ran out of premoistened towelettes.*

S        Keep a supply of diaper liners handy to use as
wipes. Have a vacuum bottle of warm water
nearby to wet the liners.

\*     \*     \*

P        *I wish I didn't have to put a cold diaper on my baby
at night.*

S        Slip a few diapers (perhaps a gown, too) under
your electric blanket or heating pad. Diapers will
be nice and warm for baby's change.

## Feeding

P        *My little one loves fresh bananas, but those little
fingers just can't hold them.*

S        Slippery banana slices can be a hassle. Roll them
in graham cracker crumbs and they'll have something to hold onto.

\*     \*     \*

P        *It never fails that when I'm feeding my "little darling" she dumps the entire bowl of food on her
head. Help!*

S        Before feeding her put a plastic shower cap on her
head. Make it a game and she won't know it's for
her own good—and your sanity.

**P**     *I need a bib for myself when I feed my little one!
It seems like more food ends up on me than in his
mouth.*

**S**     Mom should have a bib, too. Slip on a large man's
old shirt, or anything that covers most of you.

\*     \*     \*

**P**     *My youngest (eighteen months) insists on feeding
herself, and oh, what a mess at the table.*

**S**     Give the lady her own space, as the saying goes
. . . put her in a regular chair and be sure she is
secure. Then belly up a TV tray and it should be
just about her height.

\*     \*     \*

**P**     *Handling a bowl, spoon and baby too, is sometimes
a chore.*

**S**     Use a tea or coffee cup that has a handle so you
can hold onto it securely. And even if little hands
hit it, you don't have to worry about it being
dropped to the floor.

\*     \*     \*

Small plastic spoons, like the kind that come with ice cream or ice
tea are perfect for feeding a baby. They are tiny for their mouths and
the plastic isn't as hard on their gums as metal is.

An iced tea spoon is much easier to feed baby with than a regular teaspoon. The bowl is smaller and fits those little mouths.

\*   \*   \*

Baby learning to feed himself or herself? Spread strained meat from a jar of baby food on a cracker. They can hold a cracker easier than a spoon.

\*   \*   \*

P    *I can't get my baby to swallow his liquid vitamins once I get them into his mouth.*

S    From the smell of them, who'd want to! But, when baby won't swallow, just gently blow in his face. It really works.

\*   \*   \*

P    *There is no closet in my baby's room.*

S    Suspend a hula hoop toy from the ceiling and hang the clothes hangers on it.

\*   \*   \*

P    *I can't afford curtains for my baby's room, but want something "baby-looking."*

S    Buy summer receiving blankets (much cheaper than curtains) and hem an edge to slip a rod through.

\*   \*   \*

A sturdy card table covered with a mattress pad makes a nifty dressing table for baby.

\*   \*   \*

Got a huge baby gift to wrap? Why not buy a disposable plastic or paper tablecloth? It usually doesn't cost as much as a couple of packages of wrapping paper and it surely will be easier to manage! Cute, too!

*High Chairs*

P  *When visiting friends who don't have a high chair or booster seat, my small one's chin rests on a table when we eat.*

S  The phone book to the rescue (if you live in a large town). I can remember some of my best meals, sitting on top of large (fat) books with a small pillow as a cushion. There are some grandparents who have a special phone book. It's last year's edition, covered with adhesive-backed paper . . . not much extra money spent for a chair booster.

\*  \*  \*

If you don't have the time to take the high chair to the car wash for a good cleaning, put it in the shower. Let the shower run a while, and all the built-up grime should go down the drain, with a little help.

\*  \*  \*

P  *My baby's high chair gets pretty gunked up with spills.*

S  Make it easy on yourself to clean! Just stick it outside in the rain or turn the lawn sprinkler on it.

\*  \*  \*

P  *My baby slips down in his high chair.*

S  Safety pin a towel or tie a bib to the back of the seat of the chair. No slipping, and the towel will catch spills, too.

You can also put strips of adhesive tape or foam rubber on the seat of the chair for "grip."

\*  \*  \*

P  *My young son has a way of tipping over his high chair.*

S If you attach a large screen door hook to the back of the chair and when he is in the chair, hook it to the wall, you'll never fear about the tot falling over. You could even put a hook on each of the back legs for safety.

\* \* \*

P *My little girl is big enough to sit in the high chair, but she wobbles from side to side.*

S Make some bumper pads for her. You can roll up hand towels or even a bath size towel. Then just place them on the sides of the high chair and your "precious" can bob and weave but she won't wobble out.

## Injuries

P *I can't keep the little hands of my baby protected when injured.*

S Clean and bandage the area, then cover it with a baby stretch sock.

## Nailtrimming

P *My baby really protests having his nails cut.*

S Use blunt pointed scissors to cut his nails while he is sleeping.

## Pacifier

P *My baby always manages to drop his pacifier and screams until I get it sterilized.*

S Tie a pretty ribbon onto the pacifier and pin the ribbon to his clothing, or attach it to his high chair.

\* \* \*

A fussy baby in a waiting room is not much fun for mom, baby or others. Stash a few little toys or items in a plastic bag that will amuse the baby. Also, a little sweet-coated dry cereal tucked in a sandwich bag is a lifesaver at times!

### Playpen (See Baby Bed for Camping, p. 289)

P    *I "inherited" a mesh playpen which is in good condition except for looking horribly dirty and dingy.*

S    Put a solution of bleach and water in a spray bottle and spray the mesh liberally, scrub and then rinse *well.* Afterwards, if there is a remaining bleach smell, spray a little liquid fabric softener on the mesh. If the playpen is completely washable, the high pressure hose at the car wash would be great!

*    *    *

P    *My toddler aggravates his older brother who's trying to build with blocks.*

S    Try putting the older brother in the playpen out of the reach of the exploring but well-meaning brother!

### Quick Meals

Got a "starving baby" who can't wait for anyone to dress for breakfast when you're on a trip? Mix dry powdered milk (if okay with your doctor) with dry cereal. Just add hot faucet water at the motel. Jars of fruit can be added for a yummy taste. Feed baby, dress at leisure, and everybody's happy!

### Security Blanket

P    *I have a toddler who won't part with his blanket— that thing is dragged around through the dirt— yuck!*

S        Cut the blanket in half. Then, after awhile, cut the
         blanket in quarters. He can't drag the small part
         through the dirt—at least, not very easily—and an
         added bonus is that part of his beloved treasure
         can be in the wash. You'll always have a clean part
         to give to the child.

## Stroller

P        *I love to go shopping, but my little one is not old*
         *enough to sit up in a stroller.*
S        Put the baby in a plastic infant seat and then place
         the seat in the stroller. Of course, make sure the
         baby is well secured.

## Teething

P        *How can I make my teething baby feel better?*
S        Fill a sterilized nipple with water and then freeze
         it. Place it on a baby bottle and give to your baby.
         For an older baby, chewing on a piece of frozen
         weiner is sheer delight!

## Traveling

Baby fussy in the car? Pin or tape some bright pictures above the
car seat to amuse the child.

\*     \*     \*

Take along your baby's car seat on a long train or bus trip. They get
tired of being held and mom's arms need a rest, too.

\*     \*     \*

An inflatable child's swimming pool makes an excellent temporary
travel bed for a wee one.

*Walker*

| | |
|---|---|
| **P** | *My baby's walker makes marks on my walls.* |
| **S** | For bumpers, split a few short lengths of old garden hose and place on the edges of the walker. |

## CHILDREN

*Beds, Bedding and Bedtime*

| | |
|---|---|
| **P** | *My three-year-old likes to sleep on a top bunk at his cousin's house—I worry that he might slip through the rail.* |
| **S** | Take a full size bed sheet, fold it in half widthwise. Hang the sheet over the rail and tuck both ends under the mattress. |

\*   \*   \*

Ever think that when your youngster lies on the bottom bunk he or she has nothing to look at—tack some "interesting" fabric or pictures on the underside of the top bunk to brighten up the spot.

\*   \*   \*

A neat way to place bunk beds is to slide the lower bed under the upper one at a right angle (put both footboards on one bed and both

headboards upside down on the other). This doesn't take up as much room as twin beds.

\* \* \*

P     *My daughter wants a canopy bed, which is out of the question right now.*

S     An inexpensive "canopy" of nylon net may satisfy her until her dream comes true! Find an old umbrella and take the cloth cover off so you only have the skeleton left. Fold the ribs down on one side so you have only half an umbrella. Using the cover folded in half for a pattern, cut three layers of nylon net. Make two-inch net ruffles to go along the edge and along each rib.

   Now, tack the net cover on the half umbrella skeleton. Then add your ruffles around the edges and along the ribs. If you like, add a few silk or plastic flowers here and there.

\* \* \*

P     *My daughter is weary of her old headboard—any suggestions for an inexpensive change?*

S     Take the headboard down and hang woven straw mats or straw decorations above the bed, or tack a fake fur rug over the headboard for a new look.

\* \* \*

P     *My little one stays black and blue hitting her legs on the corner of the bed.*

S     Tie sponges on the bed frame legs. They won't show under the spread.

\* \* \*

P     *My son refuses to make his bed in the morning.*

S     Strip off all the sheets, blankets, pillow cases, and spread—fold them and put them under the pillow. Remaking a bed from scratch is not much fun—

two or three times of this should make him willing
to make his bed as he should.

\* \* \*

P   *My "little" boy is no longer little—any way I can
    "stretch" his twin bed to fit him?*

S   Buy some foam rubber as firm as you can find. Cut
    it the width of the bed and the depth of the box
    springs and mattress combined; make the foam
    about six inches long to extend the bed. Cover the
    foam with material. Put this on the edge between
    the headboard and the mattress, and the bed is six
    inches longer. (You might need a bed slat to sup-
    port the foam insert.) This works only when the
    bed frame is open at the foot.

\* \* \*

P   *My little boy sometimes wets the bed—and over-
    night visits make him (and me) edgy.*

S   Carry along an old waterproof shower curtain to
    slip under the sheet. The mattress will be pro-
    tected.

\* \* \*

P   *My little girl drives me "crazy" at night asking for
    a drink every ten minutes.*

S   Keep a plastic bottle of water or juice by the bed-
    side and a small plastic glass. It will save you steps
    and she can have her drink anytime.

\* \* \*

Daddy travel a lot? Have him read some bedtime stories onto a tape
recorder. Makes "missing him" a little easier on the kids. (Mom likes
to hear his voice, too . . . kinda like a long-distance phone call.)

*Car Pools*

P   *I drive a car pool with preschoolers and I fear I
    may smash one of their fingers in the door.*

S      Before you close the door, make a game of it—like "Everybody, hands on your head."

*　　*　　*

P      *My little girl is joining a car pool—she is afraid she won't remember the right car.*

S      Buy different colored toy cars to match cars in your car pool and write or tape the last three numbers in the license of that car on the toy. Each day pack the right color car in her lunch or in her school bag. Then she'll know what color car to look for in the afternoon and will be sure it's the right car by the last three numbers.

### Chicken Pox

Use your hair dryer to give relief to chicken pox itching. Put it on warm if the child feels chilly or on cool if the child feels hot. *Only you* should use the hair dryer—don't give it to the child.

### Childproofing
*(Also see Doors and Drawers in cabinets, p. 58)*

P      *My toddler locked herself in the bathroom and both of us were upset, to say the least.*

S      If you will put a thick towel over the top of the door, your child can't completely close it.

*　　*　　*

| P | *My child is always pulling drawers out and may get hurt.* |
|---|---|
| S | Stick a sock in the side for a wedge—very little ones can't pull the drawer out. |

\*    \*    \*

Do you have a curious little tyke in your household who loves to dial numbers on the phone?

Place a large rubber band over the receiver buttons to hold them down. If "Junior" decides to make a long-distance call, he can dial away but the numbers won't connect.

### Clothes/Dressing

When making or buying clothing for two or more children of the same sex, don't buy things exactly alike, no matter how cute you think it is at the time.

By the time the youngest child has gone through the oldest child's hand-me-downs, not only is the child sick of looking at the same shirt, but you are, too.

If you want to dress them alike, buy different colors of the same design. At least you'll have some variety.

\*    \*    \*

| P | *My child needs help putting on her coat.* |
|---|---|
| S | You can teach her easily this way. Lay her coat on the floor with the lining facing up. Have the child |

stand by the collar, bend down and slip her arms into the sleeves, then toss the coat over her head.

\* \* \*

**P**     *My toddler is so fussy when I'm dressing her.*

**S**     Try dressing your child in front of a full-length mirror. The mirror fascinates a child and will distract her.

\* \* \*

**P**     *My little girl's hair is too thin to hold a barrette.*

**S**     Glue a rubber band on the inside of the barrette; it will grip well and keep it in place.

\* \* \*

**P**     *Every time I cut my children's hair, they complain of hair in their eyes even though I use a cloth and am careful.*

**S**     Put one of those "sun visor" shades on them when you cut their hair. Much easier.

\* \* \*

**P**     *I have the hardest time remembering the length of laces needed for my kids' shoes.*

**S**     If you can remember the number of holes in his or her shoes, and multiply six by that number (one side only), then you've got it made.

For instance, if there are five holes on one side of the shoe, multiply five times six, which means you need to buy 30-inch laces.

\* \* \*

A prewash spray and a little elbow grease will remove most scuff marks from children's vinyl shoes.

\* \* \*

P   *My son is forever scuffing up his good shoes.*

S   Cover up those scuffs and scratches with a felt-tip pen that matches the shoes. They come in a variety of colors.

Give it a second coat of liquid furniture polish or shoe wax to bring out the shine.

\*     \*     \*

P   *My little girl has several pairs of lace-trimmed socks which go with special outfits, but I always have to frantically hunt for the matching pair.*

S   Next time, after laundering the dress and socks, pin them together. No more searching for the socks at the last minute.

\*     \*     \*

P   *I have the hardest time keeping up with my children's socks, and when they do end up in the wash, there's always a "lone" stranger with no mate.*

S   When buying socks for the kiddos, buy all the same color, or preferably solid white. That way, if you do happen to lose one, you'll still be able to have a pair.

\*     \*     \*

Socks worn out but still good in parts? Try this!

Use the stretchy tops to protect knees and elbows a little more when skating. Use the good tops as wrist and leg bands on pajamas and jacket cuffs.

A small child's worn-out knee-hi socks, when the tops are stitched together after cutting a U-shape for the crotch on each sock, make cute little pantyhose for a doll.

How about a nifty sleeping bag for a fashion doll?

What kid couldn't use a marble bag! Make a casing and add a draw string. Cut the foot off, gather the cut end and tie in a little "top knot." Roll the edge up and you have a cute "toboggan cap" for a favorite doll.

\* \* \*

P    *My little boy can't manage the zipper pull on his coat.*

S    Put a notebook ring or metal shower curtain hook on the zipper pull. He can slip his fingers in and pull.

### Emergencies

Keep an easy-to-read list of emergency phone numbers by the phone and teach your children how and when to use them. If the child is too young to read but can pick out numbers, place pictures of a policeman, fire truck, etc., with the appropriate telephone numbers in large writing next to each picture.

### Organizing Room, Closet and Supplies
### (Also see Organizing closets, p. 201)

P    *My son has decided to organize his room—he wants a storage area for his sports equipment but I can't afford one right now.*

S    Hope you were sitting down when he decided to "neatenize"! Shocks like that are hard on mom's system, right? Anyway, find a bar stool and turn it upside down. Stuff baseball bats, bow and arrow, golf club, football, etc., in that center area, and hang baseball gloves and caps on the legs.

\* \* \*

Like a nice neat closet with everything in its place? Try making some separator disks like you see in clothing stores to separate the sizes of garments. Make them out of plastic lids.

Label each, such as slacks, skirts, blouses, dresses. The kids will know right where things go, and mom can see at a glance what's needed to round out a wardrobe.

\* \* \*

When small children are unable to reach the closet rod to hang their clothes, a good learning device would be suction cuphooks attached to the inside of the closet door.

As the child grows the hooks can be moved up, but in the meantime the child can learn to hang up his or her clothes and feel a little more independent, not to mention the help mom gets.

\* \* \*

P    *My little boy collects tiny little cars and other "treasures"—I need a place to display and store them.*

S    Save large 46-ounce juice cans. Cut one end out, being sure there are no sharp or jagged edges. Paint and then glue them together (arrange them on their sides). The cans make round cubbyholes which can be hung on your child's wall or placed on a shelf.

\* \* \*

A plastic laundry basket makes an excellent toy box. No hard corners to bump heads on, and it fits easily on the closet floor out of sight.

\* \* \*

Toys all over the room? Grab an old pillowcase and have a "police call" with the kiddies.

P    *My daughter is "too big" to play with dolls but she can't quite bear to put them away yet.*

S    She can have her cake and eat it, too! Hang her dolls and stuffed animals from the ceiling. It's really cute for a young girl's room.

*       *       *

P    *School mornings are so hectic that the children are continually leaving the house without all their school things.*

S    Have each child put a cardboard box in his room in a handy place. The night before, put all homework, books, gym clothes, lunch (if possible) and school money into the box.

Next morning it's a simple task to grab everything up as they go out the door. Kinda like an "in and out" basket in an office.

*       *       *

Want a unique cover for that school textbook? Cover it with an old road map (and protect it with clear self-sticking plastic if you want).

Interesting to say the least! Especially if it's your own area. Wouldn't a city map with your neighborhood on the center front be neat! You could pinpoint all your friends' streets.

*Playtime*
*(Also see Fun Activities in Camping, p. 288)*

P    *Our apartment is a little difficult to find—how can I make it easier for my child's guests?*

S    Tie or tape some balloons to your front door to make it easy to spot.

*       *       *

Want to have a "ball" at your next party? Fill a balloon almost full with water with a few drops of food coloring added. Put in the freezer and when frozen, split the balloon off with a knife. You will have a colorful ice ball to keep the punch chilled.

\* \* \*

Smaller children love door prizes. They all like to go home with something (it needn't be expensive).

\* \* \*

P     *My child wants party favors for her party—any suggestions for an inexpensive favor?*

S     Save empty rolls from bathroom tissue and fill them with pieces of candy. Wrap the rolls in gift paper and tie both ends of the wrapped roll with ribbon.

       Make a fabric place mat and have each guest sign his or her name in pencil. Later, liquid embroidery the place mat and your child has a souvenir of the party.

\* \* \*

A good icebreaker for an older child's party is to ask each guest to bring a baby picture. Post them and have each child write down who he or she thinks each picture is.

\* \* \*

P     *My little girl wants to play musical chairs at her birthday party—almost impossible in our tiny apartment.*

S     Instead of chairs, use cardboard squares for the children to stand on—musical "squares"!

\* \* \*

P     *Pin the tail on the donkey is a popular party game but I think pins are too dangerous.*

S     Make your own version of the game. Draw a large bunny and use cotton balls (stick tape on them) to play "Pin the Tail." Safe and just as much fun!

\* \* \*

**P**      *My little boy loves to play ball but he gets frustrated*
          *because he can't catch well yet.*

**S**      Make him a "basket scoop" out of a half-gallon
          bleach bottle to catch the ball with. These games
          are very popular now.

\*    \*    \*

Even a small child can be of service to the community! They can copy
regular bingo cards on larger pieces of cardboard with large print to
donate to nursing homes for older people to use. Bottle caps could
be spray painted for markers.

\*    \*    \*

Want to delight your youngster? Poke a peppermint or other flavored
hard stick candy right through the center of an orange. The child will
have a "candy straw" to suck up the juice of the orange.

\*    \*    \*

Save those detergent bottles! Partially fill them with sand or water
to weight the bottoms down. An old rubber ball, a driveway, kids—
and instant bowling alley!

\*    \*    \*

**P**      *I need a recipe for some play clay that I can make*
          *at home for my kids.*

**S**      Put 2 cups of salt and 2/3 cup of water in a pan
          and heat slowly until near boiling. Mix 1 cup of

cornstarch and ½ cup water and add to the salt and water mixture. Stir until thickened, cool and store the dough in a plastic bag in your refrigerator.

Another recipe you may use is to mix 4 cups flour and 1½ cups salt. Slowly add 2 cups water. Mix well. You will have to knead the dough for about ten minutes, then store the dough in airtight containers and place in the refrigerator.

Food coloring may be added to both these recipes.

\* \* \*

A plain cardboard box makes a nifty desk for your child. The bottom of the box will be the desk top. Cut off the flaps. Draw and cut out a semicircle on the bottom of the long sides of the box. Your child's legs slip through this cutout and presto, instant desk!

\* \* \*

P  *My child loves to fingerpaint but I'm afraid of ruined clothing.*

S  Let her wear one of dad's old, worn-out shirts. Put it on your child with the buttons in the back. Instant painter's smock.

\* \* \*

P  *My kids love games but the game boards really get frazzled.*

S  Cover the boards with clear shellac before you give them to the kids—the coating will sure make those games last longer.

\* \* \*

P  *My kids are always "hounding" me to take them to play miniature golf—it's too expensive to go as much as they would like.*

S  If there's an area in your backyard or a vacant lot nearby, they can design their own golf course and place a few tin cans in the ground for the holes. I think they'd have just as much fun!

\*     \*     \*

Having a hard time choosing a gift for a young person? How about a "party pack"? Older children love to give parties but the family pocketbook feels the pinch. Give a supply of paper goods, some balloons for decorations, etc.

\*     \*     \*

Remember, a child with braces on his teeth often can't enjoy the refreshments you serve at your child's parties. Make sure you have something softer for them to eat—usually hard candies, apples and such are a no-no for brace wearers.

\*     \*     \*

**P**     *Serving birthday cake to a group of kids can really be a hassle.*

**S**     Use flat-bottomed ice cream cone cups and fill them half full with cake batter. Bake in a muffin tin at 350° for twenty minutes, or until done. When cool, ice them and they are easy to serve.

\*     \*     \*

**P**     *My children feel they're a little old for coloring books, but they need a quiet activity on a rainy day. Help!*

**S**     Have them cut words or sentences out of newspapers or magazines and then glue them on stationery or notebook paper. They can have "typed" letters or messages to send to their friends!

\*     \*     \*

A game for a rainy day is a coin toss. Get an egg carton and let the children take turns tossing coins in the egg cups. They could even practice their math by adding up the total number of coins that landed in the cups, and the number of pennies, nickels and dimes in the total amount.

Hours of fun can be had on rainy days playing pickup sticks using long spaghetti!

*     *     *

Make a "family" of dolls for your youngster. Save clean dishwashing detergent bottles and draw faces and hair with marking pens.

*     *     *

Wonder what to do with old Christmas or other greeting cards? Save them for "sicktime." They can be cut up to make little jigsaw puzzles (stash the pieces in a plastic sandwich bag), or they can be assembled to make an autograph book or scrapbook. Also, it's fun for a child just to cut out the picture.

*     *     *

When you leave children with a babysitter and prefer that they only watch certain programs, mark the programs on the TV schedule and inform the babysitter which programs the children are allowed to watch.

*     *     *

P     *Being from a large family with one TV, we get into arguments about which program to watch.*

S     Be democratic. Vote on the programs and the majority wins. Or take turns. You watch your favorite, then let the others choose theirs.

      Better yet, turn off the set and read a book once a week!

## Signals
(Also see Identification, child, p. 306)

P     *We go camping a lot and I once lost my child for a little while.*

S     Tie a whistle around your child's neck—if he or she gets lost, you can follow the shrill sound.

P      *I have several small children and I'm afraid one
       will slip out of the house without my knowing
       it.*

S      Put a hook on the screen door above their reach,
       or attach a bell to both the front and back doors
       so you will know when anyone opens the doors.

\* \* \*

To save a few steps while caring for a sick child, give the child a bell
to ring if he or she really needs something.

## Snack Money

P      *My kids always lose their snack money at the swim-
       ming pool.*

S      Sew a small pocket on an old towel and fasten it
       completely shut with a safety pin.

## Spills

P      *My little girl always knocks over her drink.*

S      If you are using plastics, try switching to a heavier
       weighted glass or a small mug.

## Toys

P      *My kids love to get new toys (as all kids do), but
       they soon tire of them and the toys are doomed to
       a life of neglect.*

S      "Absence makes the heart grow fonder," they say
       —and it's true with toys, too. When the child tires
       of certain toys, pack them away for a few weeks
       or months. When you drag them back out, they'll
       seem like new toys all over again. Then you can
       pack up the present group for a later reunion!

\* \* \*

**P**    *My child "collects" stuffed animals, and some of them are really getting grimy from so much love and attention.*

**S**    If they are stuffed with straw or some substance where they can't be washed, try sprinkling corn-meal or cornstarch on them and letting it set awhile to absorb the oil and dirt. Brush it out.

I've found, though, that if you will cut a small opening in the bottom of the toy and remove all the old stuffing, more than likely you can hand wash it in a cold water wash. Remove any trim, such as felt eyes, etc., that might be damaged if wet.

Dry it in the dryer, or use a hair dryer. Once dry, restuff it with a washable filler such as foam or cut-up panty hose. Stitch the opening closed, and you have a clean fluffy, ever-so-cuddly toy!

\*     \*     \*

**P**    *My toddler is allergic to stuffed toys but she refuses to part with her favorite animal.*

**S**    Remove the stuffing and replace it with nylon net

or old panty hose. You can then wash the stuffed
toy as often as needed.

* * *

If a wagon is on your list for that son or daughter, drill a couple of
small holes in the bottom to allow water to drain out.

Helps keep the wagon from rusting out.

# In Sickness and in Health

This chapter deals with those of us who can't peel an apple because of arthritis, or can't bend over and clean out the bathtub because of back trouble. The term *handicapped* doesn't only apply to those who are permanently disabled. It can mean anything from not being able to carry a cup of coffee because you are on crutches, to having a hard time hearing the phone because you are slightly deaf.

I had a fractured leg and was in a cast and on crutches for two months, and then had to walk with a cane for another two months. I was not supposed to put any weight on the broken leg for the first two months so I couldn't even put my foot down.

I learned the hard way that many things that we take for granted can be so difficult and frustrating. My biggest problem was getting my meals and especially my morning coffee into the living room so I could park on the couch for the morning.

Such a simple task—but when you can't carry anything because you have to use crutches, and can't even put your foot down, the smallest task becomes a real irritant. At first I had a relay system. I placed little TV tray tables every few feet, and then putting the cup of coffee on one, I would hobble-hobble to the next one, place the cup down, and so on until I reached the couch.

The thought of doing that more than once a day was enough to make me stop drinking coffee, or at least have only one cup. Then the light dawned. I filled my vacuum bottle up with coffee and cream, etc., put the lid on tight, and just rolled it across the floor with my good foot. I even put a cup hook on my crutches so I could hang and carry my empty coffee cup. I had three cups of coffee without ever having to get up. Do you know I still do this (although I don't roll it on the floor!) when I am sick in bed. It's great for soup, juice and even fresh ice water without ever having to put your feet on the floor.

What I am calling "home aid" is a "first-aid" section Heloise-style! I'm not going to tell you how to deliver a baby, or put a broken arm in a cast. I am going to give you information for common problems.

The problems and solutions that you find in this chapter are simple, easy things that you can do. If there is ever any doubt or questions in your mind, call a doctor. Your health and your family's health is too important to take a chance on.

I want to leave you with my favorite "home-aid" remedy for a headache. My mother used to brush my hair and then give me a neck massage . . . don't ask me why but it worked. I think it was the TLC that really did the trick!


## ADVANCE PLANNING FOR EMERGENCIES
### (Also see Sunburn Protection, p. 416)

Caution: Any first-aid hint given in this chapter is NOT intended to be all inclusive in all emergency situations nor are these complete first-aid directions. You should have an up-to-date first-aid handbook and first-aid kit. However, the problems discussed here are everyday household situations that may not require professional medical attention. If in doubt, see a doctor.

*Babysitter, information for*
*(Also see Identifying Locations, p. 357)*

| | |
|---|---|
| **Problem** | *I have just started babysitting. What information do I need to ask the parents for in case of an emergency?* |
| **Solution** | First, find out how to reach the parents or nearest relative in an emergency, and the street address and apartment number of the home in which you're babysitting in case of fire. The police and firemen have to know where you are before they can come help you. Second, if the parents cannot be easily reached, they should leave you a notarized medical release form authorizing you to get treatment for the child. Third, you should know the baby's doctor's name and phone number and any other emergency phone numbers you might need. |

### Escape Route

You and your family should have a prearranged escape route and meeting place in case of fire. Make sure any guest in your home is aware of the fire plan. Also, give your guests a flashlight—you may be able to find your way around your home in the dark but maybe a guest can't—especially in a traumatic situation.

### First-Aid Kit

You may never need it, but you should always have a first-aid kit handy . . . even if it is a lunch box, old makeup case or overnight bag filled with a few supplies. This should be labeled clearly and put in a specific place so everyone knows exactly where to go if needed. You can buy a complete first-aid kit, which I think is well worth the money. If you want to make your own, the things I have listed are the bare minimum that you should have to take care of the very minor cuts and scrapes at home:

1. Adhesive bandages of all sizes and shapes. They sell a multi-type package at the drugstore.

2. Adhesive tape to hold dressing in place.

3. An elastic-type roll to hold bandages or compresses in place or to wrap an ankle.

4. Sterile gauze that is sealed in packages.

5. Scissors that stay in the first-aid kit.

6. Soap and cotton balls. If you run out of antiseptic spray, you can gently wash a cut, etc., with a bar of soap and it will disinfect it.

7. A thermometer for taking temperature . . . this is very important if you have to report to a doctor.

8. Tweezers are a must for removing splinters.

### Flashlight

Keep a flashlight near your bed for emergencies.

### Identification, child

Teach a little one his or her last name, street address and phone number by making it rhyme.

### Identifying Locations
### (Also see Babysitter, information for, p. 356)

If you have an emergency, firemen and policemen need to be able to find you quickly. Make sure you can describe your house and its location clearly. At night, turn on the porch lights as well as the headlights and flashing lights on cars that may be parked in your driveway or at the curb.

\*    \*    \*

Always be sure your house numbers can be seen clearly from the street. Paint them on the curb with fluorescent paint so they can be spotted at night.

＊   ＊   ＊

If you live in an apartment complex or building, leave the front door open, or throw a towel over the balcony to identify your apartment. If possible, have someone waiting outside to direct the emergency help.

## Phone Lists

Be prepared for emergencies. Write phone numbers you'd need in an emergency and tape the list next to or on your phone.

## Ready Coins

It's good to write phone numbers needed in emergencies on a card and tape some coins on the back of it for pay phones—keep this card in your wallet.

## AT-HOME TREATMENT

### Bone Fractures

**P**      *What are signs of a bone fracture?*

**S**      Swelling, discloration, or painful to the touch are signs. It's important not to wait long to get X-rays and medical attention. Improperly healed fractures can cause problems down the road. So, better be safe than sorry—when in doubt, seek medical attention.

*Cuts and Burns*

P      *I don't understand the difference between first, second and third degree burns.*

S      First degree means redness with mild swelling, limited to the outer layer of the skin. Second degree means a deep-red oozing tissue with blisters, extending to the inner layer of the skin. Third degree means a loss of all skin, including glands and hairs; the skin may be charred, coagulated, or white and lifeless. With third degree burn or extensive second degree burn, or with the very young or elderly, a physician should be consulted immediately.

\*     \*     \*

P      *A minor burn is so painful.*

S      Hold the area under cold running water, or immerse it in a pan of cold water. Hold an ice cube over the spot, or keep some clean damp sponges in plastic bags in the freezer for these minor burns around the home. Cold will help relieve the pain and also keeps swelling down. Never, never put grease or butter on a burn.

\*     \*     \*

P      *How should I treat minor cuts?*

S      Check to make sure no glass, etc., is in the wound. Flush out the wound with hydrogen peroxide if available. Wash the surrounding area and the wound with soap and water. If you can't stop the bleeding, press directly on the cut with a sterilized cloth or gauze. Remember, any redness or swelling is a sign of infection—see your doctor if this occurs.

*Hot Soaks and Packs*

P          *Whenever my little toddler injures a finger it's next to impossible to get him to soak it in a pan of water.*

S          Fill the pan with the proper soaking solution, then put in some of his favorite small plastic toys or some interesting and safe kitchen gadgets for him to play with.

             The soaking time will pass a lot faster for both of you.

\*    \*    \*

P          *I have to apply hot packs frequently.*

S          Keep the solution hot in your slow cooker.

*Liquids*

P          *When my children are sick with colds and fever, I have a hard time getting them to drink the required liquid.*

S          Keep frozen popsicles made of fruit juices handy during the cold and flu season. When they don't feel like drinking from a glass, the cold popsicle is usually too tempting to resist.

             Keep popsicles handy for bumped and bruised lips, too.

             Make several different flavors so they'll have a choice.

*Medication, Giving and Taking*

Remember, medication should be kept in a place away from little hands. Although we call the cabinet in the bathroom a "medicine cabinet," if you have children in the house, it is a good idea to keep all aspirin and other medicines in a place that only adults can reach.

P    *I have a hard time remembering to take my "daily dose."*

S    Get in a routine—if you take your medicine in the morning, put it by your toothbrush or in the kitchen next to your coffee cup.

✳    ✳    ✳

P    *I have to take quite a few pills each day and I always worry about forgetting to take one.*

S    Take out the number of pills you need to take that day and place a ball of cotton back in the medicine bottle. Lay the number of pills on top of the cotton in each bottle and replace the caps. Each medicine stays in its original container and you can tell at a glance whether you took a pill.

✳    ✳    ✳

P    *I can never remember when my children are supposed to take their medicine.*

S    Put a small piece of adhesive or masking tape over the hour on the clock when it's time for the medicine. When you give the child the dose, take the tape piece off and place it over the next time.

✳    ✳    ✳

Help that wee one's hurt go away. When putting a disinfectant such as Mercurochrome on an injured knee or elbow, paint a "happy face" over the injury. Bring a smile through those tears.

\*     \*     \*

P       *My little ones drive me crazy asking "when do I have to take my medicine next?"*

S       If you have an old clock that doesn't work, set the time at the hour they are supposed to take their medicine next. Then they can "see" the hour. If you want to, you can use a working clock and set the alarm for the "correct time, please."

\*     \*     \*

P       *I'm an adult but I still have a hard time getting down unpleasant medicine.*

S       Suck on an ice cube for a couple of minutes before taking the medicine—it will numb the taste buds.

\*     \*     \*

P       *Whenever I give liquid medication to a bed patient using a spoon, I usually end up spilling it on the person or the bed.*

S    Measure the medication into a clean, plastic pill bottle and mark the correct level with a piece of tape. Then the patient can easily drink the liquid without spills.

\* \* \*

P    *I think more liquid medicine ends up on my little one's chin than in her mouth.*

S    Hold a small paper cup under her chin. Whatever dribbles into the cup can be mixed with a little water, and she can drink the rest down. Sometimes, when giving liquid medicine, every drop is important, so don't waste any.

\* \* \*

P    *Childproof caps drive me up a wall. I can't get them open—and I don't even have children in the house.*

S    You can ask your pharmacist not to use childproof bottle caps when you know there is no danger of children getting ahold of the bottle. Remember, take your time opening any bottle. Read all instructions, it really is easy to do!

\* \* \*

Do not tell children medicine tastes good or is "candy." Accidental poisonings can result. Explain what the medicine is and why it has to be taken by the child. Be honest about the taste. Give the child a little juice or cracker before and after they down the medicine.

### Stings and Bites and Rashes

Did you know that white vinegar will help stop the itching in insect bites or stings? Also, baking soda and water paste is good.

\* \* \*

P      *How do I remove a stinger?*

S      If there is a stinger, get it out using tweezers. Don't squeeze the stinger out. Then wash the sting area with soap and water. Apply cold pack (ice cubes will do) to the area.

\*    \*    \*

P      *I was told not to pull a tick off my skin—what is the right way to remove one?*

S      Don't pull the tick off because the head might not come out of the skin. Cover the tick thoroughly with petroleum jelly. Leave on for about thirty minutes. If the tick does not fall off after thirty minutes, grasp it firmly near its head with tweezers and slowly remove it. Make sure the whole tick, including its head, is removed. Wash the bite area with soap and water. Destroy it, being careful not to touch it.

*Poison Ivy/Oak*

P      *What should I do if I meet up with poison ivy or oak?*

S      As soon as possible after exposure, wash your skin thoroughly with warm water and soap and then pat on calamine lotion.

*Sunburn Protection*
*(See p. 416)*

## CASTS AND CRUTCHES

Never, never stick anything down a cast. Pencils and coat hangers are a no-no. Your skin is very sensitive and can easily become infected.

\*    \*    \*

P        *I have a cast on my arm and I can't get a blouse over it.*

S        Go to a thrift store and buy some men's shirts with deep armholes. Have someone hem the sleeves at a length you like, and square off the shirttails. These new "blouses" will do until you get the cast off.

\*     \*     \*

P        *My ugly white arm cast just doesn't go with anything I wear.*

S        Get a supply of different colored tube socks. Cut off the foot part, slide one on, then color-coordinate your cast with whatever you are wearing!

\*     \*     \*

P        *I have a cast on my leg and it itches like crazy. What can I do?*

S        Blowing air or baby powder down inside the cast with a hair dryer will usually give relief.

\*     \*     \*

P        *My toes get so cold, and I can't put a shoe or sock on because of my cast.*

S    Make mini-socks. Use some old or mismatched socks and cut off just the toe part, or at least as much that will cover your toes. You can use a little piece of tape to hold it on.

\*    \*    \*

P    *The cast on my leg gets so heavy.*

S    Always prop up your leg as much as possible to help the circulation. If you are on crutches, you can turn the crutch upside down and rest your foot on the hand grip.

\*    \*    \*

P    *My cast just looks awful–it's so dirty*

S    Grab the bottle of white shoe polish and clean your act up! You can dab here and there or do the whole thing.

\*    \*    \*

P    *I am so afraid my son's cast is going to get wet when he's out playing.*

S    Cover it with plastic wrap, or a plastic cleaning bag. Be sure and tape it well; this will also help keep it clean. Be sure and remove the wrap when he comes in, so the skin can breathe.

\*    \*    \*

P    *My friends signed my cast but now the ink is all smeared.*

S    As soon as they sign their name, let it dry and then cover with clear nail polish so it won't smear.

\*    \*    \*

P    *I have been on crutches only a few days and my hands are killing me.*

S    If you will pad the hand grip it will make it much more comfortable. You can use sponges or foam rubber. I placed a pretty piece of scrap material over the sponge, and it looked nicer, plus it didn't crumble up.

P   *The rubber that covers the top of the crutches (where it goes under your arm) is all dried out and falling apart.*

S   First, replace it with a new one, or make your own, then always cover it. A real easy way is to use the little footlet socks that women wear for tennis.

\* \* \*

P   *I can't even stand up long enough to wash a few dishes or put on my makeup—my crutches get in the way.*

S   If you can lean, you have it made. I used two old barstools, one in the kitchen and one in the bath. Just lean against them, or even sit on them and you can do a multitude of things. I even spent an afternoon potting and repotting my plants, after setting everything up on a table and sitting on my stool.

\* \* \*

P   *I can't carry anything.*

S   Attach a cup hook (like you use in your kitchen cabinets) on the outside of each crutch and bend the hook part a little. You can hang an empty coffee cup on it or an old purse for carrying various small items. Also, you can wear an apron with pockets.

\* \* \*

P   *While walking on crutches, I got aching muscles from trying to hold up my foot that was in the cast.*

S   A heavy leather belt attached to the handbar of the crutch would make a little "hammock" to hold your foot and cast when you sit down.

\* \* \*

Through with your crutches? Instead of stashing them away, why not leave them at your doctor's for a patient who can't afford crutches?

Know you're going to have surgery and be on crutches for a while?
Practice with them before the surgery. It will make all the difference
in the world!

## HELPS FOR THE ELDERLY

*Arthritis*

**P**    *I have arthritis and it's difficult for me to hold a
pen.*

**S**    Push that pen through a small rubber ball. Or,
wrap masking tape around and around until it's
large enough for you to hold.

\* \* \*

**P**    *I have arthritis and can't hold a toothbrush.*

**S**    Take a wooden spool or dowel; have someone drill
a hole large enough to insert the handle. Then glue
the handle of the toothbrush in it. The large spool
or dowel is easier to grasp.

\* \* \*

**P**    *I can't hold newspaper pages in place.*

**S**    Staple the sections where they are folded so that
they open like a book. Or, tear the paper in half
to make it easier to manage.

## Bathing

**P**    *How can I help a weak or feeble person bathe?*

**S**    Set a lawn chair in the tub and turn the shower on. A person too weak to stand under the shower or pull himself out of the tub can sit in the chair and bathe. If you think the chair might slip, put a towel under it. Also, a towel will prevent marks in the tub. A hand-held shower is super.

\*    \*    \*

**P**    *I have been ill, and the full force of the shower is too much for me.*

**S**    Attach a hand spray to the tub faucet. They are easy to regulate and you can get the water just where you want it.

\*    \*    \*

If you have to bathe and can't get a foot or leg wet, sit on a stool, and keep the foot or leg outside the tub.

## Bathroom Safety

**P**    *I want to make my bathroom safer for my elderly parents—any suggestions?*

**S**    Attach grab bars close to the tub, shower, sink and toilet to prevent falls. Use nonbreakable soap dishes and drinking glasses. Be sure medications are clearly marked (relabel them if necessary in large enough print to be easily read). Of course, put nonskid adhesive strips or decals in the tub and shower floor. Wall-to-wall carpeting provides better footing. A night-light is a must. Ideally, a telephone in the bath to summon help in an emergency would be nice.

\*    \*    \*

P        *I have difficulty getting out of the new, lower style*
         *tubs.*

S        Turn over onto your hands and knees and push
         yourself up. And take it slowly!

### Bed, getting out of

P        *I can't get out of bed in the morning—no joke!*

S        Tie a piece of rope at the bottom to the bedpost,
         tying knots at intervals to have a good grip, or on
         the side of the mattress frame. Grab the rope and
         pull yourself up! Pin the rope to the sheet or blan-
         ket at night so it's handy come morning.

### Car, riding in

P        *How can I help my disabled friend into the car?*

S        Spread a couple of plastic trash bags on the front
         seat. Help her to back up to the seat, sit down on
         the bags and slide back as far as possible. Then lift
         her feet and swing them around "frontward." It's
         also easy to get a person out of the car using the
         plastic bags to "slide" on.

*            *            *

P        *I have trouble lifting my legs to get in and out of*
         *a car.*

S        Why not wear slacks? You can use the legs of the
         slacks to grasp and pull your legs up and around.

### Cooking

P        *I'm afraid to cook on my daughter's electric range*
         *—the buttons are confusing and I can't see very*
         *well.*

S        Have your daughter mark the medium heat and off
         buttons with a fluorescent sticker or fingernail pol-
         ish so you can see them.

**P**      *I am disabled and can't peel vegetables with just one hand.*

**S**      Have someone drive a long nail through the center of a board. Just stick the potato or whatever over the nail and peel away.

\*     \*     \*

Old curtain rods make good "hookers" to reach canned goods too far back on shelves.

### Dentures

**P**      *I dropped my dentures brushing them—how can I avoid breaking them?*

**S**      Fill up the sink bowl with water before brushing them, so in case you do drop them, the water will cushion the blow—no more breaking for you!

\*     \*     \*

**P**      *My dentures never smell really fresh.*

**S**      Soak them in a small amount of mouthwash and water.

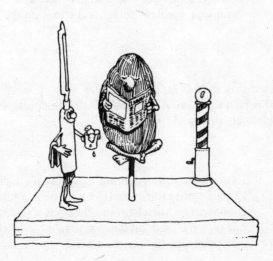

## Dressing

You can make a handy hook to help handicapped people pull up trousers, socks, etc., with a wire coat hanger.

Pull the pants hanger part to form a long handle, with the "hook" part at one end. Pinch the wires close together and wrap them with colorful plastic tape.

Put the tape on the loop end of the hook to prevent snagging clothing or scratching the skin. You'll find it to be a real handy tool for a lot of things.

*      *      *

P  *I can't bend over to put on pantyhose or stockings.*
S  Get a pair of scissor-type kitchen tongs. Cover the end of the tongs with a "snagless" material such as velvet. Use the tongs to pull up the hose.

## Eating

P  *I have to wear a bib when eating, but I can't keep a napkin in place bib-style.*
S  When you have to use a napkin bib-style, use a chain-type eyeglass holder and clip it on the napkin.

*      *      *

Use heavy dishes such as pie plates or even new, clean ash trays for a disabled person to eat on. Also, rubber mats (sink protectors) make super table mats that won't skid.

*      *      *

P  *I have a hard time seating myself at the table.*
S  Place a sturdy turntable (like you use in a kitchen cupboard) on the chair and then put a round pillow on top of that. Sit down sideways on the chair, and then turn to face the table.

*Eyesight, poor*

**P**        *I can't see regular print but I love to read—why*
             *don't stores sell books in large print?*

**S**        You may not find too many large print books for
             sale, but check at your local library. They do have
             large print books, if you'll just ask for them.

✳   ✳   ✳

Left your glasses and can't read a menu? Put a hole in a matchbook
cover or a piece of paper and look through this.

✳   ✳   ✳

When writing to someone with poor eyesight, use black ink on white
paper. If you'll write large and distinctly, and leave more space
between words and lines, the person can usually read the letter
without having to ask a neighbor or friend.

*Gifts*

**P**        *I need some gift ideas for elderly persons.*
**S**        If they're still keeping house, a gift of meat for the
             freezer is appreciated (the cost of meats really cuts

into a fixed budget). If you decide on clothing, consider warmth and ease of closing. Buttons are hard to manage for arthritics. A zipper closing in back is also hard to manage. Flowers, candy or a favorite food (check if permitted on diet) are welcome. A goldfish bowl would be enjoyed by a confined person (with fish, of course!).

## Hearing, hard of

**P**    *We love grandpa but this is driving us bananas! He is hard of hearing and when we all watch TV together he blasts everybody else out of the room.*

**S**    You can now buy a portable radio that has a TV band on it; it picks up the sound of the TV programs in your area. Since it has an ear jack on it, give it to grandpa to turn up as much as he likes, and the rest of you can listen to the TV set at normal volume.

*       *       *

**P**    *I can't hear the phone ring.*

**S**    Set it in a metal pan. Also, most phones have volume dials on the bottom of them. Be sure to check that it's turned up. If you still can't hear it, your phone company can install bells or other devices that will amplify the sound (for a fee, of course).

## Phone Calls

**P**    *I'm elderly and I love to get phone calls, but I can't move very fast and I miss a lot of calls.*

**S**    Tell those friends and family to let the phone ring twice, then hang up and call back about two minutes later. That will give you time to get to your phone and perhaps settle down in a chair.

*Strokes*

P    *How can I communicate with my dad who's had a
      stroke and can't speak or write.*

S    Give him a large mail order catalog and a cook-
      book. He can point to the item or food he wants.

*Wheelchair*

In a wheelchair? Use a pair of kitchen tongs to pick up dropped
articles.

## SICKROOM

When you are caring for someone at home, there are some very nice
things you can do to make their rest more comfortable. If you are
in bed for only a day, or a week, it's no fun. So let's make it as easy
on the sick one as we can.

*Bed*

P    *When I'm in bed, the covers are so heavy on my feet
      I feel like I am tied in.*

S    Get a large cardboard box and cut out two oppo-
      site sides. Turn this over and place it at the foot
      of the bed between the bed and the heavy covers.
      Slip your feet in the box opening and the covers
      won't mash on your feet.

\*    \*    \*

P    *The pillow slips get soiled from perspiration so
      quickly; I hate to change the entire bed.*

S    Put several pillow slips on the pillow at one time.
      You can remove one and have a fresh one right
      there without having to disturb your patient very
      much.

P   *When my little one is sick, he wants all the pillows in the house to hug and prop him up.*

S   Roll up some soft towels and put inside a pillow case. This is a great way to use your old, clean panty hose. Stuff them in a pillow case that closes, or fold over the end of your regular one and safety pin it shut.

\* \* \*

P   *When I am sick in bed my feet freeze even though I put on socks.*

S   Remember the old days when they would warm a brick, wrap it in a towel and put it in the bed to warm your feet? Use a heating pad and keep it at the foot of your bed for toasty toes. No heating pad? A hot water bottle wrapped in a towel stays warm and cozy for quite some time.

### Feeding

The sense of smell usually gets dulled when a body's under the weather. A good way to help stimulate the appetite or create some interest in mealtime is to cook up something "smelly" and let the odor drift to the sickroom. My mother always fried onions or bacon, and even if I wasn't very hungry I sure was ready to nibble when the

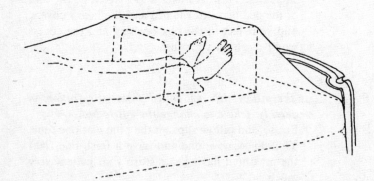

food came. Some folks can't resist salivating at the first smell of a chocolate cake or homemade cookies! It's worth the effort.

\* \* \*

When someone's sick, eating usually isn't much fun. Make mealtime as attractive as possible. For grownups, pull out the special china or pretty teacups. Most sick ones can't eat too much at one time, so use little salad or dessert plates to put food on. Colorful napkins will help make things look a little brighter.

\* \* \*

P     *It never fails—whatever I fix for my husband when he is sick and stuck in bed, it is never what he wants to eat.*

S     Give him a choice. Before fixing anything, make out a daily menu and let him mark what he wants to eat . . . works great on children and husbands.

\* \* \*

P     *It is so hard to manage a glass to drink from while lying in bed.*

S     Use a small coffee mug or anything with a handle so there is something to hold onto. Also, whenever you give someone in bed a liquid, fill the cup only one-third to one-half full and it will be easier to drink.

\* \* \*

P     *Carrying and serving soup to someone in bed is like an accident looking for a place to happen.*

S     How true! My mother always served any liquid in a gravy boat, and only filled it halfway. It is much easier to refill the "special bowl" than to worry about spilling it. The gravy boat even has a built-in spoon rest and doesn't slide off the saucer.

\* \* \*

If utensils are hard to handle, use iced tea spoons, or even baby spoons . . . much easier for sick and weak hands to hold.

* * *

Many times a tray is too large for a little one. Use a deep bread pan and place a glass and small bowl inside.

* * *

P     *No matter what I do, something on the tray spills when I am serving a meal to a sick person in bed.*

S     Place a damp hand or kitchen towel on the tray first, then put dishes on it; things won't slide around. Even if something does spill, no problem.

### Hot Water Bottle

P     *I don't have a hot water bottle.*

S     You can make a substitute hot water bottle by using a heavy-duty rubber glove. Fill it with water. Close it tightly with a strong rubber band and wrap it in a towel. A plastic bottle with a tight-fitting lid can also be used in bed.

* * *

P     *After being in bed awhile, I don't have the energy to take a tub bath or shower.*

S     Have someone put a few washcloths in hot water (maybe add a drop of light cologne), wring them out well and roll 'em up tight. You can wash face, hands, neck, etc., and feel refreshed and clean without much effort.

* * *

P     *My kids sometimes can't make it to the bathroom when they get sick.*

S     If you have someone in bed who might vomit, keep an empty trash can or heavy paper bag lined with a plastic bag next to the bed, just in case.

P      *I just can't get out of bed to shampoo my hair.*

S      Rub and pat some cornstarch or baby powder in your hair. Let it sit a little to absorb the oil; then brush, brush, brush. A little rubbing alcohol on a cotton ball dabbed around the hair line will remove most oiliness also.

         *   *   *

P      *Sometimes it is just too exhausting to get out of bed, but I sure want to brush my teeth.*

S      Give them the old navy dry brush. Put toothpaste on the brush, no water, and brush away. Then, take a sip of water and squish around in your mouth, then empty into a bowl or glass. A quick way for "fresh breath" is a dash of mouthwash in a glass of water, gargle and empty.

### Time-savers

P      *I feel like a marathon runner, going back and forth to the sickroom for a glass of this, a sip of that.*

S      Keep a filled ice bucket by the bedside. Also have fresh water, juice, and maybe a thermos with hot water and a teacup, etc. A few clean glasses and some napkins. If you have an extra thermos, fill it with soup and they can sip, sip, sip whenever you want.

         *   *   *

For anyone who is in bed and doesn't have "full-time" nursing, be it family or friend, here are a few hints for you. I try to remember these things whenever I am sick and when my husband is sick in bed, too. Sometimes it is disturbing to a sick person to be asked all the time, "Want anything?"

Here are some other suggestions if you are stuck in bed for a few days and recuperating. Along with fresh water, ice bucket, etc., I keep a few cans of little nibbles, a slow cooker to heat something if I want to, crackers, cookies, whatever I might feel like eating, by my bedside. If you don't have much room on your night table, bring in an extra table, a card table; even a sturdy wood-bottomed chair covered with a towel works as a storage place.

Most sick people don't know what they want and eating can be difficult so "finger" food is perfect. A basket of fruit, mainly easy things to eat like grapes, bananas, plums, etc., along with a knife and a roll of paper towels, makes it easy to grab a bite anytime.

It may take me a few minutes to get set up, but once I have everything I might want, I don't have to leave the bedroom.

A phone by the bed is essential; especially if you are alone you need to get to the phone easily to call for help when necessary. It also helps pass the time talking to friends. The old standbys of books, magazines and things you haven't read are good. If you feel up to it, this is the time to write a few notes or take a mental inventory of your household goods.

* * *

When you are very sick, resting, relaxing and gaining strength are vital.

Want to know Heloise's remedy for a healthy, happy family? My prescription for feeling good—A HUG A DAY KEEPS YOU THAT WAY!!!! Now remember, it's just as important to give as it is to receive. When times get bad, and no one is around to give me a hug, I pick up my dog and hug her; when she wags her tail, I feel just as good knowing I have made *her* happy!

# 12

## Pets

The wonderful world of pets! If you have any kind of animal in your household, you know that pets are a "whole other world."

I am an animal lover—and to prove the point I have four pets: two birds, one ferret, and one dog. If that doesn't make me pretty qualified to answer your questions and solve your problems about animals, I don't know what does! (Next to being a vet.)

This chapter is not a complete handbook on pets by any means. The problems that you read here are ones that millions of people have encountered over many, many years. Yes, some are very simple. But if it's the first time you have puppies or kittens in your house, you sure want to know the easiest way to take care of them.

Caring for a pet is kinda like taking care of a small child. They can't really tell you what they want or how they feel in words, but you can usually figure out what's wrong or what they need in a general sense.

The old saying about a dog being "man's best friend" sure hits close to home. Dogs and cats and birds can be man or woman's best friend. I used to think that birds didn't cuddle or show affection. Well, some of them do. The love and affection that grows between any animal and its owner is something very special. So take care of your little friend!

The following hints are about the animals that most of you have and write to me about. If I left something out about your pet boa constrictor, I am sorry but I can't cover every kind of pet so I've tried to stick with the more common varieties. Please don't be offended!

Remember, love your pets, treat them right, and they will be loyal to you and return your affection.

## BIRDS

Birds! I have two so I could fill the next pages with my own problems and solutions. But rather than bore you, I have narrowed it down to the questions I get the most.

When I say, "I know what you mean!"—boy, do I!

*Cage*

| | |
|---|---|
| **Problem** | *Cleaning the perch is the absolute pits.* |
| **Solution** | Take it outside and hose it down; then use an old sturdy brush to scrub. A suede brush is perfect. |

\*   \*   \*

| | |
|---|---|
| **P** | *The bird cage just doesn't seem to hold all that birdseed when my little bird starts eating and making a mess.* |
| **S** | If you will use a large strip of nylon net, long enough to go around the cage and about twelve to eighteen inches wide, you can wrap it around the cage, from the bottom up, and nary a seed will leave its premises. |

*Feeding*

**P**    *When I try to put water in my bird cage, the bird pecks at me.*

**S**    Use a kitchen baster to squirt the water in the dish.

\* \* \*

**P**    *I fill the feed dish full, but the bird only eats half and I have to throw the rest out.*

**S**    You can take the little dish outside and blow into it and all the hulls will go out. I only fill mine half full to start with. I may have to watch to see he has food but I think it's much easier.

\* \* \*

**P**    *How can I retrieve my bird when he gets out of the cage, without both of us ending up upset.*

**S**    I know what you mean! My cockatiel is named Fussy, and you can guess why. He thinks that we are trying to murder him when it's time to go back in the cage. The best way we have found is to throw a lightweight towel or piece of cloth over him, then gently pick him up and into the cage.

*Feeding Outdoor Birds*

To feed the birds in winter, save your fat and suet scraps and put them in mesh bags like the ones onions come in. Hang this outside and watch them flock!

\* \* \*

P      *I love to feed the birds outdoors, but birdfood costs so much.*

S      Save your bread crumbs, pizza crust, etc., in a large plastic bowl. Empty the bottom of your toaster, too, and the birds will love all the goodies.

\* \* \*

P      *Any good things I can give to the birds to help them build their nest.*

S      This is the ultimate in recycling. Save all your little strings, dryer lint, etc., and put them outside for the birds. They love it, and that's what I call "back to nature."

\* \* \*

P      *I can never tell when my hummingbird feeder is out of water.*

S      Add red food coloring to the water and you can tell at a glance when water is needed. Humming-

birds are attracted to the red color so you can paint
stripes on the feeder with red nail polish and it will
attract them, too.

## CATS

If you have some friends taking care of your cat, here are some rules
and regulations (standard for all animals) to follow:

First and foremost, leave the name and number of your vet just
in case anything happens. Take your cat's or dog's bed and familiar
things along. It helps to have a piece of your clothing for him to curl
up in; your smell is on it and the animal feels a little better.

Naturally, you want to leave as much food as the animal will need
for the length of time you are gone.

If you can, call a few days later to be sure there are no problems.
It sure doesn't hurt to tell the adoptive parents any peculiar habits
your friend has . . .

I babysat a cat and the first night he disappeared. I was frantic
thinking he got out somehow and was sick. Then he finally showed
up, inside a cabinet. When his owner returned, she said, "Oh, I forgot
to tell you he can open doors and drawers and likes to hide." Sure
would have saved me some heavy worrying!

### Caring For

P       *I'm expecting a little one, and I don't want our cat
        in the baby's room—yet I hate to keep the door
        closed all the time because I will need to hear the
        baby.*

S       Take your regular door down and put up a screen
        door temporarily. You could even paint it to
        match your baby's room!

                    *    *    *

P       *My cat's foot was injured and the vet told me to
        soak its foot for a few minutes several times a day.
        I never did figure out an easy way to do this.*

S      Put the medicine and water in a small plastic bag. Put the cat's foot in it and tape it shut. Hold your pet while the foot is soaking.

\*    \*    \*

P      *How can I make a homemade identification collar for my cat.*

S      Get a piece of elastic (it should fit loosely) and write your name and phone number on it with indelible pen.

\*    \*    \*

P      *I can't afford cat box deodorant.*

S      Shred or tear up newspapers and mix with baking soda. You are recycling the papers and they are easily discarded.

\*    \*    \*

P      *The plastic liners I buy for the litter box are too thin.*

S      Buy poly trash bags at the store—they're sturdier; the kind you use in the kitchen.

\*    \*    \*

Unused disposable diapers make great cat box liners.

\*    \*    \*

Cut several litter box liners at once.

\*    \*    \*

P      *I want to make some inexpensive toys for my cat.*

S      Make a ball of nylon net and attach a small bell, or fill a plastic pill bottle with rice and glue on the lid.

\*    \*    \*

P           *My cat needs a dry place to sleep outside.*

S           Turn an old foam ice chest upside down and place it on top of the lid. Cut a hole in one end for an entrance and add some scrap material to make it cozy. You can place the "house" on the porch or some other place. The foam is insulating and provides a dry, cozy cubbyhole.

* * *

Want a nifty house for your kitty? Build a home out of plywood scraps and *carpet* the roof. Kitty will use the carpet (hopefully) for a scratching post.

### Catproofing
*(Also see Stain Removal, Urine, p. 163)*

P           *I vacuum but I can't seem to get up all the cat hairs.*

S           Before vacuuming, dampen a broom and sweep over the area with it.

* * *

P           *Cat hairs are everywhere and just don't come off the chairs when I vacuum.*

S           Use a damp sponge to wipe them off.

P          *My cat eats my houseplants.*
S          Put a pot of grass near your cat's feeding dish.
           Hopefully, the cat will ignore your plants.

\* \* \*

P          *My cat jumps up on tables.*
S          Spray a little bit of water in its face when it jumps
           up (it won't hurt your cat). It won't take long to
           break the habit.

\* \* \*

P          *My cat claws the upholstery.*
S          All cats need to "claw." If you nail a scrap of
           carpet on a board or box, perhaps the cat will claw
           that instead. It needs *something*. Rub catnip on
           the scratching post and it should help your cat
           know where to scratch.

## Feeding

According to my vet, it's OK to give cat food to a dog; but a cat
can't survive on dog food. There are some extra things in cat food
that they must have. So don't give your kitty dog food. It's not all
the same.

\* \* \*

P          *I can't keep ants out of my cat's feeding dish.*
S          Set the feeding dish in a larger dish which has a
           little water in it.

\* \* \*

An empty cottage cheese container makes a good feeding dish for
cats. Cover any remaining food with the lid.

\* \* \*

P          *I need a feeding "trough" for my kittens.*
S          Those flying-saucer-shaped toys make super ones!

### Grooming

If your cat or small dog splashes around when you bathe them in the sink, try this. Cut a head hole and arm holes out of the bottom of a large plastic trash bag. Slip your head and arms through the holes and you have a waterproof smock. You will stay dry but will still have to mop up the floor!

\* \* \*

P     *My little cat sheds so much.*

S     Did you know you can vacuum your pet? Some animals just love it. You should start out a little at a time so they don't get scared by the noise.

### Travel

Driving with a cat and want cool water for it without a mess? Put some ice cubes in a margarine tub with snap-on lid; as they melt, they will provide water along the way. Add cubes as needed.

## DOGS

If you care for a dog, you not only take care of him, but you also love and care about him. I have a darling little 3-pound dog, Tequila, that is part of my family. So when it comes to caring for dogs, I CARE!

\* \* \*

*Before* your dog gets lost, write a complete description of him and also tuck a photograph away with the shots record.

You think you can remember each marking, but sometimes it's difficult—especially when you are upset over the pet's being lost.

### Caring For

Don't ever leave a dog in the car in hot weather. In 85°F weather outside it can become 102°F inside a car in ten minutes with the windows rolled up. Even with the windows opened a little, the temperature can reach 120° in thirty minutes. You may come back to a dead pet.

* * *

P       *I take my dog with me to the store but I have to tie him outside and several times the leash has come undone.*

S       Attach a small leather collar that will buckle to the hand strap—it's easy to attach to a pole or post.

* * *

P       *Our new puppies keep wandering away from "mama" and crying.*

S       Line a child's wading pool with old carpet or newspapers. "Mom" can come and go but the puppies can't.

* * *

P　　　*On rainy days, my dog tracks mud through the house something terrible.*

S　　　With kids going in and out, so does Rover, right? You can't be there to wipe the dog's feet every time, so just throw down some old rags or towels where the dog crosses to come in. Most of the muddy footprints will come off on the towels instead of on your floors.

\*　　\*　　\*

P　　　*How can I get dog urine stains out of my carpet?*

S　　　See Chapter five—the section on stain removal, p. 163 and p. 198. I've gone into quite a bit of detail there about petproofing.

\*　　\*　　\*

P　　　*Our new puppies whine all night long.*

S　　　An old ticking clock will sometimes do the trick. Just wrap in a towel and put it in their bed. Sometimes a heating pad or hot water bottle wrapped in a towel helps. Remember, they are used to cuddling up to something warm!

## Feeding

P　　　*Sometimes when my dog is "feeling blue" she just won't eat her dog food.*

S　　　Animals aren't the only ones . . . you like a change of taste, too. My little chihuahua will always give in to butter and sugar mixed together and rice with a little beef broth poured over. Check with your vet to be sure this is OK for your dog's diet.

\*　　\*　　\*

P　　　*My little dog has lost all her teeth! She is so fond of table scraps.*

S　　　I know what you mean. My sweet dog lost all of her teeth, too. Dog food was a complete turn-off.

My vet said anything I could feed her—as long as it was a balanced diet—was OK. So into the blender went beans, meat, veggies, etc.—and she lapped it up.

\* \* \*

**P**  *My dog doesn't like dog food and we don't have enough scraps to feed him.*

**S**  Add leftover gravy to the dry food, or some beef broth made with bouillon cubes—anything to give the dry food a "homemade" flavor.

\* \* \*

**P**  *I can't get dog food out of the can without a mess.*

**S**  Open both ends of the can and then push the food through with the lid. It'll come out clean as a whistle.

\* \* \*

**P**  *My little dog cannot eat a can of dog food in one day—it is so smelly in the fridge.*

**S**  Not if you store the can inside a coffee can that has a plastic lid.

\* \* \*

P        *My dog food always dries out before I can use up the whole plastic bag.*

S        Empty it into a jar large enough to hold one bag, add a little vegetable oil and put the lid on tight. It will stay moist and fresh.

\*   \*   \*

Remember, dry dog food stored in just the bag or an open container will attract varmints and bugs, not to mention drying out.

\*   \*   \*

P        *I get tired of dog dishes sliding all over my kitchen floor when I feed my dog.*

S        Place the dishes on a piece of foam rubber.

\*   \*   \*

P        *My bowser keeps turning over his water dish. Since there is no one home during the day, I worry about him.*

S        Dogs have to have plenty of fresh water to stay healthy, don't they! Try driving a stake or stick in the ground. Use an angel food cake pan and place the center hole over the stake.

\*   \*   \*

P        *I can't get my dog to swallow a pill.*

S        Wrap the pill in a ball of cheese, hamburger or peanut butter. Gulp and it's gone!

\*   \*   \*

P        *My dog still won't swallow a pill easily.*

S        Coat the pill in butter—have your dog's neck up —as if he is looking up at the ceiling. Put the pill in his mouth as far back as you can; hold his mouth shut and rub his neck. He has to swallow! Of course, my dog weighs only three pounds so this is easy to do!

*Grooming*

| | |
|---|---|
| **P** | *I like to bathe my small dog in the tub, but there's so much hair that gets in the drain.* |
| **S** | Put a piece of steel wool pad over the drain and it will catch the hair. Toss it away after the bath. |

\* \* \*

| | |
|---|---|
| **P** | *My dog got in some oil, and a soapy bath simply didn't do the job.* |
| **S** | Next time, rub cornmeal all in the hair first to absorb the oil. Then bathe the dog. |

\* \* \*

Take your dog in the shower with you, that is, if it is small. It's easy to soap and rinse it without a big wet mess.

\* \* \*

| | |
|---|---|
| **P** | *How can I get dog hair out of my dog's wire brush?* |
| **S** | Take a toothpick and "weave" in and out to remove the hair. |

\* \* \*

| | |
|---|---|
| **P** | *My little dog just shakes and shivers after her bath.* |
| **S** | Use your hair dryer on the lowest setting and dry her in a jiffy. Don't get too close—hold the dryer a good distance away. |

\* \* \*

Use an old sock to make your little dog a sweater. Cut off the foot part, and make two holes for the front legs.

## FISH

There is an Oriental saying that looking at water is calming. I have heard that watching fish in an aquarium is also very relaxing, not to mention interesting. If you have a family member stuck in bed for

some time, a gift of a little fishbowl would certainly help. A new
interest, something to watch (that doesn't have dials and commer-
cials) and maybe even a little companionship.

### Aquarium

**P**        *The power went off and I lost some expensive fish*
             *because the tank wasn't aerating.*

**S**        To make a temporary aerator, punch a small hole
             in the bottom of a No. 3 coffee can. Fill it with
             water from the fish tank. Set the can on the corner
             edge of the tank where drops of water will slowly
             drip back into the tank. When the can empties,
             refill it and continue the procedure.

\*     \*     \*

**P**        *My aquarium has a yucky crust built.*

**S**        After emptying, scrub the aquarium with nylon
             net and vinegar; rinse extremely well before put-
             ting your fish back.

\*     \*     \*

**P**        *The bubbleless filter siphon sucks up small fish in*
             *my aquarium.*

**S**        Cover the siphon hole with nylon net secured by
             a rubber band or string. Be sure the tube is not
             constricted.

\*     \*     \*

A lighted aquarium will soothe your child and he will have something to watch while he falls asleep. It provides just enough light to keep him from being fearful.

* * *

P  *The plastic plants I placed in my aquarium refused to stay upright.*

S  Take a circle of nylon net, place three or four marbles on it, and gather. Put the stems in the gathered net and fasten the net around the stems securely with a needle and thread. Place the weighted bag in the gravel.

### Fishbowl

P  *My little girl is too young for a fishbowl and our cat won't leave a goldfish alone.*

S  You can make her happy by giving her a little goldfish bowl on which you've glued some fish decals on the outside back. Add a little fern, some colored gravel, etc., and your little girl has her very own fishbowl!

* * *

Brandy snifters make darling goldfish bowls.

* * *

If you have an aquarium that sits against a wall, tape a pretty scene on the back glass; it will look lovely!

## HAMSTERS

P  *I have had to replace several hamster cages because of rust spots.*

S  Place a square of tile in the cage to protect the floor.

P    *Is there an easy way to retrieve an "escaped" hamster?*

S    Take a box with a lid; make a hole in the lid big enough for the "escapee" and lay a paper towel over the hole and put some food on the towel. When the hamster becomes hungry, he will go to the food and drop down in the box below. Cushion the bottom of the box with crumpled newspaper.

\*    \*    \*

P    *My kids' hamster loves to play in its treadmill—but the thing squeaks and is annoying.*

S    Oil the treadmill using vegetable oil applied with a cotton swab.

\*    \*    \*

P    *When I clean my gerbil's cage, I can't keep up with him while he is out.*

S    If you put him in the bathtub, he will stay there until you are ready to replace him in the cage. He can't climb the slippery sides of the tub.

# Index